IN THE PALM OF
YOUR HAND

THE POET'S PORTABLE WORKSHOP

To see a World in a Grain of Sand
And a Heaven in a Wild Flower,
Hold Infinity in the palm of your hand
And Eternity in an hour.

—William Blake

IN THE PALM OF
YOUR HAND

THE POET'S PORTABLE WORKSHOP

SECOND EDITION

A lively and illuminating guide for the practicing poet

STEVE KOWIT
Foreword by Dorianne Laux

TILBURY HOUSE PUBLISHERS
THOMASTON, MAINE

Tilbury House Publishers
12 Starr Street
Thomaston, ME 04861
(800) 582-1899
www.tilburyhouse.com

10 9 8 7 6 5 4 3 2 1

Library of Congress Control Number: 2017930926

Text design on Crummett Mountain by Edith Allard, Somerville, ME
Cover design by Frame25 Productions
Production and Editing: Mark Melnicove, Lisa Reece, Chris McLarty,
    Jennifer Bunting, Charles Prescott, and Jonathan Eaton
Printing and Binding: Maple-Vail, Kirkwood, NY
Printing (cover): John Pow Co., Boston, MA

Contents

The Perennial Themes

Nuts and Bolts

Foreword

I remember clearly the first evening I walked into a poetry workshop taught by Steve Kowit. I was in my late twenties, a single mother, working as a waitress at a small family restaurant. I'd been writing poems since I was twelve years old but had rarely showed them to anyone. I had no formal training in the art of writing poems, hadn't read much poetry, didn't know if what I was writing could even be called poetry. I only knew I was compelled to do something with the frayed journals I had been hiding under my bed for years. Timid and shy, I felt I had no business in a poetry workshop. I was lucky. I found a teacher.

Steve was funny and generous and kind, but he was also seriously committed to teaching us something about how and why a poem works. He did this by exposing us to as much good poetry as he could in the few weeks we had—accessible poetry, poetry of the gut and heart, world poetry, well-crafted, musical, magical poetry. Through these poems I learned about metaphor, rhyme and meter, the importance of image, revision, rhythm and language, but mostly what I learned was how to tell a story.

I had been told to write about what I knew, and what I knew was my life, a life I wasn't sure was acceptable as subject matter for poetry, a life that included instances of domestic violence and sexual abuse. In Steve's workshop I was given permission to write about that life. I was working class. I was a woman. I was a mother. Could this mundane, ordinary world be a subject for my poetry? I was told yes, again and again. I had questions, ideas and feelings about politics, philosophy, sex, religion, subjects my mother had warned me never to talk about in polite company. Could I speak to those issues? Of course, I was told, especially those issues. When I walked into Steve Kowit's poetry workshop, I was ushered in to a world that was limitless; I was welcomed into the world of the imagination.

Who knows which step will lead you into the rest of your life? I don't know if poetry can change the world, but I do know that as I read it and wrote it, my life began to change; I began to develop a feeling of intimacy with the world around me, an umbilical connection to other minds, other voices, other hearts. It was as if I were being given a map of the soul, an emotional history of the world. And as I began to feel a sense of kinship and calm grow within me, a more complex and enlivened spiritual world began to rise and take shape. The more I read and wrote, the more I knew what it was to be a human being, what it felt like to be alive and awake in a place I could begin to call my own.

I eventually returned to school full time and earned a bachelor's degree in English, raised my daughter, published two books of poetry, quit my waitress job and began teaching poetry workshops privately, putting to use much of what I'd learned in Steve's workshops. I now teach poetry at the University of Oregon and am at work on a third collection of poetry. Every time I stand up to teach or sit down to write, I hear Steve's voice, urging me on, reassuring me, challenging me.

I am deeply indebted to Steve Kowit for passing on his love of the word to a young woman in a waitress uniform with tips in her pockets and poems in her heart. I was lucky. And now, you can be lucky too. The book you hold in your hands is a gift from a gifted and inspiring teacher, a way in to the world of poetry, written by an enlightened guide who knows that world and loves it.

—Dorianne Laux

A Few Words Before Getting Started

Oh, the words, the words, the
achingly inadequate beautiful words.
—Terry Hertzler

Many years ago I spent a summer at a Catskill Mountain resort hotel as a tennis instructor. A few days after I got there the fellow who'd been hired to teach art arrived, a brilliant young New York painter named Marvin Torfield. We became fast friends and spent most of our time together that summer. Sometimes, in the evening, when everyone else was in the plush theater being entertained by silky crooners, sequined dance teams, and stand-up comedians, Marvin and I would take a rowboat and drift around on the lake. We'd play flute music together under the moon, laugh uproariously over nothing, and talk endlessly about art, books, politics, the life of the spirit, and this strange planet on which we had somehow found ourselves.

One morning I sat in on one of Marvin's sculpture classes. About twenty women—I don't think there were any men there—sat on monks' benches at a long wooden table in front of the shack where the art and lifeguard supplies were stored, while he instructed them in the rudiments of the human head. He told them to take a big hunk of clay, knead it until it was warm and malleable, and then begin shaping it into a smooth oval. Then he had them begin turning it slowly in their hands, molding it into the shape of a head. After that they started digging away at the features—those pockets for the eyes and the bones of the cheeks, and those declivities out of which a nose and lips would eventually emerge.

Marvin was a fine teacher and a serious artist, and his students were attentive and appreciative as they sat there, under the warm August sun, sculpting away. But after ten or fifteen minutes, two more women appeared, and while the others worked, Marvin went over to the far corner of the table where the new ones had found places at the bench and began quietly giving them instructions for making a human head. He told them to take a big hunk of clay, knead it until it was malleable, and then begin shaping it into a square. A few of the other women looked up from their work with evident surprise—and distress, though no one said anything—at least not at first.

Marvin went on with his lesson, walking from student to student, helping them in the strange ritual of art—of silently transforming with their bare hands shapeless clay into human heads. Now and again he'd return to the two latecomers and show them how to shape the nose or establish the arch of the neck. Everyone worked intently, silently, but it was a silence that had an edge to it and I think most everyone felt it. Finally, one broadly built woman in a large straw hat who could stand it no longer blurted out what the others had been too reticent or polite to say: "But you told us to start with an oval!" she said indignantly, like a patron in an expensive restaurant who'd suddenly discovered she'd gotten the wrong dish. Everyone looked at Marvin expectantly. Or almost everyone. I remember seeing one woman who had no doubt gotten the point of his droll lesson from the beginning, sitting there with a slight smile on her face.

"How you start and what you start from doesn't matter. You can start with a triangle if you want to," Marvin explained quietly. "Or with a hexagon. Or three shapeless blobs of clay slapped together. The trick is to shape whatever you started out with into a head!"

Though the one who had asked the question remained, for the moment, clearly outraged, and two or three others were still confused— you could see it in their faces—most of the other women laughed—the kind of short, delighted laugh that a cartoonist might portray with an exclamation point lighting up above someone's head. A tiny piece of the puzzle of artistic creation had suddenly fallen into place.

The poetry-writing exercises you are asked to complete in the following chapters are also going to be useful jumping-off points, pretexts, ways to encourage you into beginning to shape your own experience, language, and insights into poetry. They are simply there to get you to pick up the clay and begin forming it into—whatever you wish to form it into. The model poems are here to inspire you by showing you what others have done before you, and the commentaries in each chapter are here to help you see something of how they've done it—the structures and strategies of those poems—and to give you whatever techniques you will need for your own work.

If you are a highly experienced poet reading this book in order to refine your skills and generate new poems, I hope that you find the comments helpful, the exercises fruitful, and a good number of the model poems a revelation and joy. No doubt you will follow your own impulses and use this book however you think best. If, on the other hand, you have never done much writing, are timid about approaching poetry, or have little formal background in the subject, I urge you to use this book in the most active way possible. Please do not allow the spinning mind, with its inexhaustible genius for resistance, to keep you from writing the poems suggested in each chapter—or from reading this book thoroughly rather than merely skimming it. We often begin a new project with the best intentions, but easily grow distracted, frustrated, and impatient before we have hardly begun. This is really a workbook for poets, and the advantages to be gained from it will be fully realized only by those readers who use it in the most active way— those who read it closely, participate in the processes, and actually write the suggested poems. It's certainly not necessary to try your hand at all the poems that are suggested in this book, but I urge you to write as many as you can. Obviously the more time and energy you spend writing poems, the more accomplished you will become.

Hopefully, you will find yourself delighting in many of the poems that you write. But if the results of your early efforts do not seem terribly memorable or striking, please do not become overly self-critical or impatient. If you can withstand the temporary frustrations and discouragements that are likely to accompany any period of learning, you will eventually find yourself writing poems that are moving and authentic.

If writing too little to make substantial progress is one danger and the frustrations of the learning process a second, there is yet a third danger: that you will fall so madly in love with your every word that you will abandon all critical sense and refuse to rewrite and revise. Those who have little experience with serious writing often claim that "revising just makes it worse!" or "it won't feel spontaneous anymore!" That might well be true at the beginning, before you have any clear sense of what to revise and how to do it. But to write down some lines and then go on to the next poem is often to mistake one's raw inspiration for a finished work of art. Nothing will teach you more about writing poetry than the struggle to bring an early draft to perfection. Though there may be occasions when the first draft is a lucky strike and needs little or no further work, in general the secret of success in writing can be summed up in two words: tireless revision. Accomplished writers know this; beginners often do not.

But this book is about more than simply the craft of writing verse. If poetry is the art of making music out of your own life, a book about writing poetry must be, beyond language and music, a book about you; a book about your memories, dreams and sorrows; about the shapes and colors of your own imagination; about your own most personal response to this inexpressibly mysterious, beautiful and, at times, all but unbearably painful world. This is a book about making music of the things you love and long for, the memories that burn in your heart, and the fugitive images floating through your head, the things that you have always wanted to say, the things you thought you would never dare say, and the things within you that won't rest until they are finally given voice.

Since this book was first published, over a decade ago, the world of American poetry has flourished: the spoken word/poetry slam venues across the nation have increased manyfold, there is an ever-increasing number of poetry and creative writing graduate programs, and there has been a proliferation of online poetry journals and poetry sites. There has also been a shift in the wind: more and more of our serious and accomplished poets have shown a renewed commitment to accessibility, to communicating as clearly, deeply, and honestly as possible with the reader. This seems all to the good. Although many varieties of intriguingly innovative verse are represented in this small book, its author has tried not to forget that poetry is the music of the human heart and mind made manifest in language; at its most powerful and significant, it is the province not of a limited elitist coterie of "experts" and critics, but of a large, literate populace.

Poetry, in the end, is a spiritual endeavor. Though there is plenty of room to be playful and silly, there is much less room to be false, self-righteous, or small-minded. To write poetry is to perform an act of homage and celebration—even if one's poems are full of rage, lamentation, and despair. To write poetry of a high order demands that we excise from our lives as much as we can that is petty and meretricious and that we open our hearts to the sufferings of this world, imbuing our art with as luminous and compassionate a spirit as we can.

In all those efforts it is my hope that you find this little book of use.

I have always known that one day I would take this path
though yesterday I did not know it would be today.
—Ariwara no Narihari
(Japan, eleventh century)

1

How to Begin

If you are not yet an experienced writer, or if you have always wanted to write but somehow never manage to get to it, or if you can never find enough time or motivation, or are afraid to begin, or feel stuck and unable to move forward, then this chapter will prove useful for you. Read it slowly and carefully.

Many people have a hard time doing the writing they long to do. In some cases they have been convinced by their family or by society to suppress the desire to write and go about the more respectable business of earning a living and raising a family. How does one tell one's wife that what one really wants is to exchange the eight-to-five daily grind for a part-time job—and use the rest of the time to paint pictures, play the flügelhorn or write poems? For women, the problem is often harder still. In today's world most women are expected to hold down jobs and, if they are married, take care of the house and children as well. How does one tell one's husband that one has taken to writing poetry instead of vacuuming the living-room rug and stirring the risotto?

Some people get stuck for a different reason: when they were young and defenseless, they showed their work to some teacher or parent and promptly got stomped on for their efforts. Every writing teacher has encountered students who have been traumatized early on by a blow to their ego—and to their creative life. People can be stopped cold by shyness, by fear of failing, by low self-esteem. For many, to be a beginner is intolerable. It's humiliating. Some have been so thoroughly beaten down on all fronts that they are convinced they "aren't really creative." How easy it is to be wounded into silence.

A friend of mine said to me recently that he was taught from his earliest years that nothing he had to say was of value. Until he was eighteen and had left home, it was impossible to tell his parents—or admit to himself—that his real ambition was to become a poet.

If you are not comfortable letting those with whom you live know that you are writing sketches or stories or poems—putting your innermost thoughts and deepest feelings down on the page—please remember that you are under no obligation to share that part of your life with anyone. In fact, if committing such secrets and confessions to the page seems itself too dangerous, don't do it! To write honestly means that you are willing to tell the truth about your feelings and perceptions, but that doesn't mean you have to say anything about your own life that you wish not to. In the service of that honesty one may employ any devices, reach back into any memory, discuss any subject, call upon any emotion, and invent any fiction. You are not obliged to write raw autobiographical poems that reveal things you are not ready to have revealed. Honesty means, in part, to be able to feel one's anger and grief and envy and frustration, to have the courage to look at one's own life and thoughts so that one can tell the truth about how human beings think, feel and behave. It does not mean exposing yourself in ways that you do not find appropriate.

Feeling one's feelings is not as easy as it sounds. It is common for people to deny a great deal of their emotional experience. People tend to stifle their genuine feelings and deny those emotions that are not socially acceptable. For example, in our culture, women have often been socialized to avoid displays of anger. Anger is a "bad" emotion and an "unbecoming" one for women—or so they are led to believe. Many men in our culture have trouble with emotions in general, having been taught that any display of feeling (other than irritation and mild pleasure) is weak and unmanly. But if one is not permitted to feel deeply, then the chances of writing powerfully are limited. People who want to write sometimes have to struggle against the lifelong habit of shutting off their feelings. To feel relief as well as sadness at a loved one's death, to feel rage and envy at a friend's success, to feel confused and ambivalent in situations where one is conventionally supposed to feel unadulterated pleasure or sorrow is often difficult—and painful—to acknowledge.

A question that writers often face is how to find the courage to speak about the unspeakable—to delve into that maelstrom of one's past, those excruciating memories. I have already suggested that there is no need to deal with those memories and feelings—and it is probably counterproductive to do so until they are no longer so terrifying. If that material is, at the same time, boiling inside you with explosive energy, seething to be expressed, you might consider dealing with it fictively, so that the events and situations no longer appear autobiographical. If you wish to say things that are so intimate that you dare not commit them to paper, say them in the third person: make up a poem about someone else. Change the names. The genders. The locales. The circumstances. Have it take place in another country, or on another planet. Make its autobiographical genesis unrecognizable. Mask the truth the way fiction writers habitually do. Real writers talk about their own lives, their own deepest fears and terrors and passions, in the midst of telling their "fictional" tales. If that seems too difficult or awkward, leave that material alone for now.

Over the course of time, you will find yourself going more and more deeply into what you need to get said. You will make friends with your demons, learn how to lead them out of their dusty cages—teach them to sing at your bidding and for your pleasure. But for now, write about what's comfortable to write about. Let the demons lie. They won't go anywhere: they'll be there when you are ready to start taming them. Ultimately, other writers, other brave spirits, will give you the courage you need.

Only in recent years have women and men who suffered physical or sexual abuse dared to reveal their stories, and turn those torments into art. Because of those people it has become easier for young writers today to deal with such matters in their own work. Until recently, homosexuals have remained closeted—in fear for their reputations, jobs, dignity, and safety. Great writers such as Whitman, Gertrude Stein, and Hart Crane could not afford to speak openly about their sexual hungers and proclivities. It would have been, at the very least, considered "shameful," and they would have been the objects of widespread mockery and contempt. Fortunately, the tide of tolerance and acceptance is quickly sweeping such venomous prejudice away. Because of twentieth-century writers with great courage—poets like Constantine Cavafy, Adrienne Rich, and Allen Ginsberg—younger gay and lesbian writers are more and more willing to do what other writers, those who have gone before, have done: speak openly of—and celebrate— their lives.

For many writers the stumbling block is time. How does one find the time to write in the midst of so hectic a life? Some come to their art in the midst of demanding careers or the daily struggle to pay the rent and feed their family. How does one elbow some room into an already crowded day? First, it is important to remember that you are not alone: this is almost every writer's dilemma! Some writers get up early in the morning to get in an hour or two of writing before heading off to work, or they come home in the evening and have the discipline to lock themselves away for an hour or two instead of collapsing in front of the TV. There are writers who keep a notebook in their pocket and scribble at any odd moment. I have three friends, all in their fifties, who, except for short-term teaching stints, have never had full-time jobs in their adult lives. They are content with a poverty that gives them time to write and paint. They are likely to remain poor—and no doubt they will die poor. But they will get their life's work done! They have opted out of the daily grind for a life that nurtures the creative spirit. Those people, of course, have the most serious possible commitment to their art. Their creative work takes precedence over everything else. Of course not everyone who reads this book is in that position—or would want to be. But if you want to make real progress, you will have to find the time each week to devote to writing. If you have picked up this book because you wanted to start writing, or improve your skills, or because you are using it in a creative writing course, you have already taken the first step and made the first commitment.

There is a secret to a writer's commitment that is important for you to understand—for it is the key to your continued motivation. *Writers spend a lot of time at their writing because it gives them great pleasure!* It would be madness for writers to spend their lives writing poems if that activity wasn't deeply satisfying. The pleasure of writing will increase as you see your skills increasing and as you find yourself completing work that is meaningful—poems that come out of your deepest need to express yourself. The pleasures of the creative process are delectable ones, and this is true despite the fact that writing can be difficult, frustrating and anguishing. Those are simply spices in the pudding, giving it that extra tang that makes it all the more delicious!

If for any reason you had not had permission in the past to pick up a notebook and start writing, you have it now! This is the perfect time to begin. Understand that there is no "correct" way to write—no "proper" attitude, no "appropriate" or "inappropriate" subject matter or writing process. Nor do you need anything in particular to write about, any specific subject or goal. You need not have anything that you are burning to say. All you need is the desire to write—and the courage to begin. As for equipment, a ballpoint or felt-tip pen will do as well as the most powerful computer. You are free to write whatever you wish in whatever manner you wish. You may show your writing to whomever you wish or to no one at all. You may start trying to publish at once or, if you prefer, you may decide that you have no interest in publishing whatsoever—now or ever. All that's needed is your unequivocal consent. The page awaits your pleasure.

Buying a Notebook

It would be a good idea to buy a notebook that you can use for your writing—one that feels comfortable and fits your own needs. Even if you own a computer and even if it's a convenient laptop that you can take with you almost everywhere, a good notebook will come in handy. Then pick up a handful of pens that seem comfortable to you. If you don't have a computer but can afford one (you can sometimes pick up a decent used Mac or PC for under a thousand dollars), it might be a good idea to buy one. If you can't afford one, try a word processor. For four hundred dollars or so you can pick up a new word processor that will let you do almost everything in word processing (typing text) that a computer will do. The main asset of word processing, whether on a computer or word processor, is that rewriting becomes a simple chore instead of drudgery—and since rewriting and revising are essential activities for any writer, this will prove an enormous benefit.

The Writing Schedule: A Process for Creating Time to Write

Some writers find a daily writing schedule to be of great help. Even those who don't have any formal schedule usually have a good idea of when they can find time to write each week, if not each day. On a sheet of paper or in your new notebook, write down the specific times that you can set aside each day to write. Be realistic and as precise as possible. What time do you realistically have on Monday? On Tuesday? How about the weekends or your days off? There's usually a lot more free time on those days. Even a thirty- or forty-minute block of time is helpful. Thirty minutes seven days a week means three and a half hours a week devoted to writing. That can add up over the course of a few months to a lot of writing accomplished!

Better to underestimate the time you have available for writing than to bite off more than you can chew. An unrealistic writing schedule can

5

discourage you because you won't be able to keep to it. Once you have decided on your schedule, write it down in your notebook. Then pencil it in to your calendar and commit yourself to it.

Then decide where you're going to do that writing. You may be one of those people who likes to write in bed in the morning, or out in the back yard, or in that unused room that used to be the kids' room, or on the kitchen table, or out on that rock by the creek down the road, or in the coffee shop at the mall. Any place will do, as long as it's a place where you feel comfortable and will remain relatively undisturbed.

Ultimately, what you need to do is give yourself permission to write poetry—and to have fun doing it. The author of the following poem seems to understand the issue clearly:

God Says Yes to Me

I asked God if it was okay to be melodramatic
and she said yes
I asked her if it was okay to be short
and she said it sure is
I asked her if I could wear nail polish
or not wear nail polish
and she said honey
she calls me that sometimes
she said you can do just exactly
what you want to
Thanks God I said
And is it even okay if I dont paragraph
my letters
Sweetcakes God said
who knows where she picked that up
what I'm telling you is
Yes Yes Yes

     —Kaylin Haught

Speak,
Memory

2

I Couldn't Stop Watching

Memory from Childhood

A chilly and overcast afternoon
of winter. The students
are studying. Steady boredom
of raindrops across the windowpanes.

It is the schoolroom. In a poster
Cain is shown running
away, and Abel dead,
not far from a red spot.

The teacher, with a voice husky and hollow,
is thundering. He is an old man badly dressed,
withered and dried up,
who is holding a book in his hand.

And the whole child's choir
is singing its lesson:
one thousand times one hundred is one hundred thousand,
one thousand times one thousand is one million.

A chilly and overcast afternoon
of winter. The students
are studying. Steady boredom
of raindrops across the windowpanes.

Antonio Machado
(Translated by Robert Bly)

Poems are often generated by memories that haunt us—
memories that suddenly return out of the blue, or memories that are

familiar companions and part of the fabric of our lives—memories that are too precious and sweet not to be recorded, or that are so painful they cry out to be exorcised.

Antonio Machado, one of the great Spanish poets of the twentieth century, evokes not just the dullness of his childhood classroom, but something too of the magic in which even unpleasant memories of the past are likely to be draped. The poster of Cain and Abel; the withered teacher with his book; the children chanting their numbers; the rain beating against the windowpanes: how oppressive it all is, and how vividly it has been evoked.

The poem is not filled with generalized phrases such as "school days long ago," "Bible pictures," and "inclement weather." But it is a particular day, the weather is chilly and overcast, there are raindrops across the windowpanes. There is not simply some poster or other on the wall but a particular poster, one that is briefly—and evocatively—described. The old teacher is sketched in quickly with specific details: he has a husky and hollow voice, he is withered and badly dressed, and he is holding a book in his hand. The students are not simply studying their lesson but are studying a particular lesson, one that the reader hears them reciting. Concrete, sensory details such as these allow readers to form vivid pictures in their minds of what is being described. That is how writers bring a scene to life.

Notice how simple the poem is. Neither the vocabulary nor the phrasing is at all complex or unusual. If you had imagined that poetry required exotic and dramatic subject matter, this poem should convince you that the most commonplace experiences can be transformed into powerful writing.

Keep in mind that this is an English translation of a Spanish poem. The translator, Robert Bly, has decided to sacrifice the original poem's *end-rhymes*—the rhymes that come at the ends of lines—so that he can duplicate its language and flavor more accurately. A good translator would far rather sacrifice the end-rhymes than any of the poem's specific details.

The following poem, also culled from a childhood memory, is similarly filled with details that bring the scene to life:

Power

No one we knew had ever stopped a train.
Hardly daring to breathe, I waited
Belly-down with my brother
In a dry ditch

9

Watching through the green thickness
Of grass and willows.
Stuffed with crumpled newspapers,
The shirt and pants looked real enough
Stretched out across the rails. I felt my heart
Beating against the cool ground
And the terrible long screech of the train's
Braking began. We had done it.

Then it was in front of us—
A hundred iron wheels tearing like time
Into red flannel and denim, shredding the child
We had made—until it finally stopped.

My brother jabbed at me,
Pointed down the tracks. A man
Had climbed out of the engine, was running
In our direction, waving his arms,
Screaming that he would kill us—
Whoever we were.
Then, very close to the spot
Where we hid, he stomped and cursed
At the rags and papers scattered
Over the gravel from our joke.

I tried to remember which of us
That red shirt had belonged to,
But morning seemed too long ago, and the man
Was falling, sobbing, to his knees.
I couldn't stop watching.
My brother lay next to me,
His hands covering his ears,
His face pressed tight to the ground.

—Corrine Hales

Both Machado and Hales have told their stories with simplicity and clarity. The belief that good poetry is necessarily dense and obscure is a misconception. To the contrary, lucidity is almost always a great virtue in writing.

Many inexperienced poets also imagine that the language of poetry must be ultra-romantic and theatrical, but a poetry which is too richly embellished with hyperventilated language, inflated sentiments, and abstruse verbiage is in grave danger of sounding artificial or just plain foolish. Hales' poem is written in our real language, one that approximates the way we speak: she finds no need to resort to an heroic, poetic or overblown style.

Narrative: Getting the Story Told The poet Dylan Thomas defined poetry as "the rhythmic, inevitably narrative, movement from an over-clothed blindness to a naked vision." Certainly most poetry, no matter how concerned it is with music, voice, image, and language, depends to some extent upon storytelling. Like many successful storytellers, Corrine Hales manages to hook the reader's attention by opening her poem with an intriguing line—one that immediately makes us want to keep reading. Throughout the poem we see the details vividly. We experience the excitement the narrator was feeling not because she *tells* us she was excited but because she describes things in a way that makes her excitement real to the reader. It is generally more effective to imply an emotion through a physical description ("My fists tightened," "he gritted his teeth," "her face went pale") than by telling the reader the emotion ("I felt angry," "he was frightened," "she was shocked"). It is unlikely that writing will be successful if it does not convey to the reader strong emotion. If we do not know what the characters are feeling and are not ourselves moved to feel much of anything, then the writing is likely to fall flat.

Narrator and Author It is useful to remember that when poets or fiction writers seem to be speaking of their own experiences, we cannot take for granted that they are really being autobiographical. For all we know, the story Hales has told is simply a fiction, a story that she made up. The "I" of a poem refers to the poem's narrator and *not* necessarily to the author.

Conflict and Suspense Good storytelling often contains the elements of conflict and suspense. We know what the narrator and her brother are doing and we know it is dangerous. Will they get caught? Will someone get hurt? Why have they done it? What is the man who is running toward them going to do? Suspense is that quality of storytelling which keeps the reader wanting to know what will happen next. Conflict implies that a character in a story has a problem. If there is no problem, there is probably no real story. If a man is thirsty in a restaurant and the waiter brings him a glass of water, there is no conflict, but if a man is thirsty in the middle of the Sahara desert there might well be a life-threatening conflict. Conflict leads to suspense, for the reader wants to know how the problem will be resolved. Will the man find water or will he perish of thirst? If nothing is at stake for a character, the reader may not be terribly interested in that character's fate. But if a life-or-death issue has been raised, we are likely to read on, wanting to know if the character will succeed or succumb. Machado's poem

"Memory of Childhood" is not a narrative in which much seems at stake. Its power is its ability to evoke the past with a few well-chosen details. It is true that the poster of Cain and Abel hints at the tension between the innocence of the schoolroom and the real world of violent conflict, but that conflict is represented too tangentially to add suspense to the poem. Although the portrait of the old teacher has great charm, no real story emerges. The pleasures of Machado's poem are not narrative ones. In contrast, "Power" is very much a narrative poem. The reader first wants to know how the children intend to stop the train and if anyone will be hurt when they do so; then, we want to know if the children will be caught and what the engineer will do. Those questions add suspense to the storytelling.

The Power is in the Details No matter how suspenseful her story, had Corrine Hales begun "Power" in the following manner, her poem would have fallen flat:

> One day my brother and I managed to stop a train
> by putting a fake person made out of different stuff
> on the railroad tracks. We watched the train come
> to a stop and then some guy got out who was very angry....

Can you see how ineffectual such writing is? No details are given, and consequently no vivid scene is created in the reader's mind. It is unlikely that such a poem will have much emotional punch. Here we are simply *telling* about the incident rather than doing what Corrine Hales has done—*showing* the scene with specific and concrete descriptions. Hales does not say: "The train hit the stuffed dummy that we had set on the tracks"; instead, the author *shows* us this situation by finding those details that allow the reader to see, feel and hear what is happening: "A hundred iron wheels tearing like time/ Into red flannel and denim, shredding the child/ We had made...." The phrase "a hundred iron wheels" creates more of a picture in the reader's mind than does the word "train," just as the word "train" would be more concrete and vivid than the word "vehicle."

Showing us through vivid detail—specific sights and sounds—does not mean that the poet is being roundabout or evasive. To the contrary, most of Hales' poem is perfectly clear. If, at the poem's end, we are not told explicitly what the young girl was feeling as she watched the man sobbing on his knees, that is probably because the narrator couldn't distinguish the complex mesh of emotions she herself was feeling at that moment. The reader senses, however, that she's watching the sobbing engineer in a kind of spellbound awe. At the same time, there is probably fear, guilt, an exhilaration born of her excitement and newfound power and, beyond those feelings, a strong dose of shock. Good writers often try to capture the complexity of human emotion, rather than settling for an easy and simple label.

Memories Too Painful To Share There are, of course, memories more traumatic than the ones that form the subject matter of "Memory from Childhood" and "Power." Such memories are often difficult to write about. Here is a poem that suggests an excruciatingly painful childhood experience—the sort that a poet may have a fierce need to write about and yet finds, because of the anguish involved, difficult to get down on paper. It takes courage to open old wounds, though it can be liberating to do so:

The Tooth Fairy

They brushed a quarter with glue
and glitter, slipped in on bare
feet, and without waking me
painted rows of delicate gold
footprints on my sheets with a love
so quiet, I still can't hear it.

My mother must have been
a beauty then, sitting
at the kitchen table with him,
a warm breeze lifting her
embroidered curtains, waiting
for me to fall asleep.

It's harder to believe
the years that followed, the palms
curled into fists, a floor
of broken dishes, her chainsmoking
through long silences, him
punching holes in his walls.

I can still remember her print
dresses, his checkered taxi, the day
I found her in the closet
with a paring knife, the night
he kicked my sister in the ribs.

He lives alone in Oregon now, dying
slowly of a rare bone disease.
His face stippled gray, his ankles
clotted beneath wool socks.

13

She's a nurse on the graveyard shift.
Comes home mornings and calls me.
Drinks her dark beer and goes to bed.

And I still wonder how they did it, slipped
that quarter under my pillow, made those
perfect footprints...

Whenever I visit her, I ask again.
"I don't know," she says, rocking, closing
her eyes. "We were as surprised as you."

—Dorianne Laux

In the course of describing one joyful experience, the author has also managed to suggest the story of her whole brutalized childhood. To do that she has chosen just a handful of details. For the violence and terror, she has given us "palms curled into fists, a floor of broken dishes," and "the day I found her in the closet with a paring knife, the night he kicked my sister in the ribs." A few dozen words and the entire environment of her childhood—or, more accurately, one aspect of her childhood—has been laid bare. Once the element of conflict has been established, the suspense is heightened. The reader wants to know what will happen next.

What a striking contrast the poet has created by framing the story of her abusive childhood in an affectionate memory about parental love and childhood innocence. Moreover, that story about the tooth fairy was probably of help in getting the story of those abusive years told, for it gives the poem a narrative structure—a beginning and an end—and establishes the narrator's point of view—not just her memory of those horrible years, but her pity and love for her mother. Notice too how beautifully the author has caught the poem's final moment, that touching and believable portrait of her mother: " 'I don't know,' she says, rocking, closing her eyes. 'We were as surprised as you.' " The quality of appearing to be true to life, of capturing a person or occasion with such accuracy that the reader recognizes it as true, is called *verisimilitude*. Here we can say that Laux has captured the mother, in that final scene, with fine verisimilitude.

Scene The first two of the poems we have read in this chapter describe a single scene; the action takes place at one location and during one brief period of time. But in "The Tooth Fairy" there are several different scenes: the parents tiptoeing into the child's room, her

14

mother and "him" sitting at the kitchen table, fragmentary images and events that took place over several years, the abusive figure dying in Oregon, the mother home from work drinking her dark beer, and the narrator's conversations with her mother during her visits.

It is generally more difficult to write a short poem that involves several scenes than a poem that focuses on only one, but "The Tooth Fairy" is just as coherent and well-structured as the other two. That is due, in part, to the fact that the incident with the "tooth fairy" begins and ends the poem, neatly framing what might otherwise have been a sprawling array of fragmentary memories.

The Gentle Art of Lying What Machado, Hales, and Laux wish to do is tell us the truth—not necessarily the literal truth, but the emotional truth. If "Power" is autobiographical, it is perfectly possible that the author has not told the story precisely as it happened. A poet often takes a memory and after beginning to shape it into a poem finds certain details need to be changed or invented. Perhaps there were other children involved in their plot, but the poet decided to leave them out so that she could simplify the story—and turn it into a better poem. If "The Tooth Fairy" is autobiographical, it's possible that it wasn't the author but her sister who found their mother in the closet with a knife. But the poet might have decided to alter the facts so that the narrator could speak of the knife more vividly, from firsthand knowledge.

Theme and Point of View To write about your childhood you needn't pretend to be a child. None of these poems is written from the child's point of view. Though both "Memory from Childhood" and "Power" give us clear and believable pictures of children, the point of view and the language employed are not those of children.

The poem's theme or main idea is also, ultimately, a matter of the author's viewpoint, for it is an interpretation imposed upon the story by the author. "The Tooth Fairy" might have been written as a poem about the strength to survive, or the author might have discussed her residual bitterness, or how the experience of that brutal childhood wounded her irrevocably, or she might have used that memory to speak of what one learns from pain. It is not inconceivable that the very same material that Dorianne Laux uses could have been turned into comedy or utilized as a political metaphor. The raw memory does not have a built-in meaning but, rather, is interpreted by the author to fit her purposes. We understand events in different ways at different times. Often enough a poet does not know when beginning a poem what it "means," what significance it has, what the theme will be, how it will be focused

15

so that the poem moves in one direction. In that sense a writer invents—or discovers—the meaning of her material. The "meaning" of a poem is often discovered or invented by the writer during the process of the writing itself. Once the writer understands what he or she wishes to say, the poem can then be successfully focused and shaped.

A Process for Recovering Memories

Sit down with your notebook and jot down a few words or phrases for each memory that comes to you as you answer the following questions so that you will have an abbreviated record of the incidents you recalled. Something as brief as "crazy man in green hat" would do nicely. If some of these memories bring with them strong emotions, so much the better. The stronger the emotions the "hotter" the material! If a question fails to call forth an answer, that's okay too: just skip it and move to the next question. The incidents that you come up with do not have to be memories from your childhood.

1. Recall a pleasant time in the past.
2. Recall a building in which you once lived.
3. Recall a secret you once had.
4. Recall a magical person from your childhood.
5. Recall an incident that filled you with dread.
6. Recall something dangerous you did when you were young.
7. Recall something sinful or bad you did as a child.
8. Recall something that happened during a school vacation.
9. Recall something that happened in a classroom or schoolyard.
10. Recall something that happened many years ago near a body of water.
11. Recall your first romantic infatuation.
12. Recall something funny that made you laugh happily.

Taking Notes for the First Poem

Choose one of those incidents, one that calls up strong emotions and which might have had consequences for your emotional life, but also one that has a story that would be interesting to tell. Now close your eyes and go back to the beginning of that particular incident. Replay the "film" of it through to its end. Don't analyze or interpret but just watch it pass through your mind. Curiously, this will often take no more than two or three minutes no matter how charged or complex the experience is.

Then jot down as many specific details as you can recall: not simply a decorated classroom wall, but a poster of Cain and Abel; not simply a train coming to a halt but "the terrible long screech of the train's braking"; not just a man with a disease but "ankles clotted beneath wool socks." Write down what things looked like, smelled like, felt like; what someone said, how someone gestured or moved or wept. Was there a doorknob gleaming in the sun, a dog barking on the corner in the snow, did someone's dry cough punctuate the silence? If you wish, replay the incident again. You will probably find new details emerging, things that hadn't emerged in your first run-through. Write those down too. If you find yourself writing a paragraph or a couple of pages describing the incident, that is perfectly okay.

When you have done that, ask yourself what impact the incident had on your life. Why do you remember this? That is a question that is not always easy to answer. It is possible that your poem, like "Power," will be about an initiation, a rite of passage, a moment when you grew or changed or learned something important about yourself or the world. Perhaps, like "The Tooth Fairy," it will be about something that wounded you deeply, or something that has partially shaped who you presently are. Although a poem's theme, what one is to make of a particular incident, is often one of the discoveries that occurs in the process of writing rather than before the writing begins, it is a useful question to ask from the beginning, for the answer will help to focus the poem, determining the appropriate mood and how most effectively to organize and shape the material. In a sense it is a question of knowing—or deciding—what your own poem is about, what moral or truth it points at, what it says about your life or life in general.

Read the following three suggested poems and choose the one that seems to fit most comfortably the memory with which you are dealing. As you read the other two suggestions you might find that other memories brought to light by the exercise would fit those formats. Needless to say, it would be fruitful to write all three of the suggested poems.

Poem 1: A Childhood Memory

Out of all the details and facts you have written down, choose the ones that will permit you to write a poem of no more than thirty-five lines, telling your story as effectively as you can. Tell it in a manner that makes the reader continually want to know what happens next. Make sure the incident is held to one scene—one physical location. Sometimes this means you will have to choose one particular incident out of many. If the memory that you recalled while doing the memory process jumped around from locale to locale, find the one that seems the most vivid and intense, the one filled with the most action, drama and conflict. Be sure it is one that will permit you to reveal, with a minimum of explanation and background, what you want to show us. As indicated earlier, that focus, what it is you want to show us, often emerges in the process of writing itself. Good writers can give us necessary background quickly and painlessly, without seeming to interrupt the flow of the story. A poem that begins "Again he took out his strap and hit me" lets the reader know, simply through the use of the word "again," that this has happened before. Starting with the action rather than with a lot of background information is an important storyteller's device. The reader must know what the poem's narrator (the "I" of the poem) is feeling. The more intensely you can get us to feel, the more successful you have been. It is important to remember that the power of poetry rests to a large degree on the emotional intensity it generates. Try to make the reader feel the humor of the situation or its pathos or the narrator's grief or something of the mystery of the world, or the small, significant triumph of a character's life—or whatever it is you wish to call forth from the reader's emotions.

Remember to show us rather than tell us: use vivid, expressive details to give the reader the picture you want us to see before our eyes. Concentrate on *describing* the action in such a way that the reader will understand the feelings of the characters without having to be told them.

If thirty-five lines doesn't seem like enough space in which to tell your story, so much the better: the more concise you are forced to be, the more likelihood that you will select your details carefully and maintain the narrative and emotional intensity that you want.

Do not use end-rhyme (rhyming words at the ends of lines) in this poem. Far from making a poem more musical, in inexperienced hands end-rhyme often forces the author to write awkwardly, keeping a poem from becoming musical and graceful. Instead of rhyme, let the compression, precision, and clarity of your phrasing, the accuracy of your descriptions, the drama of your narrative, and the intensity of the emotion shape this into a powerful poem.

Poem 2: Working With Structure

Take one of the memories generated by the exercise and write a poem based on the structure of Machado's "Memory from Childhood." That poem evokes the mood of a place and time in the poet's past by choosing just a few details. This form might be appropriate for a memory of something that happened over and over, or a continuous action over a long period of time, or one that is significant to you without being particularly dramatic or fraught with conflict. Perhaps it will be about the two years you spent in Idaho or the three years when you lived with your grandmother, or the winter you spent in Alaska when your mother was dying. You might make each *stanza* a different scene at a different locale.

First, gather four distinct sets of details about the occasion and use one in each of four stanzas. A stanza is a verse paragraph, separated from the remainder of the poem by an additional space. Machado, for example, discusses the weather in the first stanza, the schoolroom in the second, the teacher in the third, and the students in the fourth. The final stanza repeats the first. You will observe that the poet tells the reader in the first stanza what the emotion of the poem is. If it works gracefully in your poem, try the same thing. But even if you don't tell us explicitly what the mood is, that mood must quickly and clearly be made known to the reader.

Each stanza of "Memory from Childhood" is four lines long. Keep yours the same length. Also, repeat the first stanza as the last as Machado does—or, as an alternative, make the last two lines a repetition of the poem's opening two lines.

Poem 3: Family Secrets

If there is a dramatic story that cannot be told as one incident but surveys an entire period of your life, you may wish to use the strategy that Dorianne Laux employs, framing the story with one small anecdote which appears at the poem's beginning and conclusion. Maybe your story is also about a family secret—about alcoholism or drug abuse or incest or violence or debilitating illness. Whatever the larger story you wish to tell, find a specific incident that you can use to frame it. Do not try to tell us all the things that happened but, like Laux, find the three or four details that will bring the situation to life for the reader. Since you may be encompassing the events of many months or years, try to pick out just the right details, ignoring a wealth of others that you might have the impulse to tell us. Keep this poem to a maximum of thirty-five lines.

Revising the First Poem

After you have finished writing a first draft of one of these poems, look it over and see if you have actually told your story clearly and effectively. Often inexperienced writers find it hard to separate what they know about an incident from what they have told the reader, with the consequence that crucial information never gets conveyed. An additional problem is that the excitement of writing down one's memory and creating a poem is sometimes confused with a sense that the poem, since it delighted you, will surely delight the reader.

Sometimes in a second or third draft, dissatisfied with their previous attempts, writers will start the story at a different point in time or find better details for their purpose. Perhaps there is not yet enough suspense or emotion, or you got bogged down in background material that was inessential. Perhaps your word choice is not precise or trenchant enough to bring a scene to life. Perhaps the reader is given too few clues to the emotions the characters are feeling or cannot tell what emotion they themselves are supposed to be feeling.

Looking over your draft a few days later is often an effective way to see the poem with fresh eyes.

3

Little Poems in Prose

Something must have been bugging my father the day I asked him for fifty cents in the upstairs kitchen, because although he was always a sweet and gentle man and gave me most everything I asked for, this time he turns around from the sink where he is washing dishes and starts swinging at me fronthand and backhand, again and again, his face contorted with a rage I never saw before or again. I shrivelled into the chair by the kitchen window sobbing and begging this stranger to stop. Eventually he does, and the silence of the rest of our lives swallows the moment forever.

—Fred Moramarco

Three sentences about a moment that changed one's life! Is this a vignette, a tale, a short-short story, a sketch, an anecdote? We could call it any of those—or we could call it a little poem in *prose*.

That it is written in prose doesn't mean it isn't poetry; it only means that it isn't *verse*. Poetry and prose are not in every case distinguishable, and twentieth-century poets often write poems in prose. By prose we designate that writing which extends to the right-hand margin; verse, on the other hand, breaks each line at a place not determined by the margin of the page. The nineteenth-century French poet Charles Baudelaire was largely responsible for popularizing the *prose poem* through his collection *Paris Spleen*, which he subtitled *Petits poèmes en prose*. Since the formal requirements of the prose poem require nothing more than writing an effective paragraph, it is often a comfortable way to approach poetry for those who have little experience with verse.

The following could be called a short-short story, but it could just as easily be called a prose poem:

The Gift I Never Got

It was not unusual in my house for the phone to ring once, just once, and then fade away into silence. It was not unusual in my house for my father to suddenly announce after one of these calls that he had some errand to run. Often it was a trip to the store, or some forgotten task at work. It was a usual day in my house: the phone had just rung once, my father had just left to go to the store, and I was eight years old. Christmas was near and I was searching the house for presents. Under my parents' bed is where I found it. It was a bright red toy car with real rubber tires and plastic pipes that looked like real chrome. I couldn't control myself and soon I was pushing it along the floor. I could feel my heart thumping in my head and my hands were slick with perspiration. Later that night I dreamed about the car: it would be my favorite toy. On Christmas morning I bypassed the Stretch Armstrong doll, I totally ignored the Dr. J Basketball, and went looking for the car. It was some cruel joke. "Where is it?" I cried. I ran into my parents' bedroom, rifled under their bed, but it wasn't there. My mother had followed me. "What are you looking for?" she asked. "The car! The car!" I screamed. The phone rang once—and I heard the door close as my father left to go to the store. "There is no car," she said. "Yes there is, yes there is!" I screamed back. "It's just like when the phone rings you always say it's no one. Well it wouldn't ring if it wasn't someone." She didn't speak for a long while after that. She just looked at me. Finally she said, "Alright, we'll ask him about the car. We'll ask him about the phone that only rings once. We'll ask him about all those trips to the store."

—Vincent Draper

How cleverly the story of a father's marital infidelity has been revealed beneath this story of a boy's disappointment at a missing Christmas gift. Though we are not told explicitly what the young boy is feeling at any moment, the details and descriptions are so well chosen and designed that the reader has no trouble feeling his excitement and bitter disappointment. And we know perfectly well, without having to be told, what the boy's mother is feeling when she agrees to confront her errant husband.

It is useful to note that the story is told through *action* and the use of specific details. We see the young boy searching for presents, finding the toy car, ignoring the other presents in search of the one that he has already decided will become his favorite toy. Notice too that the author has not saved the husband's infidelity for a surprise ending—something that an amateurish writer might have done—but presents that fact to us, through implication, from the beginning. If you're more comfortable thinking of this sort of piece as a short-short story, that is fine. But poetry or fiction, it is a tale concisely and effectively told.

Though there is no hard and fast boundary between the two, short stories usually involve a number of related incidents extended over a period of time, while the narrative element in poetry often concentrates on one incident briefly conveyed. The following prose poem is less narrative than descriptive, a series of continually inventive pictures of a common object, a portrait that becomes, as the poem proceeds, ever more evocative and magical:

Considering the Accordion

The idea of it is distasteful at best. Awkward box of wind, diminutive, misplaced piano on one side, raised braille buttons on the other. The bellows, like some parody of breathing, like some medical apparatus from a Victorian sick-ward. A grotesque poem in three dimensions, a rococo thing-am-a-bob. I once strapped an accordion on my chest and right away I had to lean back on my heels, my chin in the air, my back arched like a bullfighter or flamenco dancer. I became an unheard-of contradiction: a gypsy in graduate school. Ah, but for all that, we find evidence of the soul in the most unlikely places. Once in a Czech restaurant in Long Beach, an ancient accordionist came to our table and played the old favorites: "Lady of Spain," "The Sabre Dance," "Dark Eyes," and through all the clichés his spirit sang clearly. It seemed like the accordion floated in air, and he swayed weightlessly behind it, eyes closed, back in Prague or some lost village of his childhood. For a moment we all floated—the whole restaurant: the patrons, the knives and forks, the wine, the sacrificed fish on plates. Everything was pure and eternal, fragiley suspended like a stained-glass window in the one remaining wall of a bombed-out church.

—Al Zolynas

The author creates an accordion for us by making a number of comparisons: an accordion is compared to a box of wind, a piano and a braille alphabet. It is called a parody of breathing and a Victorian breathing apparatus. Then there are two more comparisons, more abstract and fanciful: the accordion is a grotesque, three-dimensional poem and a rococo thing-am-a-bob. To give us a picture of how he looked with an accordion strapped to his torso, the narrator creates two more evocative comparisons and that charming incongruity: the gypsy

23

in graduate school. The narrator then comments about the nature of such incongruity: how one finds "evidence of the soul in the most unlikely places," and launches into a vignette about the music of an old accordionist in a California restaurant who transformed an ordinary moment into something "pure and eternal," an observation made concrete by that wonderful analogy at the poem's conclusion in which the author evokes the tragedy of post-war Eastern Europe by suggesting that the moment was suspended with the fragility of "a stained-glass window in the one remaining wall of a bombed-out church."

The Poem as Epiphany The accordion, which the narrator disparaged at the poem's beginning, becomes, in the hands of an old European musician, the agent of a moment of illumination, of a moment that we tend to speak of as an epiphany. An epiphanic moment is one in which there is a revelation, either for the reader, the narrator, or a character— or some combination of the three. In its larger connotation it implies that the world is momentarily beatified, made sacred or marvelous, seen with a suddenly enlarged vision. To some extent Al Zolynas's poem does for the reader what that accordion did for the patrons of that restaurant: it opens the listener to the world of the transcendent and sublime.

Writing Prose Paragraphs

Writing prose is excellent practice, for here your effectiveness will be determined by how well you tell your story, how precise and effective your descriptions are, the grace and poise of your word choices and phrasing, and by your insight and emotional depth— characteristics that in large measure determine the effectiveness of all writing.

For those who feel uncertain about their ability to write very well in general, writing prose is likely to prove of great use. For those a bit uneasy about writing verse, not knowing, for example, where to end each line or how to make one's language musical enough to be considered a "real" poem, it would also be an excellent idea to begin by writing short prose paragraphs, for if you can write an effective and graceful paragraph it is not unlikely that you can learn to write excellent poetry. Write, rewrite, and polish short prose descriptions until you begin to feel comfortable about the level of your writing skills. Describe things that you see around you: the house in which you live, the appearance and character of someone with whom you work, the physical appearance of your kitchen table after breakfast, the view from your bedroom window, the sights you see as you walk or drive through your neighborhood, encounters you have during the day. Describe a store window, a doctor's waiting room, a local gas station, secondhand store, all-night restaurant. Do not try to be fancy; try rather to be accurate and to write with liveliness and precision. Go back and polish these paragraphs until they are finely described and gracefully expressed.

You will find other prose poems by Arthur Rimbaud, Virginia R. Terris and Aimé Césaire in later chapters.

A Process for Uncovering Traumatic Memories

The following exercise should help you uncover more material from your past. Do not limit yourself to memories from childhood. Again, jot down a few words or phrases for each recollection so that you will remember what those memories were after this process is completed. If a particular memory seems too painful to write about, leave it be for now. On the other hand, the more you are able to uncover and deal with traumatic memories, the easier it will be for even deeper memories to emerge without causing you inordinate distress. Such a process can be enormously therapeutic for people who have terribly painful material buried in their past.

1. Recall an incident from your past that filled you with sadness.
2. Recall an incident that you would be reticent to share with others.
3. Recall an incident involving a parent or guardian that still angers you.
4. Recall an incident in which you felt betrayed.
5. Recall an incident that ended in great disappointment.
6. Recall an incident in which you felt humiliated.
7. Recall an incident in which you felt love for someone.
8. Recall an incident that was emotionally wrenching.
9. Jot down any memory that popped into your mind but which you have suppressed while doing this process.
10. Recall an incident that was joyful.

Poem 4:
The Three- or Four-Sentence Prose Poem

Take one of the experiences that you want to write about but which you feel can be done with great conciseness and tell the entire story in three or four sentences. This will probably mean that you will have to write a couple of relatively long sentences, which in itself is good writing practice. But don't make those sentences awkwardly long and overburdened with information and details. Look back at that traumatic scene from childhood by Fred Moramarco and notice how the author handles the first sentence, which is seventy-three words long. Observe how colloquial and natural the sentence sounds—despite its length.

Though your impulse may be to go into great detail about this incident in your life, in order to get it into three or four sentences you will be forced to condense the material radically, to set down its very essence. Remember to center the telling on an action and to charge it with emotion. Revise those three or four sentences until you feel you've said them as well as you possibly can, and that your story has been forcefully and memorably told. If this short prose poem proves successful and stimulating, try your hand at another. Make this one five to eight sentences long.

Poem 5:
Working With the Other Side of Your Brain

Here's an exercise that was first described to me by the poet-teacher Donna Hilbert. For some people, it's likely to produce surprising results. Utilizing one of the incidents from the preceding process or the process in Chapter 2, write a prose poem with your opposite hand—the hand you do not use for writing. You may find that the writing is primitive and hard to read, the letters oversized and shaky, that you get only a few words on a line and only a few lines on a page. That is perfectly okay. Write out the entire first draft with that opposite hand while letting your mind return again and again to the experience itself so that, in a sense, you are replaying the internal film and taking notes about what you see, hear and feel. If you make discoveries about the incident or about your emotions as you go, let those enter the narrative. If the draft starts moving off in directions you did not expect, or if the exercise suddenly triggers a still earlier, more deeply buried memory, that's all to the good. Allow yourself to follow where your hand and mind lead. For some people this technique permits access to memories and feelings that are otherwise unavailable and the experience can be revelatory.

Poem 6: The Object Poem

Try writing a poem in the manner of "Considering the Accordion." Take an object that you find before you in your room or home—perhaps an object that has been with you for many years and that has a special significance, or some object that you've never paid much attention to before but which holds a quiet place in your affections. Put the object in front of you and look at it closely. Touch it, feel its heft, notice specific things about it that you had never taken note of before. Get into as close and empathetic a relationship with the object as you can. Then jot down five comparisons, things that the object looks or feels like or in some way resembles. Be as imaginative and far-ranging as Zolynas. If the object is a shell, write "The shell is (like) a ———." Fill in the blank with five imaginative comparisons. Don't worry if those comparisons are far-fetched. Now jot down three or four phrases about what the object means to you, its place—however humble—in your life or memories. If you have any specific memories of that object—some role it played in your past—write them down too.

Now begin a prose poem in which you try to describe that object with as much sympathy as possible. Bring it to life with your comparisons and allow it to become luminous both for you and your reader by feeling its nature and presence as deeply as you can and following the poem wherever it leads you. If it feels right to do so, try to end with some epiphany—some sense of transcendence, illumination, new knowledge either of the object, yourself, or of the universe. Sometimes this is done, as in the example by Al Zolynas, by shifting us into a magical sense of time or place ("For a moment we all floated—the whole restaurant: the patrons, the knives and forks, the wine, the sacrificed fish on plates"). It can also be done with an image that moves the reader's mind to an altogether different setting ("Everything was pure and eternal, fragiley suspended like a stained-glass window in the one remaining wall of a bombed-out church"). A shift in perspective, viewpoint or focus can signal this widening of perception.

Revising Your Poems

It is terribly difficult to see what is and is not effective in one's own poems. That is why many serious writers listen closely to the comments they get from a trusted circle of friends—people who are fully supportive of the author's efforts and, for that very reason, willing to share with the author their honest evaluation of the work. A good, trusted friend who is willing to play the role of sympathetic reader and supportive critic can be of great help in moving you from a work's early drafts to its completed form. Your friend might be a spouse or other family member, or simply an acquaintance who loves poetry or who is a fellow writer, or simply a person whose taste and judgment you respect. If the friend's only response is praise and admiration, you will have to let that person know that you wish support on a different level. If that doesn't work you will have to find someone else. A husband or wife might *not* be willing to be critical, preferring the easier and more comfortable path of telling you how wonderful a poet you are. Although that's always nice to hear, it won't go very far in helping you improve the poem in the next draft.

Let your supportive critic know that the piece you are sharing is an early draft and that you have every intention of revising and improving it. Do *not* in any way explain to your friend the intentions of your poem. People often reveal such information in subtle ways in order to provoke the response they are looking for. But if you give your friend that information, you won't be able to get the kind of accurate criticism you're after. If you tell your friend that the poem is about the death of a neighbor's child, and that the event stunned you into a childhood memory about the death of a beloved household pet, you will never be able to learn if your poem was clear enough to convey that basic infor-mation on its own. If the poem is supposed to be an ironic comment on contemporary values, you won't know if the reader understood the poem's point of view if you reveal in advance what the attitude of the poem is. So give your friendly critic the poem without any hints and then listen closely to the comments you get. Do not explain or clarify anything. Just listen. That's awfully hard for writers to do when their work is being discussed. The ego always wants to defend itself. But if you listen closely, and ask enough pertinent questions to get specific responses ("What did you understand about the boy's feelings from the lines about the rain beating on the roof? Did anything seem awkward or confusing?"), you can learn a great deal about what is and is not effective in that early draft.

Of course you do not have to accept your friend's criticisms and suggestions. If you show the poem to five people you may well get five different responses. But if your readers are people whose opinions you respect, it is likely that each one will give you at least one comment or suggestion that will assist you. It is not unlikely that you will immediately agree with some of the negative comments, knowing full well that the passage they are talking about still needs work. There might be other comments that you will have to mull over before determining if they are useful. Finally, there are likely to be comments that you can safely dismiss because you remain confident that that particular line or section is already effectively handled.

There will be a great deal more information about getting feedback from workshop groups in Chapter 28.

4

Shards of Memory:
Playing With Time

Some of the memories that writers make use of are unforgettable, life-changing experiences, but many others are likely to be those vagrant, momentary encounters that are memorable for no apparent reason: experiences that are part of the fabric of our ordinary daily lives but that for some reason remain significant enough to be remembered. Here's an odd and engaging poem in which the poet makes use of scattered, fugitive, and seemingly disconnected memories.

How I Knew Harold*

Around 1981 we run into your old girlfriend on an elevator. She's wearing black leather pants and a tank top. She asks how I like New York. We are all sweating bullets. I want to say it sucks, but the doors open and she's gone. We miss our floor.

Around 1953 Mom tells the family she's pregnant. My brother bounces around the living room with a pillow on his head wailing "it will change our whole lives!" This story is recounted each year around my birthday.

Around 1978 I leave home to move in with Jack. Dad and I are standing in the driveway. They don't want me to go. He's Jewish. Mom packs ham sandwiches and slips me two twenties. I move back in three months.

Around 1979 my friend Sandy plays taps at a funeral gig, so I go along. I walk up to the casket in my boots and fur jacket. I'm checking out the deceased when a woman grabs my elbow. She wants to know how I knew Harold.

Around 1972 my sister tells me and my parents she's gay. Dad
says it's unnatural and they start arguing. I keep
quiet. Mom goes to the kitchen to make sundaes.

Around 1962 my brother feels like scaring the hell out of me
and chases me around the house with a butcher knife.
I hide behind Dad's suits. It smells like Old Spice.

Around 1969 I tell my parents over dinner that I'd live with a
man before I'd marry him. Dad says it's unnatural. I
tell him to get his own dessert.

Around 1963 Grandma gives me ten bucks for learning the
times tables.

Around 1957 Dad and I sing My Darlin' Clementine every
morning on the way to school.

Around 1968 Patty Bryant and I run out on the check at
Woolworths.

Around 1964 Mom colors her hair—starts wearing eye
shadow and mascara. She's standing over a steaming
sink in a pale green mohair singing "Edelweiss." She
looks absolutely radiant.

(*with thanks to Terence Winch)

—Deborah Harding

The fact that these incidental memories are not sorted chronologi-
cally gives the inventory a surprising and quirky flavor. The writing
seems so casual one has the illusion of listening to a series of disjointed,
casually organized, but interesting reminiscences—incidents that have
simply popped into the poet's head. There's an innocence to the telling
that lends the piece a personable charm—and there is an added charm
in the form itself, the parallel constructions created by beginning each
item with the same word, which gives the poem a satisfying aesthetic
structure while keeping it from looking or sounding like a poem in any
traditional sense.

The poet establishes her casual and chatty style in the very first
stanza with such phrases as "sweating bullets" and "it sucks." Notice
the humor she gets out of that second, surprising use of "Dad says it's
unnatural." This is very much a family album with quick but telling
portraits of her parents, her brother and sister and, of course, herself.
We are given a series of personable domestic details. Her brother, for
example, "bounces around the living room with a pillow on his head,"
and her mother stands over "a steaming sink in a pale green mohair."
It is a collage of memories out of which the poet has created an appeal-
ing self-portrait.

It is not at all unusual for poets to take their inspiration from other poets: a rhythm stolen from Yeats, a phrase adapted from Sappho, an idea picked up from Marvell. Poets so inspired by other writers' works are usually delighted to credit their sources. Terence Winch, to whom the poet gives credit in a footnote at the end of "How I Knew Harold," is an innovative contemporary poet whose poem "I Am Dressed as a Gondolier," which also used an achronological series of informally related incidents, was Harding's inspiration.

Contemporary poets often delight in creating surprising structures. Here's another series of memories shaped into a poem that is at once disarmingly simple and formally innovative:

People Who Died

Pat Dugan....my grandfather...throat cancer....1947.

Ed Berrigan....my dad....heart attack....1958.

Dickie Budlong....my best friend Brucie's big brother, when we were
>>> five to eight....killed in Korea, 1953.

Red O'Sullivan....hockey star & cross-country runner
>>> who sat at my lunch table
>>> in High School....car crash...1954.

Jimmy "Wah" Tiernan....my friend, in High School,
>>> Football & Hockey All-State...car crash...1959.

Cisco Houston......died of cancer......1961.

Freddy Herko, dancer...jumped out of a Greenwich Village
>>> window in 1963.

Anne Kepler...my girl...killed by smoke-poisoning while playing
>>> the flute at the Yonkers Children's Hospital
>>> during a fire set by a 16 year old arsonist...1965.

Frank....Frank O'Hara....hit by a car on Fire Island, 1966.

Woody Guthrie....dead of Huntington's Chorea in 1968.

Neal...Neal Cassady...died of exposure, sleeping all night
>>> in the rain by the RR tracks of Mexico...1969.

Franny Winston...just a girl...totalled her car on the
>>> Detroit-

> Ann Arbor Freeway, returning
> from the dentist...Sept. 1969.
>
> Jack...Jack Kerouac...died of drink & angry sicknesses...
> in 1969.
>
> My friends whose deaths have slowed my heart stay with me
> now.
>
> —Ted Berrigan

Like the previous poem, this one by Ted Berrigan has a surprisingly simple formal structure, being nothing more than a list of people who died and a brief statement about each one's death. Only the last line has any of the formal eloquence we associate with traditional poetry—and yet, despite that, it is an authentic, disarmingly moving elegy.

A Process for Recovering Fugitive Memories

1. Jot down a list of some of the places where you have lived.
2. Jot down a list of some of the jobs you've had. Include the weirder ones.
3. Jot down a list of old friends, people you don't see much of anymore.
4. Jot down two embarrassing things you've done and a lie you once told.
5. Jot down one triumph and two failures.
6. Jot down a list of remembered kisses.
7. Jot down the names of someone who hurt you, someone who helped you, and someone you admired.
8. Describe a piece of clothing you once loved, name a piece of music you still love, and two old movies you still remember.

Poem 7: Shards of Memory

Write a poem with the same structure as "How I Knew Harold." Begin each line with the phrase "Around 19—" or some variation on it. Plug in a few choice items from the above exercise, each of them sketched briefly with a few well-chosen details. But as other memories are triggered, get them down too, at least for the first draft. Make sure to jumble the chronology so that the memories don't move in a clear progression but jump back and forth. Make sure, too, that at least three of the items interconnect, if only tangentially. Perhaps one item can give a bit more of the portrait sketched in an earlier one. For example, when Harding says "I'd live with a man before marrying him," the subject is continued when she writes "I leave home to move in with Jack." Make sure, however, that the poem does not seem consciously organized in any sequential and obvious way—that it does not tell a single coherent story. Instead, take the memories in the order they come or organize the poem intuitively. Find an order that seems right to you, juggling items around to suit yourself. Make sure you hold to a chatty voice. In a poem like this, you do not want to get self-consciously eloquent or lyrical.

This kind of poem has the virtue of allowing inexperienced writers to write in a tradition closer to the prose sentence than to the poetic line. However, in "How I Knew Harold," the interesting result that Harding gets cannot be divorced from her ability to write a good, well-balanced, richly detailed English sentence. If someone had written either of the following items we would probably not continue reading:

> About 1991 from high school I remember how I would try to convince my teacher of negative numbers. Without the care to explain it she simply ignored it.

> Around 1987 Dad and I get ourselves into a wrestling type fight in which when we get into the front yard I flip him off and he embarrassedly tries his darnedest to put me back into the house. I really guess neither of us actually won that fight.

Both memories could have been sketched in engagingly had the authors spent time finding appropriate details and polishing their sentences. Remember that a well-polished sentence can still sound colloquial, casual and spontaneous. Revision and polishing do not mean that you must work for a higher level of diction or more eloquent phrasing. Sometimes you want a line or a whole poem to have a rough, unworked appearance. To make a sentence or poem seem unworked often takes hard work!

In "How I Knew Harold," the length of the items varies. Some are one or two lines long and others are more detailed and lengthy. Make some of your items only a sentence long, and others three or four times that length. But make sure none of them is longer than five lines long.

If your poem's formal resemblance to our model poem bothers you, try deleting some of the dates and placing a few others in the middle or at the end of the item. Another alternative is to leave out the dates completely. What you will be left with is a series of autobiographical vignettes about your life. You may wish to number the stanzas and call the piece something like "Fifteen Little Poems about My Life."

Poem 8: A List Poem

Write a poem based on "Those Who Died." It might be "Those I've Kissed," or "People I've Hurt," or "A Few of My Failures." Keep each item spare, but vary them enough that the poem never gets monotonous. End each item with a date if you wish, but in the final draft you may wish to leave out the dates altogether. You may wish to vary your lines more than Berrigan does, so that they do not all start with the name of a person. Here, for example, is the beginning of a poem called "The Ones I've Kissed":

> My mother, the first kiss, red cheek and rubbery nipple
>   and breast soft as my own,
> And my dad with his tickle-face prickle I'd wait for at dusk
> And Timmy Arno, smelling of mushroom and soap who
>   couldn't find my lips,
> and Mark Hampell. At 14, sweet Mark. His lips a bolt
>   through my belly, a shorted-out wire humming with
>   sparklers. I kept my eyes closed and cried afterwards—
> Then those awful dates with boys whose faces have
>   vanished. Laughter and sighs in the back seats of souped-
>   up Chevys and Hondas....

> —Cristy Matlock

A First Principle When working on these poems—or any other poems—remember that there is ultimately only one essential rule for writing: *it must be interesting to read!* Cross out anything that isn't interesting to read and replace it with something that is!

The Secret
of Writing

Understand that you can have in your writing no qualities which you do not honestly entertain in yourself. Understand that you cannot keep out of your writing the indication of the evil or shallowness you entertain in your self[.] If you love to have a servant stand behind your chair at dinner, it will appear in your writing—or if you possess a vile opinion of women, or if you grudge anything, or doubt immortality—these will appear by what you leave unsaid more than by what you say. There is no trick or cunning, no art or recipe, by which you can have in your writing what you do not possess in yourself.

—Walt Whitman
(Journal entry 1855-56)

5

Awful Poems

The Missing of You Hurts

O you who were there all the time
to show how much you truly cared,
so that I knew you'd evermore be true,
and gladden my heart like the sun-kissed clime

But left me like the tide that goes out
and we can never stop it or get it repaired,
You are the only one I care so much about
and yet where is to be found another like you

when I look within myself or even out?
I often cry thinking of you know who,
and your last goodbye
And yet it is indeed to me a huge question mark why

you left me here to feel this way
like I am dead inside
making it the one and only happy day
where I can see your sweet hazel eyes and face.

So I wish you would come back to me
and the two of us wander the beach, happy and free,
for you know I still carry you in my heart
no matter even if you did that day depart.

Had enough? One trouble with this love poem is that it could have been said more effectively in a sentence of ordinary prose. It is an example of telling us the feelings instead of showing us the scene that conveys the feelings. To make matters worse, the sentiments are expressed almost entirely in dull, commonplace language. "You truly cared," "you'd evermore be true," and "sun-kissed clime" are pretty pedestrian and awful attempts at poetic language.

And perhaps most damaging of all is the fact that so many of the clauses and sentences are awkwardly constructed. The title itself is written in garbled English. "When I look within myself or even out" is anything but graceful English. Awkward writing is awkward writing whether in prose or verse.

Avoiding Trite Language The author is using a language made up almost entirely of clichés—stock phrases and conventional tags that quickly convince a reader that the poet thinks superficially, has no intention of revealing real emotions and experiences, and has little ability to use language with either precision or originality. Trite expressions such as "You are the only one I care so much about," "gladdened my heart," "I am dead inside," "the one and only," and "I still carry you in my heart," will make this verse heavy going for the unfortunate reader. Remember, the writer's job is to wake us up, not put us to sleep!

Rhyme at Any Cost Another problem is the rhyme. For the sake of finding a rhyme word, the author is willing to say almost anything, however silly or nonsensical. The idea of getting the tide "repaired" is ridiculous. The word was only used so that our poet could have a rhyme with "cared." "Where is to be found another like you/ when I look within myself or even out" is another example of nonsense. What on earth could it mean to find another person like one's lost lover by looking inside oneself?

Abandoning all sense for the sake of a rhyme is a sure sign of a versifier who imagines that poetry is a lot of foolish nothings that sound pretty. If that's your ambition you would be better off becoming a political speech writer, where a talent for high-flown rhetoric, clichés, and pomposity might earn you a decent living. Rhyme used well can charm the reader, but good poets don't sacrifice real insight or graceful phrasing to come up with rhymes. Sloppily used, rhyme can be fatally destructive to a poet's intentions, for it makes serious feelings sound foolish and inauthentic.

Avoiding Archaic Words and Poetic Inversions The word "evermore," which the poet must have imagined made line three more poetic, is archaic and its use here renders the line so artificial that it destroys rather than enhances any impact the statement might have had. The word "clime" in line four is also archaic. The phrase "Within myself or even out" and the attempt at a poetic inversion of syntax (changing the normal order of words in a phrase) in the final line, "if you did that day depart," are similarly artificial and unintentionally comic in their attempts to sound poetic. Far from being more genuinely poetic, such phrases have just the opposite effect: they create bathos and insincerity where the poet wants genuine feeling and believable expression. Throughout, the poet has chosen an easy, soppy, prettified language of the sort that people (who don't read poetry) sometimes imagine is quintessentially poetic.

So another rule of thumb—and one of fundamental importance: *don't try to sound poetical! It will just end up making your poem sound silly.*

Sentimentality: Emotional Slither Self-pitying declarations of grief and gushy declarations of love will probably sound boring whether in verse or prose. The writer of our model poem is either unwilling or unable to tell us anything more interesting or true about the loss of his beloved or his emotional response to that loss than that he feels badly and wants her back. It is all generic, vague and superficial when what the reader wants is a believable voice creating believable portraits and scenes. How much more effective it would have been for the author to present us with a scene that conveyed his confusion and sorrow in such a way that we could see it and feel it for ourselves.

The less you talk *about* emotions in general terms, the better. The more you describe events that *convey* emotions, the more effective your writing will be. To say "When my sister told us she was gay it was a wrenching moment for all of us" is less effective than to say—as Deborah Harding has done in "How I Knew Harold"—"Around 1972 my sister tells me and my parents she's gay. Dad says it's unnatural and they start arguing. I keep quiet. Mom goes to the kitchen to make sundaes." That one word, "sundaes," eloquently conveys the mother's desperate and pathetic attempt to hold on to the illusion of innocence while the narrator's silence is a no less poignant indication of her state of shock and anguish. Having been given these details, we can sense the grief, distress and confusion of that moment for ourselves.

Honesty Sometimes poets are seduced by current fashion, conventional expectations, or their own language and inventiveness into asserting things which, although they may sound clever or provocative, they don't really believe. It is a danger to be guarded against. In the introduction to his *Selected Poems*, the American poet Robinson Jeffers wrote:

Another formative principle came to me from a phrase of
Nietzsche's: "The poets? The poets lie too much." I was
nineteen when the phrase stuck in my mind; a dozen years
passed before it worked effectively, and I decided not to tell
lies in verse. Not to feign any emotion that I did not feel; not
to pretend to believe in optimism or pessimism, or unre-
versible progress; not to say anything because it was popular,
or generally accepted, or fashionable in intellectual circles,
unless I myself believed it; and not to believe easily. These
negatives limit the field; I am not recommending them but
for my own occasions.

Here's another problematic poem for your inspection:

Attic Revelation

Minerva, anguished goddess of tormented years!
Before the darkened altar of my soul's quiescent solitude
twined my childish hand around the dusty magic
of that puissant knight.
But sharing treasure leads, I learned too late,
to slapping atavistic violence.
Grabbed from my trembling hands into her own,
resuscitated memories unflinched her eyes.
My aging face even today replays
the inarticulate response, and reddens still
from the unreconcilable and suicidal past.

The author is probably under the misapprehension that poets must
not say anything clearly for fear of having their poetic license revoked.
To describe the language of this piece of verse as vague, confused, and
utterly indecipherable would not be overstating the case. Confusion
and suspense are *not* the same thing. The more you confuse the read-
ers, the less likely they'll be to remain interested in what you are trying
to relate. Advised by a workshop of friendly critics to clarify the narra-
tive, the poet might have come up with a second version:

The Picture

She was as saddened as a boatless winter lake
when all of it had taken place.
The darkened attic of that ancient house
was where I played alone and where I found
that dusty, cobwebbed oil-painted portrait.
Maybe not the pirate's chest of gold
I had longed to find up there

41

in that mysterious upper room—my secret playground,
but something nonetheless distinctly magical,
this painted figure of a handsome man
with his old-fashioned mustache and brown eyes.
As swift as Hermes and excited as a frog in rain
I brought it down to show my mom
who at the time was in the kitchen
singing to herself and baking
those thick chocolate brownies that I used to love.
But nothing could prepare me
for the dreadful nightmare of the moment
when she saw what I had carried down.
She grabbed it from my trembling hands
and tore it up and slapped me
as hard as the slap of water must have crossed
the doomed Titanic's broken hull.
Astonished (I was innocent at twelve)
it's hardly a surprise that I didn't understand
that picture was a portrait of my dad
who had killed himself some three months
before I had been born. How was I to know
that I had done something wrong?
I cried myself to sleep that night,
and even now I still remember that sad time.

Although the author has managed to get his story told, more or less, it has been drained of all drama and immediacy. We get the fact that a boy has discovered an oil portrait of his father in the attic and is slapped by his distraught mother, but the scene never comes to life. It seems confused in its telling, filled with arbitrary figures of speech that add nothing, and awkwardly expressed.

Adjectivitis Notice that many of the nouns in both of these versions are preceded by an adjective—no doubt to add color and texture to the writing. The attic is darkened, the house ancient, the treasure cobwebbed, the painting dusty, and so on. There is nothing wrong with the occasional use of adjectives, but be careful of relying on them too heavily. Overused, they tend to weaken phrases rather than strengthening them.

Inappropriate Imagery Nor do the images seem particularly appropriate. Though a "boatless winter lake" might, in another context, effectively suggest isolation and sadness, nothing in this poem has anything to do with water or boats. The images of the Titanic and the frog in rain are similarly inapposite. Those images of water, boats, and frogs might be useful in a poem about a fishing village in the rainy season, or about a boy whose father was lost at sea, but here they are out of place.

The Misuse of Allusions and Mythology Inexperienced poets love exotic words and the Greek gods, imagining that such decorative elements add poetic luster to their writing. If you have nothing that genuinely requires the presence of Minerva or Hermes, do not drag them into your poems. Let those poor old retired gods rest in peace.

Clarity, Simplicity and Directness Had the poet been asked to write a new draft in half the words, sticking to the core of the story he wished to tell, and to tell it more straightforwardly, the poem would no doubt have improved. Had he been encouraged to tell his story in a way that would grab the reader's attention from the beginning, it would have helped considerably. The poem that follows tells the same story—the one buried beneath all the verbiage of the previous effort. It was written by one of America's outstanding poets, Stanley Kunitz. Notice with what dispatch and effectiveness the poet gets his story told, how well focused it is, how clear, simple, and moving:

The Portrait

My mother never forgave my father
for killing himself,
especially at such an awkward time
and in a public park,
that spring
when I was waiting to be born.
She locked his name
in her deepest cabinet
and would not let him out,
though I could hear him thumping.
When I came down from the attic
with the pastel portrait in my hand
of a long-lipped stranger
with a brave moustache
and deep brown level eyes,
she ripped it into shreds
without a single word
and slapped me hard.
In my sixty-fourth year
I can feel my cheek
still burning.

—Stanley Kunitz

Stanley Kunitz tells his story in fewer than half the number of words used in "The Picture." There is no attempt to fashion a "poetical" language or to obscure what is being said. The sentences are graceful, the details well observed, and the figurative language—that "deepest cabinet" of his mother's life in which the young boy could hear his father thumping—is perfectly appropriate to this domestic scene.

Notice how much information is packed into that first sentence. It is a suspenseful and intriguing line creating the sort of suspense that will keep a reader reading. The first sentence of "The Picture" also contains suspense, since the reader wants to know why the woman was sad and what it was that took place. But it is inelegantly said. The poet begins in the simple past tense and then inappropriately shifts to the past perfect tense in line two. And who is the "she" we are introduced to at the poem's beginning? That is never clarified, though by the time we reach the end we can pretty much guess that it's the boy's mother. Inexperienced writers love to hold back essential information, thinking that they are thereby increasing the suspense. But good writers are careful to utilize the element of suspense and avoid needlessly confusing the reader. Stanley Kunitz is straightforward, but that doesn't mean he tells us explicitly what his characters are feeling. Rather, he *shows* us what they are feeling by describing their actions. The narrator does not tell us that his mother was furious at seeing the portrait nor that at the age of sixty-four the incident still burns in his memory. The first he shows through her action of ripping the portrait into shreds and then slapping his face; the second he conveys by saying that he can feel his cheek still burning. In this poem you will find no sentimentality, no adjectivitis, no excessive language, no inappropriate figures of speech, no attempt to be labyrinthine or oblique, nothing to confuse or distract the reader. Instead, the story is told with control, economy, and admirable narrative skill.

Keeping the Ego Out of the Way Poetry that is self-aggrandizing usually has the same effect as people who are self-aggrandizing—an unpleasant one. Trying to impress with one's erudition or vocabulary or in any other way is likely to backfire. Here is an amusing poem by a poet well aware of the silliness of the inflated ego—a silliness he uses to delicious effect:

I Like My Own Poems

I like my own poems
best.
I quote from them

from time to time
saying, "A poet once said,"
and then follow up
with a line or two
from one of my *own* poems
appropriate to the event.
How those lines sing!
All that wisdom and beauty!
Why it tickles my ass
off its spine.
"Why those lines are mine!"
I say
and Jesus, what a bang
I get out of it.

I like the *ideas* in them,
my poems;
Ideas that hit home.
They *speak* to me.
I mean, I understand
what the hell
the damn poet's
talking about.
"Why I've been there,
the same thing," I shout,
and Christ! What a shot it is,
a shot.

And hey.
The words!
Whew!
I can hardly stand it.
Words sure do not fail
this guy, I say.
From some world
only he knows
he bangs the bong,
but I can feel it
in the wood,
in the wood of the word,
rising to its form
in the world.
"Now, you gotta be good
to do that!" I say
and damn! It just shakes
my heart,
you know!

                    —Jack Grapes

Exercise—Critiquing a Poem

Here is an early draft of a poem by a student learning his craft. It has many of the faults we discussed in the poems "The Missing of You Hurts," "Attic Revelation," and "The Picture." Read the poem critically and think about what is keeping it from being effective. What problems do you find with individual lines and phrases? Be as specific in your criticisms as you can be. Then follow the directions given below.

Tracks of the Wandering Mind

I want sometimes naught but to weep
As standing by the trestle deep
I long to follow that railroad train
To a realm of dream that's free of pain.
What an urge I have to stray somewhere
On a train that's bigger than a bear
which climbs up toward old mountain peaks
And watch the sea for days and weeks.
A train to some vast tropic isle
Where swaying beauty makes me smile.
But the trains of reality just skitter off
And my city home where pollution does cough
Doesn't let me see the pyramids
Or drink till dawn with memory's kids,
Or ride off to the Orient
To get away from this discontent.
But today something inside me went through a shift
And gave my spirits that needed lift,
And I bid adieu to my dreams of escape
while the train roared through like a ghostly shape.

1. Circle the archaic word in the opening line.
2. Circle a phrase in line two that seems artificial because it is inverted in a way that is unnatural to modern English.
3. What is silly about line six? Why do you think the poet wrote that line?
4. Circle two phrases near the end of the poem that seem stale.
5. Rewrite the first sentence (the first four lines) in graceful English.

Exercise—Creating Images and Scenes that Convey Emotions

Here are five statements that tell us what someone was feeling. Replace them with brief descriptions that convey rather than state the emotions. You will have to invent specific situations, five little scenic moments that a reader can visualize. For example, the phrase "I felt so happy" might be replaced with "I grinned despite myself and rushed to greet him."

1. She felt very sad.
2. That summer at camp he missed his mother.
3. The letter confused her.
4. He felt angry.
5. She begged him to stay.

Poem 9: A Rewrite

Go back to a poem you have already written or have been trying to write, one that you can now see has one or more of the failings that we have been discussing in this chapter—or other problems that you have become aware of. Rewrite the poem to get rid of its shortcomings. If you have to start from the beginning and simply discard the old version, that's okay. Sometimes just saving one or two lines or a good image or an excellent phrase—or nothing but the idea and starting from scratch—will be easier and more effective than repairing a poem with serious flaws. On the other hand, you might not feel that your poem needs so radical a re-visioning.

If you have not done so in the original version, be sure to present to your readers a vivid scene—a specific moment in time that tells your story for you.

6

The Art of Revision

In poetry everything is permitted.

With only this condition, of course:
You have to improve on the blank page.

—*Nicanor Parra*
(Translated by Miller Williams)

It's true enough that some poems come quickly and that it's possible to get lucky and write a real one, a good one, at a single inspired sitting. On the other hand, it is much more common for a serious and accomplished poet to work for days, weeks or years before feeling that a particular poem is finished. If there is any "secret" to writing, it is rewriting—a process that can be every bit as exciting as getting that first draft down on paper.

Writers who consider their poems done as soon as the first draft is finished probably won't develop as quickly as those who are able to separate the delicious first flush of creative excitement from the knowledge that a poem is perfected. If you don't yet have any desire to rewrite, you probably haven't been able yet to take a cold, critical look at your poems and see where they go limp. Rewriting entails an ability to look at one's own work critically—to decide what is working and what needs to be rethought and revised. If, like most writers, you cannot look at your poem with objectivity immediately upon finishing a draft, you would do well to put the poem aside for a day or two and then go back to it. The less emotionally attached you are to what you have written (though not necessarily to the material about which you're writing), the easier it will be to see it objectively.

You will probably agree that "Tracks of the Wandering Mind," the poem you were asked to critique in the previous chapter, is sorely in need of revision. Here it is again:

Tracks of the Wandering Mind

I want sometimes naught but to weep
As standing by the trestle deep
I long to follow that railroad train
To a realm of dream that's free of pain.
What an urge I have to stray somewhere
On a train that's bigger than a bear
which climbs up toward old mountain peaks
And watch the sea for days and weeks.
A train to some vast tropic isle
Where swaying beauty makes me smile.
But the trains of reality just skitter off
And my city home where pollution does cough
Doesn't let me see the pyramids
Or drink till dawn with memory's kids,
Or ride off to the Orient
To get away from this discontent.
But today something inside me went through a shift
And gave my spirits that needed lift,
And I bid adieu to my dreams of escape
while the train roared through like a ghostly shape.

As we have already suggested, the phrase "naught but to weep" in the first line is a mistake, indicating to the reader that the author is trying to sound poetic instead of trying to create music out of our real language. In the second line, "trestle deep" was probably stuck in only because the author needed a rhyme with "weep." The inverted syntax—placing the adjective "deep" after the noun—probably sounded "poetic" to the original author, though to a reader it simply sounds artificial, "poetic" in the worst sense. That forced rhyme at the very beginning of the poem raises the question of whether or not we should look for better rhymes in the next draft or abandon end-rhyme altogether. A decision must be made early on in the revision: Is one going to work with *rhymed couplets* (two successive lines that rhyme), as in the first draft, with some other verse form, or with no conventional form at all?

Perhaps a particular poem you are working on seems to cry out for a formal structure. On the other hand, having tried rhyming with little success in a first draft, you might make an entirely different decision and rewrite it without rhyme. Let's try that, concentrating on what the poem really wants to say and how we can best say it.

Let's try a simple rewrite of that first sentence, using the real language of our time. We'll refrain from telling the reader that we want to weep, refrain from having the narrator standing by the trestle (a detail hardly realistic), and get rid of the platitudinous and generalized fourth line. Our revision might read something like this:

> When the Amtrak hoots by in the morning
> I sometimes want to be on it, heading to Tucson,
> Austin, Oshkosh—anywhere but here in this
> awful life I've been leading...

Well, that's going in a more interesting direction already. For one thing, we've gotten in some specific details and set a tone that's less soppy and more convincing. Naming the train the Amtrak makes it specific and gives it some color. Then too, naming those cities makes the train more real. "Hoots" also helps a bit. On the other hand, perhaps "here in this awful life" is a bit vague. And the phrase "I sometimes want to be on it," might need to be punched up, made more emotionally graphic. Perhaps placing the speaker in a specific location will help:

> When I hear the Amtrak hoot by at 6:34 in the morning
> I groan, still half asleep, and draw the sheet over my head,
> and dream of what life might be like in Tucson, Austin,
> Oshkosh—anywhere but here in this life with its bitter
> coffee, and dusty streets and measly paychecks. Wherever
> that train is going I want to go too!

Not bad—but too many words. We've lost some of the jaunty rhythm we just had. Here's another stab at it:

> When the Amtrak hoots by at 6:34 I groan,
> half-asleep, drawing the sheet over my head
> in this city of dusty streets and lousy paychecks
> and wish I was anywhere else—Tucson, Austin,
> Oshkosh. Wherever that Amtrak is going
> I want to be on it!

Better. But why mention Amtrak twice? Doesn't that seem redundant? And "half-asleep" might be assumed from the time of day and the sheet being pulled over the head. Let's keep at it:

> When the 6:34 hoots by I groan,
> drawing the sheet over my head,
> and wish I was elsewhere—Tucson,
> Austin, Oshkosh. Wherever that Am-
> trak is going I want to go too!

50

Let's think about that "hoot" for a moment. It sets up a good sound-echo with "Tucson" and "too." But maybe we can expand on it a bit to get that train more vivid for the reader. Also, that coffee from the earlier draft seemed like a good move and might be worth putting back in:

> When I hear the 6:34 hooting and clacking,
> panting over the trestles like ~~an excited~~ a frantic
> lover, I roll ~~on~~ to my other side, groan,
> pull the sheet over my head—and wish
> I was snuggled in one of her sleepers:
> Carson City, Austin, Oshkosh...wherever
> that Amtrak is going I want to go too!
> To hell with ~~the~~ my bitter coffee at 7,
> the bloodthirsty paper, the dusty streets
> and the filthy traffic my life has become...
> To hell with my landlord, my boss,
> my measly and laughable paycheck:
> I want to head for the ~~Painted~~ Desert, [white-
> water country,] the Great Lakes, the Rockies....

Well, the "snuggled inside one of her sleepers" might justify that image of the train panting like an excited lover—though it could easily prove a false lead, a dead end. Or we can follow its lead and eroticize the poem's imagery more: after all it's about a fantasy while lying in bed! The opening still seems a bit weak, a bit too passive. Perhaps it's partially the fault of that "I hear the..." construction. That lovemaking image should at least give some pace and energy to the opening. "Carson City" seems a good move, the name has nice character, nice color, though "the filthy traffic my life has become" might be a bit much. But the voice is beginning to emerge now. Let's try it again:

> When the 6:34 hoots up its head of steam
> in the morning, screaming over the trestles...
> panting like somebody's lover,
> I roll over groaning, pull the sheet
> over my head and wish
> I were snuggled inside her—
> Carson City, Austin, Oshkosh.... To hell
> with my coffee at 7, the bloodthirsty
> morning *Gazette*, the godawful 8 am traffic.
> I want to head for the Desert, whitewater
> country, Tucson, Oshkosh—
> Wherever that Amtrak is going I want to be on her!

The line break after "to hell" seems to be right, since it makes Hell one more place the narrator is willing to go (like Carson City, Austin and Oshkosh) until you move to the next line where its real meaning becomes clear. It presents a nice little surprise there.

At this point it would probably be a good idea for the poet, who now has some sense of the poem's voice and movement, to move on to the next section. It's not that these opening lines have been perfected, but they are stable enough to let us move forward. Where does the poem go from here? That's up to the individual poet. No two people will compose the same poem. One might leave the piece just as it is and say: yes, that's it, that's the whole poem. Another might find that it's only beginning, and think of these lines as the opening section of a relatively long poem, while another might find it needs just one or two touches more, and resolve to bring the whole thing home within another half dozen lines.

If we look back at the first lines of that first draft, the one done in rhymed couplets, it should now be easy to see how banal and simple-minded they were. Although the rewriting might still be at an early stage, it should be clear that it is turning this into a real poem—full of passion, complexity, wit and the emotional energy that will keep a reader engaged. The polishing will take place after all the pieces of the puzzle are in place.

Rewriting in this case did not mean fiddling with a word or two here and there, but redrafting the poem from scratch, that is, actually *finding* the poem that was buried under that first ineffectual version. It is an act of discovery in which we find the language and the meaning at the same time.

Remember that this is simply one person's rewrite. You might decide that you want a loftier, more eloquent tone, that slang and casual phrases don't fit the mood that you want to establish for the piece. Or perhaps you want the movement to be slow and meditative, or you want to maintain the rhymed couplets, or some other more intricate and demanding rhyme pattern for the poem. Or perhaps you want a long-lined poem to emerge, or one that gets told in half the number of lines, or one intense with language, or lyrical and quiet. There is no one right way to write or rewrite a poem!

A Guided Rewriting Exercise

If you are not in the habit of doing extensive rewriting and revising, the following process might be a revelation for you. Take out one of your recent poems—one that is not yet as perfect as you'd like it to be—and follow these directions:

Read your poem over to yourself as objectively as you can. Then underline one passage, line or phrase that seems very good to you. Now circle a line, phrase or section that seems unsuccessful. Perhaps it is too commonplace, or it's awkwardly stated, or the word choices seem dull or inaccurate. Perhaps there is simply no voice behind the passage, or a voice that is not consistent with the tone you had been trying for. Maybe it seems a bit muddled or overly complex and you sense that readers would probably not understand what you're talking about. Maybe it's corny and simple-minded, or you see that you haven't really said what you wanted to. It's not always necessary to analyze the reason why a piece of writing doesn't work: just recognizing that it's not effective is all you need to get you started.

Now that you've broken the ice, try finding other passages that could be improved. Once you begin to get critical, you are likely to uncover other weak spots that you did not notice when you first started this process. Circle them, too.

Sometimes poets find that their real poem starts somewhere other than where their most recent draft began and the material in the first few lines is either unnecessary or better used elsewhere in the poem. Sometimes the most effective ending is several lines—or stanzas—earlier than the poem's current ending.

Rewriting can be facilitated by comments from others. One often can't see the problems in one's own poem, the places where it goes dry or loses its voice or becomes muddied or false. If you haven't done so yet, this might be the time to approach friends or family members whose judgment you trust, and ask them if they'd be willing to look at a poem and give you suggestions for improving it.

An Exercise in Rewriting Prose

If rewriting poetry is difficult for you, the habit of perfection might be easier to engender in prose, a form with which you are likely to be more familiar. Earlier, we suggested revising and polishing your short prose poem. An even simpler exercise would be to write a brief letter to the editor of your local newspaper on a subject that's currently newsworthy—one that you're passionately interested in. Revise and polish the letter until it's beautifully expressed—clear, persuasive, and graceful. Remember, letters to the editor are usually fewer than 200 words in length. Since newspapers want to publish letters that are timely, you will have to get it to the newspaper relatively quickly. Nonetheless, send it out only after several rewrites and only after you've polished it to such a gloss it all but squeaks.

The process of revising a straightforward, persuasive letter should then allow you to begin using the same process with your poetry. It is a safe bet that the more you are willing and able to revise your poems, the more accomplished a poet you will become.

Music and Metaphor

7

After-Glow:
The Interior Music:

After-Glow

The dusk of evening comes on. Earlier a little rain
had fallen. You open a drawer and find inside
the man's photograph, knowing he has only two years
to live. He doesn't know this, of course,
that's why he can mug for the camera.
How could he know what's taking root in his head
at that moment? If one looks to the right
through boughs and tree trunks, there can be seen
crimson patches of the after-glow. No shadows, no
half-shadows. It is still and damp....
The man goes on mugging. I put the picture back
in its place along with the others and give
my attention instead to the after-glow along the far ridge,
light golden on the roses in the garden.
Then, I can't help myself, I glance once more
at the picture. The wink, the broad smile,
the jaunty slant of the cigarette.

—Raymond Carver

In this chapter, rather than talk about a poem's meaning or
the process that transforms memory into poetry, we will concentrate on
the music that a poem creates. For whatever else poetry may be, like all
art it "aspires towards the condition of music," as Walter Pater once
suggested. In a more literal sense, music—a stimulating, moving or
pleasing pattern of sounds—is at the very heart of what we mean by the
word "poetry."

One of the main musical devices of all English poetry, but particularly important in an age which has largely abandoned the earlier convention of end-rhyme, is *internal rhyme*, a device used to good effect in "After-Glow." The poems of Raymond Carver usually have a "prosy" feel to them and an untrained reader going through this poem without much consciousness of the musical qualities of the language might well wonder what makes this a poem rather than a piece of prose broken into verse lines. If the reader knew that Carver had been one of America's finest contemporary short story writers, the impression that this is really prose might well be reinforced. But Raymond Carver was as serious a poet as he was a fiction writer—and his poetic ear was a fine and well-trained one. Knowing that, it will be worth our while to look more closely at this poem's internal rhymes so that we can appreciate the rich orchestration of sounds in this poem that on the surface seems so colloquial and prosy.

Assonance In the first two lines we find a great deal of sound repetition. For example, in line one, *dusk, of* and *comes* have the same vowel sound. In line two we have the same sort of vowel repetition in *fallen* and *drawer*—an identical "awe" sound, a sound that is repeated once more two lines further in *course*. In like manner, the last two words of that line, *find* and *inside*, share that long *i* sound. If you trace the long *o* sound through the poem, you'll find it cropping up a dozen times, beginning with *open, photograph,* and *knowing* in lines two and three, and ending with *golden* and *roses* in the fourth line from last. This technique of forming a partial rhyme by using identical vowel sounds is called *assonance* and is one of the most important musical devices in English language poetry.

Repetition All those *o* sounds reinforce what is, arguably, the central word in this poem, *know*; for the poem is about a man who is looking at a photograph of someone who does not know he is going to die soon. (In light of the author's history, it is likely that it's a picture of himself.) The word appears, in one form or another, three times in the poem—after which come two uses of its homonym: *no*. The technical name for the repetition of words or phrases in a poem is *repetend*.

Alliteration The repetition of consonant sounds also plays an important role in the internal music of poetry. The phrase "I put the picture back in its place" contains three words that begin with the letter *p* and one that begins with a *b*, a letter that has a very similar sound. The phrase "The man goes on mugging" takes some of its grace from the repeated *m* sounds, just as the final phrase, "slant of the cigarette" takes some of its grace from the repeated *s* and *t* sounds. *Alliteration* is the repetition of the initial consonant sound in words or syllables. More loosely we can say it is the repetition, for musical effect, of any consonant sound in words.

These lines from Corrine Hales' "Power" have many alliterative *b*'s and *d*'s, *g*'s and *w*'s:

> Hardly daring to breathe, I waited
> Belly-down with my brother
> In a dry ditch
> Watching through the green thickness
> of grass and willows.

While reading them aloud you probably also became aware of the assonant rhyme made of *breathe* and *green*. The *ing* of *daring* also partakes of a similar sound.

Rich Consonance In "After-Glow" there is another technique of internal rhyme that is more rare but useful to know. The word *root* in line six and *right* at the end of line seven both begin and end with the same consonant sounds but have a differing vowel sound between them. This device is known as *rich* or *full consonance*. Other rich or full consonant rhymes with *root* and *right* would be *rat*, *rate*, *wrote*, and *rout*.

Partial Consonance A more common sound device than rich consonance is *partial consonance*, more generally just called *consonance* and sometimes called *terminal alliteration*. It denotes the identity of the final consonant sound in two or more words. In the first line of "After-Glow," the words *fallen* and *open* share the same *en* sound at the end. In the line "light golden on the roses in the garden," the words *golden* and *garden* are also an example of partial consonance because of their final *en* sound. Those two words are also highly alliterative, sharing an initial *g* followed by a *d* at the end of that syllable. The fact that there is an *l* in the middle of one word and an *r* in the middle of the other keeps it from being an example of rich consonance. The music of that line is, of course, further enriched by the assonance of *golden* and *roses*.

Emily Dickinson often used partial consonance instead of full end-rhymes. Note the consonant rhymes in lines two and four and in six and eight in the poem below:

> There is a pain—so utter—
> It swallows substance up—
> Then covers the Abyss with Trance—

> So Memory can step
> Around—across—upon it—
> As one within a Swoon—
> Goes safely—where an open eye—
> would drop Him—Bone by Bone.
>   —Emily Dickinson

Up and *step* are examples of partial consonance; so too are *swoon* and *bone*. But there is a good deal more consonance in this brief poem. Look at all the words that end in the *n* sound: *pain, upon, one, within, swoon, open,* and *bone*. In the first three lines assonance can be heard in the short *u* sound that appears in *utter, substance, covers,* and *up*.

If you are inclined to think that such repetitions of vowel and consonant sounds are inevitable, given that there are a limited number of sounds in the English language, you are quite right. Any passage of ordinary prose will also exhibit these characteristics. But because poets tend to make conscious use of these devices for musical effects, you will find such repetitions of vowel and consonant sounds considerably more frequent in poetry than in prose. Often when a passage from a poem sounds lovely to your ear, it is precisely because of these devices we have been discussing. These repetitions of sound tie the phrases together musically and create a pleasure more subtle than, but similar to, that which we take in ordinary end-rhyme.

We should not leave Dickinson's poem without noting its brilliantly incisive and idiosyncratic perceptions about the nature of intense pain. Dickinson was a master of the poem that attempts to define or delineate—with precision and acuity—particular states of consciousness.

Anaphora Another musical and rhetorical device, one that is closely related to repetend, is anaphora (pronounced a-na´-phor-a), which designates the repetition of the opening word or phrase in several successive lines. It was a favorite device of Walt Whitman's, used extensively in his long lists. The following passage from his greatest poem, "Song of Myself," is typical of the power that can be achieved by this technique:

> Where the humming-bird shimmers, where the neck of the
>   long-lived swan is curving and winding,
> Where the laughing-gull scoots by the shore, where she
>   laughs her near-human laugh,
> Where bee-hives range on a gray bench in the garden half
>   hid by the high weeds,
> Where band-neck'd partridges roost in a ring on the
>   ground with their heads out,

> Where burial coaches enter the arch'd gates of a cemetery,
> Where winter wolves bark amid wastes of snow and
>   icicled trees,
> Where the yellow-crown'd heron comes to the edge of the
>   marsh at night and feeds upon small crabs,
> Where the splash of swimmers and divers cools the warm
>   noon,
> Where the katy-did works her chromatic reed on the walnut-
>   tree over the well...

Beginning each clause with the word *where* gives tremendous thrust to the lines, impelling them forward with great energy. As you should be able to see for yourself at this point, Whitman's lines are also extraordinarily musical because of the techniques of assonance and alliteration, the repetition of vowel and consonant sounds. For one example among many, notice the *bird/curving* assonance in the first two lines and the alliterative *w* sound in "Where winter wolves bark amid wastes of snow." If you recite this Whitman passage aloud you will hear the rich music created by those repeated sounds.

Diction and Sentence Grace These techniques are not the only means by which a poet produces musical lines and sentences. In English there are harsh sounds and softer ones, phrases that seem quick and energetic and others that are slow, deliberate, meditative or mournful, while still others might seem to have a humorous and playful lilt. Every phrase has its own peculiar tone and pace, an effect that is made up of the specific words and their sounds combined. Imagine if Carver had opened his poem this way:

> As the somberness of evening takes place
> and after it had been raining for a while
> but now the rain had stopped,
> you open up a drawer in which, behold,
> you find the photograph there of a man and that man
> you know has, alas, got only two more years in which to live.

This writing is dreadfully awkward, punctuated by distracting rhetorical mannerisms and gives the reader none of the feeling that Carver is able to establish at the beginning of "After-Glow." One is likely not to finish reading a poem that begins with such poorly made phrases. One immediately distrusts the author's literacy and, fairly or not, one is less apt to take his remarks seriously. The poor writing simply gets in the way of what is being said and with any pleasure we might take in how it is being said.

To some extent, we are talking about nothing more than the ability to shape phrases and sentences gracefully and well. Serious poets are concerned with every syllable they set to paper. They will search for just the right word or phrase, rewriting their lines over and over until they have just the sound they are after. They know that the right sound combination will help establish a particular voice, or tone, or pace, or shade of meaning. Perhaps the line you are working on calls for a particularly harsh or jarring sound, or a sense of urgency, or a sense of quiet resolution. Perhaps it is a particular word that you need with just the right connotation, or the right number of syllables, or a word that has an accented syllable in just the right place for the rhythm you're after.

Both a dictionary and a good thesaurus are handy tools for writers. A thesaurus is not used for finding exotic synonyms, words that you imagine will make your writing sound more eloquent and learned, but to remind you of the whole spectrum of common words that have the meaning you're looking for. A good rule of thumb is never to use a word that you're proud of. If you're not certain of a word's connotations or precise usage, you are better off avoiding it until it is more familiar. Two excellent thesauruses are *Sisson's Synonyms* by A.F. Sisson and *The Synonym Finder* by J.I. Rodale.

An Exercise in Recognizing Alliteration and Internal Rhyme

Go through the rest of the Whitman passage finding the alliteration and assonance. Then go back to "Power" and "The Tooth Fairy" and find the internal rhymes in those poems created by these same devices.

An Exercise in Describing Scenes and Brief Encounters

Whitman habitually kept a notebook with him, and we can trace the inception of many of his poems and prose writings to those notebook entries. Keep your notebook with you for a week or two and write down brief descriptions of anything that catches your eye—or heart—in the manner of Whitman's list of birds, animals, and events. Describe various objects and creatures around your house, yard, street, and/or neighborhood, trying to hold each to no more than two or three lines.

Make your descriptions as accurate and richly evocative as you can without muddying them with excessive language. Try to keep from getting too adjectival, too flowery, too rhetorical. Rather, make your descriptions as concrete as possible. Use sensory detail: sights, sounds, smells, and textures. Don't get lazy and generalize. Imagine, for example, if Whitman had written:

> Where people go into cemeteries
> Where animals cry out during the winter

instead of the two magnificent lines from the passage quoted above:

> Where burial coaches enter the arch'd gates of a
> cemetery,
> Where winter wolves bark amid wastes of snow and
> icicled trees...

In his version, the reader can almost hear wolves barking and see those icicled trees and wastes of snow. How much more vivid such pictures are in the mind than those produced by that vague, generalized language.

If you look again at the Whitman passage, you will observe how often the animal or object is described in two segments: the beehives are on a gray bench in the garden *and* they are half hid by the high weeds; the partridges roost in a ring *and* their heads are out; the heron comes to the edge of the marsh *and* feeds upon crabs. Try the same technique with some of your sentences. Moreover—and no less important—each item of the Whitman passage is a genuine observation: the product of having looked, seen and recorded. However simple that might seem in the abstract, it is not quite so easy in practice. We are usually too fast asleep to notice our environment with accuracy. But such careful observation is a habit of ultimate use to a writer—one well worth nurturing. If in looking about you this week you notice things that you have never taken note of before, good! That too, is part of the writer's craft.

Try not to be too judgmental in your choice of subjects. A tiny bug well observed, an object that you've had for years, an old pair of shoes that should have been thrown out long ago but that you still love, the bit of dying shrubbery outside your window, dust particles suspended in a ray of light, a bicycle leaning in the shadows against a wall, a patch of wild flowers, or broken glass, or scattered leaves—all are fit subjects. Cultivate a taste for the homely, the commonplace, the familiar. Make sure that you use assonance and alliteration. But use alliteration moderately. Too much of it will make a passage sound labored and self-conscious.

It is possible that you will find that some of the descriptions you have written, no matter how short, stand by themselves as complete poems. Here is a two-line poem by Whitman: a description followed by an observation that expands the description into a large perception about reality:

> I last winter observed the Snow on a spree with the north
>   west wind;
> And it put me out of conceit of fences and imaginary lines.—

If you analyze these two lines closely you will find both alliteration and a surprising amount of internal rhyme—some of it ordinary rhyme and some of it assonant rhyme.

Poem 10: An Anaphoric List Poem

As for the other brief descriptions that you have gathered, the ones that do not stand up as poems by themselves, try connecting several into a longer poem, employing the device of anaphora. If all those scenes are located in one physical area, you might want to use the word "where," to begin each new item, as Whitman does. Or you might start each line with something like "I see the..." or "And here is..." or "How seldom I see..." and then go on with your list of descriptions. Whitman ends one list with "All these I feel or am." In another section he ends a list with "All this I swallow, it tastes good, I like it well, it becomes mine." You might want to use a repetitive phrase to begin two-thirds of the lines rather than every one of them in order to give the poem more variety and make its language less predictable. Other anaphoric poems in this book include Jack Marshall's "Forced Entry," and the passages from Harold Norse's "In November," Aimé Césaire's "Notebooks of a Return to the Native Land," and Christopher Smart's "Jubilate Agno." You may wish to look at those poems for additional models.

Once your descriptive lines are together in a single poem, do whatever rewriting is necessary to make it all cohere both logically and musically. Use as much internal music as you can without the poem sounding cluttered, artificial or silly. Also try for those other essential qualities of poetry—precision, emotion, grace and honesty. Whatever you do, don't get "poetic" or wordy. Keep your phrases free from decorative or artificial language. Your job is to convince us and move us—not to impress us.

63

8

Lonely as a Leftover Thumb:
Figure and Image

Girl in the Doorway

She is twelve now, the door to her room
closed, telephone cord trailing the hallway
in tight curls. I stand at the dryer, listening
through the thin wall between us, her voice
rising and falling as she describes her new life.
Static flies in brief blue stars from her socks,
her hairbrush in the morning. Her silver braces
shine inside the velvet case of her mouth.
Her grades rise and fall, her friends call
or they don't, her dog chews her new shoes
to a canvas pulp. Some days she opens her door
and musk rises from the long crease in her bed,
fills the dim hall. She grabs a denim coat
and drags the floor. Dust swirls in gold eddies
behind her. She walks through the house, a goddess,
each window pulsing with summer. Outside,
the boys wait for her teeth to straighten.
They have a vibrant patience.
When she steps onto the front porch, sun shimmies
through the tips of her hair, the V of her legs,
fans out like wings under her arms
as she raises them and waves. Goodbye, Goodbye.
Then she turns to go, folds up
all that light in her arms like a blanket
and takes it with her.

      —Dorianne Laux

Figurative Language   Like many other fine contemporary poems, "Girl in the Doorway" takes a good part of its power from its rich and imaginative use of figures of speech. The expression "tight curls," which the poet uses to describe the phone cord, also evokes the young girl herself, since "tight curls" is a phrase more commonly heard in reference to hair than to telephone cords. It is an example of the complex use of *imagistic language* which works on both a conscious, explicit level and on a level that is subconscious and implicit. *Ambiguity* is the word usually used for this technique of using a word or phrase so that it has multiple meanings or implications. Ambiguity is an important aspect of language and an important device in poetry.

The "thin wall" between the mother and daughter is at once the literal wall between them and the wall of non-communication that adolescents so commonly erect between themselves and their parents—that is to say, it is a *metaphoric* wall as well as a literal one. A *metaphor* is a comparison that does not state that it is a comparison. To say there is a wall between two people is a way of saying there is such a lack of communication between them it is *as if* there were a wall between them. When the poet says "She walks through the house, a goddess," the use of *goddess* is metaphoric. The reader knows that she means the young girl walks *like* a goddess—with the beauty, poise and self-assurance that a goddess would display.

The phrase "her voice rising and falling as she describes her new life," is also richly evocative, the "rising and falling" suggesting the volatile moods of a typical twelve-year-old. And, of course, seen in a larger perspective, that is precisely what the excitation of a young woman's incessant phone calls are, manifestations of her need to describe her new life. This is a girl at puberty, a child turning into a young woman, and the telephone frenzy of her life at this age bears witness to that transformation. The "rising and falling" will be repeated a few lines later with reference to her grades, signaling the mother's sardonic and exasperated humor.

How interesting and imaginative to use the static electricity from her socks and hairbrush to allude to the "sparkling" nature of her youthful energy, the constant excitation of her spirit. Since the narrator is standing at the dryer, the static electricity coming from her daughter's socks is a realistic detail; nonetheless, the description of the girl surrounded by stars makes her visually into a goddess, an image that becomes explicit only later in the poem. And yet those stars at her feet and in her hair are also a kind of "static," a word that connotes interference, bad communication, trouble. "Don't give me any static," we say idiomatically. It's also a word that one thinks of in terms of phones, isn't it? The word, as used in this poem, is richly ambiguous. That doesn't mean it's unclear, but that it contains a complex of meanings.

"Her silver braces shine inside the velvet case of her mouth" is a strikingly unusual and effective image. The mouth is seen metaphorically as a "velvet case" which allows the reader to see those braces as expensive silver jewelry being exhibited. From a parent's point of view, given their cost, that's just what the child's braces are! The narrator-parent, with some exasperation, then thinks of her daughter's grades rising and falling, the phone calls she waits for expectantly, and her dog "chewing her new shoes to a canvas pulp." At this point it is worthwhile to note the objects that the poet has chosen to use to characterize the daughter: a phone in a room with the door closed, socks, a hairbrush, braces, erratic grades, equally erratic friends, a dog, and new shoes in ruin. They are well-chosen items, ones that are perfectly representative of the life of an adolescent American girl. Indeed, except for the boys—who are about to enter the poem—they are the central facts of her life.

The musk rising "from the long crease in her bed" is again well imagined—at once erotic, adolescent, and a way of somewhat humorously characterizing the disheveled condition in which the narrator's daughter leaves her room.

The denim coat dragging the floor again characterizes the girl—but here too there is that underlying suggestion of the goddess, this time with the train of her gown sweeping the ground behind her. The dust that "swirls in gold eddies behind her" is another image that both characterizes a typical teenage girl with her careless and sloppy habits and sets the stage for, or *foreshadows*, the figure of the next line, the explicit image of her as a goddess.

When the narrator tells us that each window is "pulsing with summer," it is surely that young, vibrant girl to whom that phrase refers, as much as it does to the heat of the day. It is also, certainly, the young boys to whom that pulsing alludes, those boys who "wait for her teeth to straighten." So that simple phrase becomes rich with implication. And how right that "vibrant patience" is in the phrase that follows.

Outside, about to leave, the sun shimmering through her hair and the V of her legs, the daughter raises her hand to wave goodbye, and the light "fans out like wings under her arms." Here the light has not been turned into wings but is explicitly compared to wings. We call this kind of explicit comparison a *simile*. Had it been a metaphor, the poet would have said that the light *was* wings fanning out under her arms.

The image of the wings is an effective and meaningful one because the reader understands that she is flying off into her own life. She "folds up/ all that light in her arms like a blanket/ and takes it with her." Folding the light *like* a blanket is another simile. It is a stunning conclusion, the young goddess waving goodbye to her mother and taking all of her light with her.

How much color and light there is in this poem: blue stars, silver braces, gold eddies, until at last, outdoors, she—and the poem—are bathed in sunlight. But there are also textures and smells in the poem— velvet and musk. Note as well how active are the poem's verbs: the cord *trails*, static *flies*, her braces *shine*, dust *swirls*, the window *pulses*, the sun *shimmies* and *fans out*. In all, the language is rich, active, specific, precise, evocative. It is this sort of language from which powerful poetry is made.

The Poem's Internal Rhyme If you have read the previous chapter, you were probably paying more attention than usual to the internal music of the poem. If so, you will have noticed that the rich music of "Girl in the Doorway" depends to a large extent on an abundance of carefully used internal rhymes—assonance and alliterative sound patterns. In the first half of the poem we have the assonance of *door, cord, hall, morning, hall, wall, falling, fall,* and *call*. There are numerous assonant rhymes based on the long *i* sound in *dryer, rising, describes, flies, shine,* etc. Notice the alliterative *c*'s in: "her room/ closed, telephone cord trailing the hallway/ in tight curls"; and the alliterative *s*'s and *b*'s in the line, "Static flies in brief blue stars from her socks." It would be worthwhile to look through the poem and pick out as many of those sound echoes as you can, for it is in large measure just such repetitions of sound that make this charming poem so musical.

Here is another engaging contemporary poem that is filled with effectively used figures of speech:

I Went to the Movies Hoping Just Once The Monster Got the Girl

He was as hungry for love as I. He lay in his cave
or castle longing for the doctor's lovely nurse,
the archeologist's terrific assistant while I hid
in my bedroom, acne lighting up the gloom like
a stoplight, wondering if anybody anywhere would
ever marry me.

I was hardly able to stay in my seat as the possibilities
were whittled away; her laughter at his clumsy gifts,

her terror at his dumbness and rage, his final realization
synapses lazy as fly balls connecting at last as he
stands in the rain peering through her bedroom window
she in chiffon and dainty slingbacks he looking at
his butcher shop hands knowing he could never unsnap
a bra

and in comes Jock Mahoney or Steve Cochran and takes
everything off in a wink and she kisses him over
and over, wants to kiss him has been waiting to kiss
him while the monster feels his own lips big as eels
or can't find them at all or finds four.

I almost shouted into the dark that life with Jock
or Steve was almost something to be feared. Couldn't
she see herself in a year or two dying at a barbecue,
another profile nobody with his tongue in her ear?
Wouldn't she regret that she had not chosen to stay
with someone whose adoration was as gigantic as
his feet?

I went to the movies hoping that just once somebody
would see beneath the scales and stitches to the huge
borrowed heart and choose it, but each time Blob
was dissolved, Ogre subdued, Ratman trapped, Giant
Leech dislodged forever and each time Sweater Girl
ran sobbing into those predictable rolled up sleeves
I started to cry too, afraid for myself, lonely as
a leftover thumb.

"What's the matter with him?" the cheerleaders asked
the high scorers as they filed out.

"Nothing. He's weird, that's all."

—Ronald Koertge

Koertge's poem utilizes a number of original and amusing *tropes*, or figures of speech. Since the narrator of the poem wanted to be invisible by hiding in his room, the idea of his acne "lighting up the gloom like a stoplight" is at once funny, sad and psychologically evocative. Magnified by his self-consciousness, his pimples glow red in the dark, and act, in effect, as a stoplight to his social life. That pimples, no matter how red and shiny, can light up the gloom "like a stoplight" is pure *hyperbole*—that is to say, conscious exaggeration for effect. Saying pimples are like a stoplight is, of course, a simile—one of Ronald Koertge's typically outrageous ones. "Synapses lazy as fly balls" is another simile (similes usually contain the word "like" or "as"). Since the narrator of the poem is remembering his adolescence, an image drawn from baseball is an especially appropriate one. The word "lazy" is also a perfect choice. To call a synapse or a fly ball "lazy" is an example of *personification*, projecting a human characteristic onto an inanimate object.

"Lips big as eels" is another unusual simile, giving us a sense not only of their enormous size, but of a slimy and unappealing texture. A simile such as "someone whose adoration was as gigantic as his feet" seems marvelously right. "Lonely as a leftover thumb" is another strikingly appropriate simile, reminding us of film monsters put together from spare body parts. It suggests the notion of being "all thumbs" while associating the separation of the thumb from the other fingers (and an extra thumb surely even more alienated yet) with the loneliness of the poor creature whom the narrator so wants to see win the girl.

The metaphoric phrase "butcher-shop hands" makes us imagine fat, bulky, insensitive hands that could easily be employed in meat-hacking slaughter.

The phrase "high scorers" near the end of the poem is another example of ambiguity, a device that, like metaphor, is at the very heart (metaphorically speaking!) of poetic language. "High scorers" means both those who are successful athletes—that is, those who score a lot of points in basketball or football games—and those men who are frequently successful at getting dates and/or sex, those who "score" with women. The ambiguity, then, elegantly serves to characterize the other boys as both jocks and studs. Keep in mind that when used effectively in poetry, this sort of ambiguity does not lead to vagueness or confusion, but to an enrichment of the meaning.

Metaphor and Common Language The word *stud* that was used a moment ago is itself a metaphor—a comparison of a sexually active and potent male with a stallion used for breeding. But the word *stud* is so common in this extended usage that we forget that its root is metaphoric.

We call these unconscious comparisons made in ordinary speech *dead metaphors*. The word *dead* in that phrase is itself a dead metaphor, since it is being used figuratively but is so common in that usage that we usually don't recognize its metaphoric nature. *Root* in the sense that we have just used it is also being used metaphorically. But because it is so common to use the word in that manner, you probably didn't think of it as a metaphor. Literally it means the underground branching of a plant or tree, its foundation and connection to the nutrient system of the surrounding earth. But by extension we speak of the *root* of a problem, or the *root* causes of a depression. We could have said the *basis* or *genesis* of a problem rather than the root, but language tends to find concrete ways of talking about abstractions, often by employing metaphors. Thus it is not surprising that metaphoric language is often used by poets to make abstract concepts concrete. For example, here is a couplet by Charles Reznikoff:

> My hair was caught in the wheels of a clock
> and torn from my head: see, I am bald!

What a wonderfully imaginative and vivid way to say that the passage of time has trapped him into old age! Here the substitution of something tangible, the "wheels of a clock," for the abstract concept of time, is brilliantly employed, the couplet evoking all the anguish of age—the violent sorrows of growing old made concrete by his hair having been torn from his head by time.

Here is a brief and haunting passage from a poem titled "Album of Dreams" by the Polish poet Czeslaw Milosz and translated by the poet and Lawrence Davis:

November 23

> A long train is standing in the station and the platform
>   is empty.
> Winter, night, the frozen sky is flooded with red.
> Only a woman's weeping is heard. She is pleading for
>   something
> from an officer in a stone coat.

It is a cold, foreboding set of images, is it not? All of the details conspire to chill us: one thinks of Eastern Europe in the mid-twentieth century, of police states, fleeing refugees, desperation, poverty, exile. How bloody that frozen sky is and how evocative and formidable that officer with his stone coat. What a brilliantly effective metaphor! If we were to analyze that "stone coat" literally, we would say something like this: it is a long, heavy coat thick enough to seem inflexible, unmoving in the wind. It seems, on the man's shoulders, powerful, looming, immovable, and itself reminds one of the cold from which it protects him. It is grey or dun-colored or some sort of earth color. Perhaps from wear it glistens a bit as worn fabric will, is shiny as a wet stone in the moonlight. Given all that, the coat is like one made of stone.

But that word *stone* reveals so much more: it tells us everything we need to know of the officer's face, demeanor, heart. It characterizes not just the officer but the whole oppressive, unyielding state system under which that woman and officer live. At the same time it does something to the picture itself, that picture which had been so simple and realistic. A stone coat! And suddenly the picture is disturbingly askew, unreal, dreamlike, distorted—itself a statue made of stone. By that one word the scene has been removed from the commonplace and familiar, from the ordinariness of ordinary life.

Although images often rely on visual details, good writers bring the other senses into play, recreating the sounds, smells and tastes of things as well. Here are a series of images from the poem "Fortress" by Brenda Hillman. Notice that they do not paint visual details but auditory ones, the sounds of early morning in a big city:

> Few natural noises here. The wet thwack
> of the paper at 5:00 A.M. The foghorn's two-note
> tired bass viol behind the fast entrance of the garbagemen;
>
> and every morning, the favorite sounds:
> the clatter of junk mail, paper on iron,
> the helmeted sparrow's transcendent song...

A talent for metaphoric language, the ability to describe one thing in terms of another (a foghorn as a "two-note tired bass viol"), and for describing sensory details in precise and evocative language ("the wet thwack of the paper") are the tools needed to create haunting images.

The word *thwack* is an example of *onomatopoeia*, the technique of naming something by its sound. The word *thwack* is an imitation of the sound of something being hit or slapped. The words *boing*, *clunk*, and *pow!* are also imitations of sounds. When children call a clock a *tick-tock*, they are using this device of onomatopoeia. In Chapter 10, "Myth, Legend and Pop Icon," there is a poem titled "Gretel" by Ronald Koertge with the line "Bam! went the big door." Clearly, *bam* is another example of onomatopoeia.

Haiku and the Epiphanic Image Haiku, a Japanese poem of seventeen syllables, uses a single, striking image to illuminate one or another facet of existence. It was developed out of an earlier verse form called the *tanka* or *waka*, a thirty-one-syllable poem, two examples of which you will find in the poems of Izumi Shikibu later in this book. Brought to its aesthetic and philosophical peak by Matsuo Basho, the haiku is a poem that combines utter simplicity with some larger understanding of the world. Haiku takes the commonplace world for its subject and the mystery and grandeur of creation for its theme. The haiku usually works not through metaphor but through a single image or relationship between images that creates a poignant, charming, and significant moment:

71

Perfect moon for love!
You and I, O my sweet quilt—
against the night's frost.

—Sanpu

Until the word "quilt," the poem gives every indication of being a love poem—which indeed it is. But it is not a lover who will keep the narrator warm through the cold night. Though we are not used to praising loneliness, the ability to appreciate that emotion—and the joy buried within the essential loneliness of life—is not lost either on Sanpu or on the author of the following haiku:

Loneliness—which makes
the Autumn evening hues seem
deeper...lovelier...

—Buson

And here is one simple picture—but one resonant with the eternal, reminding us that forms emerge out of emptiness and fade back into emptiness; that the landscape before us is exquisite in all its seasonal transformations—at once impermanent and a participant in the cosmic play:

Summer's green mountains
and valleys, now simply white
snow— empty... silent.

—Joso

The poem too partakes of emptiness and silence—the emptiness into which all dissolves—the beautiful, ugly, good, and evil, those man-made categories of which the universe seems to take indifferent note:

A mountain temple:
The sound of the misstruck bell
dissolves in the mist.

—Buson

Did the relationship fail? Did winter bury the landscape in emptiness? Did the ringer of the temple bell strike true? No matter. In either case the sound reverberates for an instant and then is lost.

Here is a haiku at once serious and full of humor, a poem which tries to express the inexpressible—the beauty of the Matsushima landscape. Basho, left with its inexpressible beauty, can do no more than utter its name again and again. It is one of the few poems that needs almost no translation:

> Matsushima ya
> ah Matsushima ya
> Matsushima ya

We can render it into English with only a few changes:

> Matsushima!
> Ah, Matsushima!
> Matsushima!

The poem is, of course, not only about the beauty of this landscape but about that sense of awe that leaves us speechless, a feeling with which poets are intimately familiar.

To capture, through images of ordinary life, the sense of the eternal, and to do it in seventeen syllables! That is the challenge of the haiku. Another of its great masters is Issa, whose awareness and compassion extended to the smallest of creatures. He understood that they have their own lives, their own dreams, their own anguish:

> Not in the least moved
> by such beautiful flowers,
> the foxes cry out.

How well Issa understood that this life is transitory, that he himself, admiring the world, would soon be lying under the ground—those few feet of earth separating the living from the dead:

> Six feet above Hell
> I walk through this world gazing
> at lovely flowers.

Issa, a Shingon priest, did not imagine his own fate to be different from the fate of his fellow earth-bound mortals. His life too, he knew all too well, was fragile, impermanent:

> Made of dust,
> I am as light
> As the mosquito net
> Made of paper.

Notice that this last translation, done by Nobuyuki Yuasa, renders the poem in four lines instead of three, though the translator holds to the seventeen-syllable count.

The "spiritual structure" of haiku is described by the poet who brought the form to its fruition, the great seventeenth-century haiku master Matsuo Basho. His statement, translated here by Nobuyuki Yuasa, is more properly about the spiritual structure of all poems that

73

identify with their subjects:

> You can learn about the pine only from the pine, or about bamboo only from bamboo. When you see an object, you must leave your subjective preoccupation with yourself, otherwise you impose yourself on the object, and do not learn. The object and yourself must become one, and from that feeling of oneness issues your poetry. However well phrased it may be, if your feeling is not natural—and if object and yourself are separate—then your poetry is not true poetry but merely your subjective counterfeit.

Here is a haiku by the American poet and novelist Jack Kerouac that captures some of the same flavor, the same ability to grant beingness and reality to our earth-born compatriots, but at the same time makes no attempt to imitate the feel of the Japanese. It is a very American haiku:

> In my medicine cabinet,
>   the winter fly
> has died of old age.

Allen Ginsberg, in his book *Cosmopolitan Greetings*, has included a section he calls "American sentences." These are seventeen-syllable sentences that, like Kerouac's haiku, have an entirely American flavor. Ginsberg doesn't bother with the division into three segments but presents his images and epiphanies as ordinary sentences. Here are some American sentences done by young contemporary writers who have been inspired by both traditional haiku and by Ginsberg's poems:

> Pulling tissues from a box, the baby builds an igloo on
>   her head.
>   —Nina Garin

> The phone, coiled like an ancient serpent, whispers vague
>   threats and promises.
>   —Terry Hertzler

> White Cessna and seagull cross in a sky unconcerned with
>   birds or men.
>   —Will Boland

> At their raucous meeting the pacifists start fighting
>   among themselves.
>   —Malika Fusco

A Warning Some poets are so enamored of figurative language that they will sacrifice all sense of proportion and felicity to decorate their poems with similes and metaphors, no matter how destructive to the overall effect. Figurative language, well used, can help turn an indifferent poem into a wonderful one—but beware of cluttering your poems with numerous figures that detract from, rather than add to, their power! This delightful piece by Ogden Nash is a clever comment on that predilection:

Very Like a Whale

One thing that literature would be greatly the better for
Would be a more restricted employment by authors of
      simile and metaphor.
Authors of all races, be they Greeks, Romans, Teutons or
      Celts,
Can't seem just to say that anything is the thing it is but have
      to go out of their way to say that it is like something
      else.
What does it mean when we are told
That the Assyrian came down like a wolf on the fold?
In the first place, George Gordon Byron had had enough
      experience
To know that it probably wasn't just one Assyrian, it was a
      lot of Assyrians.
However, as too many arguments are apt to induce
      apoplexy and thus hinder longevity,
We'll let it pass as one Assyrian for the sake of brevity.
Now then, this particular Assyrian, the one whose cohorts
      were gleaming in purple and gold,
Just what does the poet mean when he says he came down
      like a wolf on the fold?
In heaven and earth more than is dreamed of in our
      philosophy there are a great many things,
But I don't imagine that among them there is a wolf with
      purple and gold cohorts or purple and gold anythings.
No, no, Lord Byron, before I'll believe that this Assyrian
      was actually like a wolf I must have some kind of proof;
Did he run on all fours and did he have a hairy tail and a
      big red mouth and big white teeth and did he say Woof
      woof woof?
Frankly I think it very unlikely, and all you were entitled to
      say, at the very most,
Was that the Assyrian cohorts came down like a lot of
      Assyrian cohorts about to destroy the Hebrew host.
But that wasn't fancy enough for Lord Byron, oh dear me
      no, he had to invent a lot of figures of speech and then

interpolate them.
With the result that whenever you mention Old Testament
    soldiers to people they say Oh yes, they're the ones that
    a lot of wolves dressed up in gold and purple ate them.
That's the kind of thing that's being done all the time by
    poets, from Homer to Tennyson;
They're always comparing ladies to lilies and veal to venison,
And they always say things like that the snow is a white
    blanket after a winter storm.
Oh it is, is it, all right then, you sleep under a six-inch
    blanket of snow and I'll sleep under a half-inch
    blanket of unpoetical blanket material and we'll see
    which one keeps warm,
And after that maybe you'll begin to comprehend dimly
What I mean by too much metaphor and simile.

An Exercise In Using Figurative Language

A. Create effective similes—striking and apt comparisons—by filling in the blanks in the following sentences. Your solution might be a single word or a short phrase, or it might be a lengthier, more complex description:

    1. In his rage my father would bang on the wall like a ——.

    2. Among her new in-laws the young wife was as nervous as ——.

    3. I paced the room as restless as a ——.

    4. Like a ——, his smile suddenly collapsed.

    5. It was the old sycamore in the front yard, swaying like a——.

B. Now create evocative images—strong descriptive language—to complete these sentences:

    1. I loved the —— of the wash on the line in the summer morning.

    2. I was afraid of his ——, his drunken, ungainly walk.

    3. I will not forget the —— of your lips, your skin's ——, or the ——
       of your eyes.

    4. She wished to draw me deeper into the —— of her life.

C. In three or four sentences that sparkle with linguistic invention, describe:

1. a rundown house

2. an old table, desk, bicycle, car or truck

3. a particular potted plant

4. someone working in a kitchen or garden

5. a small incident seen in the street or in a store.

Make your descriptions come alive using precise, charged language. The goal, of course, is to describe each item accurately, vividly and engagingly.

Poem 11: A Brief Descriptive Poem

Take the metaphor, simile, or descriptive passage that you like best from the above exercise and use it as the basis of a short poem—one that is no longer than seven lines. If you have described a house in four sentences, see now if you can turn that passage into a poem, concentrating on precision of language, internal music, and rhythmic grace. Needless to say, it should not be a less effective composition as a poem than it was as a prose paragraph. If you used the line "I shall not forget the —— of your lips..." perhaps only one additional sentence would be needed to turn it into an effective love poem. If you create additional similes and metaphors for your poem, be careful not to load it with so many figures that it seems cluttered. Remember that figurative language must, in the final analysis, be at the service of the overall effect that the poem makes and not simply stuck into the poem for its own sake.

Poem 12: An Object Poem Using Metaphors

If you have written the poem inspired by Al Zolynas's "Considering the Accordion," then you have already experimented with writing that uses metaphors and similes to describe an object imaginatively. But now that we have investigated figurative language more fully, it might be worthwhile to write another poem of that nature. Take an object that you have nearby—perhaps a ring, or piece of pottery or paperclip or lipstick—and place it in front of you. Spend a few minutes looking at it quietly and calmly. Notice things about it that you never noticed before. Allow yourself to feel it, smell it, observe it from various angles. Write four metaphors turning it into four different things: "The paperclip is a silver whirlpool...." Next, four similes: "The lipstick is like a fleshy purple bullet...."

Now write a poem about the object employing some of those figures of speech. Let the poem go where it wants to, its direction determined more by the inventive play of language than by your conscious efforts.

Poem 13: Haiku and Hike-U

Write two traditional haiku. Each is a three-line, seventeen-syllable poem that uses common language, deals with the natural world, suggests the season, and expresses an insight about the world. There should be five syllables in the first and third lines and seven in the second.

Then write half a dozen American haiku by composing seventeen-syllable sentences in the manner of the Kerouac poem and the four American sentences. These are perfect poems to compose while walking or driving, perfect poems to write while you hike (hence the name) up in the mountains, stroll around a park, or sit at a bench waiting for a bus. They're perfect for writing on your lunch hour, and if you're bored at work and the boss isn't looking over your shoulder, try your hand at some more. Make sure they sound more like sentences than poems—and that no one would guess that they are all seventeen syllables long.

Suggestions for Rewriting Go back to a poem that doesn't yet work and see if you can't enrich its texture with more evocative descriptions and with at least two interesting metaphors or similes. Don't worry if the poem becomes something completely different from what it was—as long as it becomes more lively and effective.

9

Speeding Home in Reverse:
The Controlling Metaphor

What She Wanted

was my bones. As I gave them
to her one at a time she put
them in a bag from Saks.

As long as I didn't hesitate
she collected scapula and
vertebrae with a smile.

If I grew reluctant she pouted.
Then I would come across with
rib cage or pelvis.

Eventually I lay in a puddle
at her feet, only the boneless
penis waving like an anemone.

"Look at yourself," she said.
"You're disgusting."

　　　—Ronald Koertge

We've all known people whose expectations we could never satisfy—to whom, no matter how deferential, sacrificing, generous, and solicitous we were, it was never enough. Sometimes it's a parent whom we can never sufficiently please. Young women often find that the young men they date have a desperate need to dominate and make them feel small and foolish. And of course there are women who manage to do the same thing to the men they are with.

Koertge has found a pointed and funny way of describing such a relationship. It is not that there are metaphors within Koertge's poem about a domineering and emasculating woman: rather, the entire poem *is* a metaphor, much the way a fable or parable can be said to function metaphorically—the story expressing some greater truth about our lives or the world around us.

In ordinary conversation one could imagine someone saying: "She wanted everything I had, my money, my dignity, my pride... she would have yanked my bones right out of my flesh if she could have gotten them!" It is as an extension of that sort of metaphoric discourse that Koertge's poem functions.

"I Went to the Movies Hoping Just Once the Monster Got the Girl," which was written by the same poet, also uses the device of a *controlling metaphor*, that is to say, a symbolic story. The young man rooting for the ungainly monster is of course rooting for that other awkward bumbler, himself. One might say, more loosely, that Czeslaw Milosz's "November 23" is also a metaphor—that the scene presented "stands for" the tyranny of Eastern Europe under totalitarian communism: the woman weeping, the officer in the stone coat, the cold winter evening, the train in the station with its hint of another world beyond the oppressive one that the lines present.

Here's another poem that works on the same principle, creating a little dreamlike fantasy in order to explore human relationships—in this case the relationship between husbands and their abandoned wives:

The Divorcing Men

Their wives are these heart-shaped
metallic balloons that got loose
and bobbed up high over
the jammed intersection where
the divorcing men sit at the wheel
with a bumper at either end.
The hearts glint like a second prize,
are seamed at the sides, with deep
creases of vexation and a string
for holding, except who
has arms that long anymore?

—Suzanne Lummis

How dreamlike these images are—or rather, how much like a disquieting nightmare: the wives transformed into heart-shaped balloons over the jammed intersection, anchored only by strings that their errant husbands cannot—or will not—reach up to hold. The image of the husbands in their cars "with a bumper at either end" is emblematic of people stuck in a world of spiritual gridlock. And the anguish of that final image, those arms of the husbands not being long enough, represents perfectly the anxiety of relationships in which strong commitment is chronically wanting.

Although there are metaphors within the poem—wives as heart-shaped balloons, for example—it can be argued that the entire poem functions as a complex metaphor, exploring, through this little fantasy, the psychologically complex dynamics of contemporary relationships.

Here is another poem that functions as a metaphor, a poem about a character with a penchant for savagery and destructiveness, the sort of person who might be called a she-wolf or man-eater. In the poet's hands it becomes a grimly humorous horror story:

Untitled

she was the perfect woman
until he discovered she had a mania for flesh
he'd come in late at night. she'd be gnawing away at it
    under the covers

she kept jars of it in the medicine cabinet
and when she kept telling him she had a headache
he would lay there looking at the ceiling, knowing what
    she was really doing

sometimes she'd snatch a bite in public
one day they were visiting mutual friends
she dropped her purse and it fell open
all that red bloody black flesh on the carpet. it was
    embarrassing
so that night he decided to tell her that it was no good,
    over, finished

and as he mounted the dark stairwell leading to her living
    quarters
he hesitated. but no, he thought. she loves me

she had crouched behind the door, and as he walked past,
    she sprang

she stored some of the fresh meat in the drawer by her
    typewriter
she put some chunks of it in the bowl by the bed stand so
    she could munch on it while she watched tv
she wrapped the rest of it carefully in tin foil and stuck it in
    the freezer

looking into the mirror she let out something like a bark.
well, she thought, i never lie to them. i always tell them
   what i am.
they never believe me.

                   —Wanda Coleman

And here is a poem whose protagonist suffers not from savagery but from innocence and trust. It illuminates a kind of personality pattern that is difficult to describe but which most of us will be able to recognize at once:

The Farewell

They say the ice will hold
so there I go,
forced to believe them by my act of trusting people,
stepping out on it,

and naturally it gaps open
and I, forced to carry on coolly
by my act of being imperturbable,
slide erectly into the water wearing my captain's helmet,
waving to the shore with a sad smile,
"Goodbye my darlings, goodbye dear one,"
as the ice meets again over my head with a click.

                   —Edward Field

Surely at one time or another we have all been shamed, goaded, or cajoled into doing something that we dreaded doing, putting on a brave smile and acquiescing—simply because we were too trusting or because it would have been socially awkward to have refused. What trouble we have all gotten into at one time or another by our "act of being imperturbable." Edward Field has managed to embody that ticklish situation in a story at once funny and touching. That sad smile, the absurd captain's helmet, and the audible click at the end are perfect details and bring the scene and situation vividly to life.

If you have ever wished that some event in your life had never happened, you will understand at once the clever metaphoric use the author of the following poem has made of the amusing spectacle of a film running backwards:

Retreat

Before she can deliver
the cruncher,

I stride away backwards.

My car door opens,
I fall in
as the engine fires.

I speed home in reverse,
unshave, unshower,
plop down in my easy chair

where, picturing what a good
night it's going to be,
I slowly spit up

a manhattan—dry—
just the way
I like it.

      —Charles Harper Webb

All the poems we have exhibited thus far in this chapter have been fantasies. But of course incidents in one's actual life can also be seen as metaphors that illuminate some situation that would be otherwise difficult to describe. The following poem is a straightforward description of an actual event—a child's first solo bicycle-ride. But the title of the poem tells us that the incident stands for an event currently troubling the narrator's life:

To a Daughter Leaving Home

When I taught you
at eight to ride
a bicycle, loping along
beside you
as you wobbled away
on two round wheels,
my own mouth rounding
in surprise when you pulled
ahead down the curved
path of the park,
I kept waiting
for the thud
of your crash as I
sprinted to catch up,
while you grew
smaller, more breakable
with distance,
pumping, pumping
for your life, screaming
with laughter,

the hair flapping
behind you like a
handkerchief waving
goodbye.

—Linda Pastan

Only that final simile, the child's hair "flapping behind you like a handkerchief waving goodbye," and the poem's title, signal that the incident described in the poem is emblematic of the more painful and complex experience of a daughter leaving home. Here, too, the narrator finds her daughter growing smaller and "more breakable with distance." Thus the poet has managed to describe her current anxiety through an ostensibly simple memory of her daughter joyfully outdistancing her on a bicycle years before.

Here is a poem that manages, through a brilliantly conceived simile, to describe how the narrator bears the burden of an intolerably heavy grief—the death of his beloved:

Michiko Dead

He manages like somebody carrying a box
that is too heavy, first with his arms
underneath. When their strength gives out,
he moves the hands forward, hooking them
on the corners, pulling the weight against
his chest. He moves his thumbs slightly
when the fingers begin to tire, and it makes
different muscles take over. Afterward,
he carries it on his shoulder, until the blood
drains out of the arm that is stretched up
to steady the box and the arm goes numb. But now
the man can hold underneath again, so that
he can go on without ever putting the box down.

—Jack Gilbert

Poem 14: Reanimating Dead Metaphors

Think of some common figures of speech and how, if taken literally, they might turn into little fantasies. Perhaps the pool in which you are swimming is beginning to boil—a literal embodiment of the figure of speech "to be in hot water." A poem about finding your tongue tied in knots can become a statement about being—you guessed it—tongue-tied. A poem about parts of your body cracking off can be used to indicate a sense of your life falling apart or coming unglued.

84

A poem in which a mask keeps slipping off your face might indicate your unsuccessful attempt to keep up a false front or put on a good face about some unpleasant situation. Similarly, one could write a poem about giving someone the gate (or the axe, or the finger), about eating crow, being torn in two directions, having one's heart broken, skating on thin ice, sticking one's foot in one's mouth, or walking on cloud nine. What would the literal story be of some awkward person who has two left feet, or some woman who has her boyfriend wrapped around her little finger, or some poor dreamer who's always building castles in the air? Use one of these examples—or one of your own—and, after dreaming up an appropriate story, begin writing a short poem about that person or situation. Be careful not to rely on the comic equation between your story and the maxim to do all the work. The poem will have to be interesting in its own right. Part of the trick of such a poem is to make the symbolic or metaphoric intention perfectly clear without ever having to explicitly tell the reader what you're trying to say. Linda Pastan doesn't have to tell us the relationship between her daughter's leaving home and the memory of her daughter learning to ride a bicycle. Charles Webb doesn't have to tell us that he's using the analogy of a film running backwards.

Poem 15: A Fable

Another way to approach the same sort of poem is to think of situations in your own life that would be worth exploring in poems and then dream up stories that embody those situations. Jack Gilbert found a striking analogy for his overwhelming grief. Do the same for a situation in your own life that would otherwise be difficult to express. A sense of confusion or danger might be equated with swimming in water that's suddenly too deep, too full of treacherous weeds and tangled plants. That same emotional complex might be equated with walking into a forest or maze of alleys and getting lost. What fantastic situation could you dream up to describe a relationship that pretends to be loving but is filled with barbed hostility? Or one in which you always end up being in the wrong? Or one in which one person always manages to manipulate the other?

Among those little tales that you have just invented, some will probably seize you with their possibilities, and details will start revealing themselves in your head. When the most promising has fleshed itself out sufficiently, start writing the poem. Make sure you present it with specific, concrete details—without getting cute or vague.

Another method of writing such a poem is to begin with a fantastic story that appeals to you and in the process of writing, discover or invent its significance for you. In this case, you should concentrate on the story while continually asking yourself what it means, what it all comes to. Eventually its meaning should become clear, and at that point you will be able to begin reshaping your story to fit its meaning. Though this is a more intuitive and less cognitive approach, it is also one that writers commonly employ.

Poem 16: An Autobiographical Metaphor

Can you find a concrete experience in your past that can function as a metaphor for an event that is more complex and recent in your life? Jack Gilbert has found a simple metaphor—an experience of shifting a heavy package from one position to another—for the complex predicament of bearing a heavy grief. Can the description of burying a dead bird when you were twelve be used to express the burying of a relationship, or trying to bury a painful memory? Is there an experience you can describe that will stand for some larger, more abstract situation, one that would be difficult to articulate without the analogy that you are creating between the two events? Recalling how someone stole a childhood toy might be used to explore the betrayal of a relationship that you might not otherwise have been able to speak about. Make sure the two stories, the one told and the one implied, are considerably different either in kind or in importance—yet somehow analogous. Otherwise, the controlling metaphor will have little punch. You may let the reader understand what the real subject is by a well-chosen title and at least one line in the poem, as Linda Pastan does. On the other hand, the significance of your story might be revealed to the reader in an entirely different way. That is a problem that is unlikely to be solved except in the course of writing the poem itself.

Poem 17: The Dream Metaphor

Dreams often function as complex metaphors. Use a particularly vivid dream of your own as the basis for a poem. Do not tell us it's a dream but simply relate it as powerfully as you can, making us feel what you felt during the dreaming. If you understand the dream—that it was a metaphor for your anxiety about your new job, or fear that you will fail at a new relationship, or resentment at not being able to make a lot of money—the poem is likely to be more successful. But don't tell us explicitly what the dream means. You must tell your story in such a way that the significance is implicit in the tale itself. Don't hesitate to deviate from the actual dream if you feel like it—simplifying, leaving elements out, altering whatever you need to in order to create a powerful poem.

10

Myth, Legend, and Pop Icon

Come Muse, migrate from Greece and Ionia,
Cross out please those immensely overpaid accounts...
—Walt Whitman

Lot's Wife

The just man followed then his angel guide
Where he strode on the black highway, hulking and bright;
But a wild grief in his wife's bosom cried,
Look back, it is not too late for a last sight

Of the red towers of your native Sodom, the square
Where once you sang, the gardens you shall mourn,
And the tall house with empty windows where
You loved your husband and your babes were born.

She turned, and looking on the bitter view
Her eyes were welded shut by mortal pain;
Into transparent salt her body grew,
And her quick feet were rooted in the plain.

Who would waste tears upon her? Is she not
The least of our losses, this unhappy wife?
Yet in my heart she will not be forgot
who, for a single glance, gave up her life.

—Anna Akhmatova
(Translated by Richard Wilbur)

The story of Lot and the destruction of the wicked cities of Sodom and Gomorrah are part of our cultural and religious heritage. That Lot's wife was turned into a pillar of salt for the sin of glancing back at Sodom as she was fleeing that burning city is known even to people who have little interest in the Bible.

But Anna Akhmatova is not simply retelling the biblical story; rather, she is using it to express her anguish at the destruction of her native Russia and at her sense of alienation—her spiritual exile—from the police-state created by Joseph Stalin. Akhmatova, one of Russia's greatest twentieth-century poets, saw her son imprisoned and her husband and closest friends murdered by the Soviet terror apparatus. Her dear friend Osip Mandelstam, another of the great Russian poets of the age, was banished to a gulag, where he eventually died, for having written a poem mocking Stalin. Instead of choosing exile, as did so many members of the Russian intelligentsia who were lucky enough to have survived the terror, Akhmatova remained in the Soviet Union and bore witness to the misery of those terrible decades. Despite the fact that her poetry was banned and was not again published in Russia until after her death (before the revolution she had been one of Russia's most widely read and admired poets), she became a symbol for the Russian people of the silent, agonized resistance to the decades of Stalinist tyranny.

Here, Lot's wife is not that Old Testament figure "looking back" with fondness on the life of sin and corruption that the biblical city of Sodom represents, but simply a woman who looks back at her native land—and at the life of fellowship and love that she cherished. How human the story becomes in her hands—how real this desperate figure of ancient legend becomes to the reader!

Richard Wilbur has used four-line stanzas of rhymed verse, a structure not unlike that of the original Russian poem, for his brilliant translation. Notice, however, that the formality of the structure does not impede him from writing with lucidity, power and grace; neither the rhymes nor the rhythm seems at all forced or artificial. In Chapters 16 through 20 we will discuss the formal and metrical structure of poems such as this. For now, simply observe that the poem rhymes and that every line has a similar length (most lines are ten syllables long), and similar rhythmic pattern.

Here is another poem in which a familiar tale is transformed:

Gretel

said she didn't know anything about ovens
so the witch crawled in to show her
and Bam! went the big door.

Then she strolled out to the shed where
her brother was fattening, knocked down
a wall and lifted him high in the air.

Not long after the adventure in the forest

89

Gretel married so she could live happily.
Her husband was soft as Hansel. Her
husband liked to eat. He liked to see
her in the oven with the pies and cakes.

Ever after was the size of a kitchen.
Gretel remembered when times were better.
She laughed out loud when the witch
popped like a weenie.

"Gretel! Stop fooling around and fix
my dinner."

"There's something wrong with this oven,"
she says, her eyes bright as treasure.
"Can you come here a minute?"

—Ronald Koertge

Plot and characterization combine, along with some wonderful phrasing, to give us an amusing revisionist version of Gretel. The poem's delicious humor should not keep us from noticing how expertly the narrative is constructed. It takes the author just six lines to retell the familiar story, and in those lines he not only gives us the main features of the fairy tale but manages to create a vivid portrait of Gretel as a young woman of calm determination and fairy-tale power. "Bam! went the big door" reveals her no-nonsense decisiveness while setting the jaunty tone of the entire piece. Given that characterization, her final act is completely believable—within, of course, the context of this cartoonish fantasy. For any woman who believes that for too many centuries "ever after was the size of a kitchen," the social commentary behind this poem will not be lost. It is worth noting that Koertge manages to do the whole thing in just twenty lines.

Here's a little poem by Billy Collins that uses a contemporary "mythological" figure. Like the Koertge poem, it is at once funny and chilling:

Flames

Smokey the Bear heads
into the autumn woods
with a red can of gasoline
and a box of matches.

His hat is cocked
at a disturbing angle.

The moonlight catches the teeth

of his smile.
His paws, the size of catcher's mitts,
crackle into the distance.

He is sick of dispensing
warnings to the careless,
the half-wit camper
the dumbbell hiker.

He is going to show them
how a professional does it.

No one runs after him
with the famous lecture.

—Billy Collins

Just as Ronald Koertge managed to create a surprising version of
Gretel, Billy Collins has turned Smokey on his head. Notice how the
poet manages to characterize his protagonist with a few masterly
strokes. The second stanza, with one well-chosen detail—"His hat is
cocked at a disturbing angle"—gives us a chilling picture of this darker,
sociopathic version of Smokey the Bear. Indeed, the entire disconcert-
ing story has been told from a "disturbing angle."

It is often difficult to speak of the social and political world without
sounding like someone on a soapbox mouthing political platitudes. But
here's a poem that avoids such a pitfall by playing with a well-known bit
of mythology in order to create a controlling metaphor that illuminates
the poet's sense of political frustration. Any political activist who's ever
grieved over the lack of front-line support can identify at once with
LoVerne Brown's poem and the implications of its clever metaphor:

A Very Wet Leavetaking

Comrades, I regret to inform you
I'm about to abandon this project.
The city cannot be saved,
does not deserve to be saved,
does not want to be saved—
since our warning cries went unanswered,
since, though the night was clear,
they chose to remain
with Merv and Johnny and carcinogenic beer.

Our own involvement was simple,
a matter of timing.
These holes appeared in this dike
and we were here.
We remembered that big-thumbed kid,

the hero of Holland,
and thought we could hold back the sea
till the townsmen came.

Well, the night's half over;
it's plain that they're not coming;
the tide is high and
the holes in the dike grow larger.
My arm is too small a cork
and floats in the flood,
and I must tell you
with shame but in all honesty
I am not yet fully committed
to sticking my head in.

—LoVerne Brown

When we think of the use of mythology in poetry, we often think of a poet alluding to some biblical character or Greek myth, such allusions being one of the adornments of English poetry. But the mythy world of folk and fairy tales, of comic book heroes, soap opera characters, and old movies, can also be used by contemporary poets—indeed, those pop-mythology characters are often more effective figures because their significance is more fully a part of our popular culture. That is not to say one can't take inspiration from the figures of Hecuba weeping before the ruined walls of Troy or Iphigenia, about to be sacrificed, bidding farewell to her mother. But the idea that the use of myth is limited to such figures is to fail to see the possibilities of using material from our own culture. It makes perfect sense for the plays of Euripides to be filled with Greek legends and for the works of contemporary American poets to be filled with American ones.

Poem 18: Apocryphilia

Choose a character with whom you are familiar and whom it might be provocative, inspiring, useful, or fun writing about: Wonder Woman, Rambo, Job's wife, Attila the Hun, Lilith, Betty Crocker, Ozzie and Harriet, Bart Simpson, Sitting Bull, Goldilocks, Madonna, Beetle Bailey, Snow White, Al Capone, Rapunzel, Pinocchio, Mickey Mouse, the Prodigal Son, Dagwood Bumstead—or any of scores of other figures whom you might be interested in reinventing.

Find an unexpected situation in which to place your character and an unexpected personality behind the stock figure we are all familiar with. Anna Akhmatova gives us a Lot's wife who is a refugee looking back on a country she has been forced to leave. Ronald Koertge projects Gretel into an unhappy marriage. Billy Collins creates a Smokey the Bear entering the woods with a can of gasoline. You might consider, for example, Dagwood Bumstead's eating disorder. What might happen if Barbie the doll became a radical feminist? How would Beetle Bailey react if he were suddenly in a real war and saw his friends getting killed? Did the third little pig, the one who built his house of bricks, eventually become a land developer? And what did Noah's wife feel like after the flood? Once you put your character in an unexpected situation, you can discover what happens next. For this poem, do *not* worry about your "theme" or idea; let that reveal itself to you in the course of the writing. By the end of the first or second draft, you should have a clear idea of the poem's thematic direction. From that point on, consciously steer the poem so that it all moves in a single, coherent direction.

Like the poets you have been reading in this chapter, try to surprise the reader while keeping the story logical. For example, Barbie might be a closet anorexic while Lazarus might return from the dead with some terrible secret that only the dead know. Those are perfectly "logical" situations, considering the characters.

Rather than give in to the impulse to write at length, see if you can do it all concisely—in fewer than twenty-five lines. That will force you to search for the one detail that will speak volumes. If you have difficulty keeping it so short, go back and reread the poems in this chapter, paying attention to how the writers manage to keep their stories to a single scene and how the details quickly bring character and setting to life.

If you are writing a comic, light-spirited poem, be sure that your humor is not sophomoric and obvious. On the other hand, there is no reason for this poem not to be as serious and significant as the Akhmatova poem with which this chapter began. Comic or serious, your object is to write a poem that is crisp, quirky, admirably wrought and memorable.

11

Family Secrets:
The Poem as Photograph

Mementos, I

Sorting out letters and piles of my old
  Canceled checks, old clippings, and yellow note cards
That meant something once, I happened to find
  Your picture. *That* picture. I stopped there cold,
Like a man raking piles of dead leaves in his yard
    Who has turned up a severed hand.

Still, that first second, I was glad: you stand
  Just as you stood—shy, delicate, slender,
In that long gown of green lace netting and daisies
  That you wore to our first dance. The sight of you stunned
Us all. Well, our needs were different, then,
    And our ideals came easy.

Then through the war and those two long years
  Overseas, the Japanese dead in their shacks
Among dishes, dolls, and lost shoes; I carried
  This glimpse of you, there, to choke down my fear,
Prove it had been, that it might come back.
    That was before we got married.

—Before we drained out one another's force
  With lies, self-denial, unspoken regret.
And the sick eyes that blame; before the divorce
  And the treachery. Say it: before we met. Still,
I put back your picture. Someday, in due course,
    I will find that it's still there.

            —W.D. Snodgrass

The experience of coming upon an old photograph and being moved by it, being swept up in memories of a time long gone, is surely a common one to most of us. W.D. Snodgrass maintains a relaxed and "talky" tone of voice while imposing on that ordinary speech a good deal of end-rhyme and internal music. The end-rhymes, a mixture of full rhymes, assonant rhymes (*slender/then, daisies/easy*), and—in one case—full consonance (*stand/stunned*), help create the poem's lovely music. The internal music is no less rich. Notice all the alliterative *l*'s and *c*'s in the first three lines and the repeated *e* sound in letters, checks, yellow, and meant.

The statement of the poem is a touching one, the imagery is often strikingly effective—like that simile comparing the narrator's shock at finding the photo to that of a man coming upon a severed hand—and the affection and humanity behind the poem, the refusal to use the occasion for self-justification or complaint, make it a trustworthy document about human suffering.

Here is another poem about a photograph. Though its surface is simple, it reveals a family's secret life:

My Wicked Wicked Ways

This is my father.
See? He is young.
He looks like Errol Flynn.
He is wearing a hat
that tips over one eye,
a suit that fits him good,
and baggy pants.
He is also wearing
those awful shoes,
the two-toned ones
my mother hates.
Here is my mother.
She is not crying.
She cannot look into the lens
because the sun is bright.
The woman,
the one my father knows,
is not here.
She does not come till later.

My mother will get very mad.
Her face will turn red

and she will throw one shoe.
My father will say nothing.
After a while everyone
will forget it.
Years and years will pass.
My mother will stop mentioning it.

This is me she is carrying.
I am a baby.
She does not know
I will turn out bad.

       —Sandra Cisneros

The poet steps outside the photograph to tell her story and then
returns to the snapshot in the surprising concluding lines. In effect, the
entire poem becomes a photograph. What an interesting shock the last
line leaves us with, and yet it is somehow right—for, in fact, life does
not turn out the way we imagine it will and the happy family portrait
often hides the seething lives of its subjects. Cisneros' title, by the way,
is also the title of Errol Flynn's autobiography.

Here's a poem about a photo that becomes an emblem of something
touching, mysterious and unnameable:

The Hat in the Sky

After the war,
after I was born,
my father's hobby
(perhaps his obsession)
was photography.
New fathers often become
photographers, it seems.
But he took pictures of many things
besides me,
as if he suddenly felt it all
slipping away
and wanted to hold it forever.
In one of the many shoe boxes
full of photographs
in my father's house,
one photo sticks in my mind,
a snapshot
of a black hat
in midair,
the kind of hat fashionable in the forties,
a fedora—something
Bogie would wear.
Someone has thrown it

into the air—
perhaps my father himself,
perhaps someone in an exuberant moment
at a rally or gathering.
It's still there,
hanging in the sky
as ordinary and impossible
as a painting by Magritte,
and it's impossible
how it wrenches my heart, somehow.
At odd moments in my life,
that hat appears to me
for no discernible reason.

—Al Zolynas

This is not a poem that describes a photograph so much as one that uses a photograph to give us a sense of the mystery of photography—and of the past—and of life itself. Note how simple the language is and how mysterious the photo of the hat is acknowledged to be. The poem is perfectly clear and yet the feeling with which it leaves the narrator—and reader—is similarly mysterious, mysterious in its ability to capture life's unspeakable sadness in words that are more than the sum of their parts.

Here is another poem about a photograph that becomes engagingly mysterious, a poem in which the author finds a way of animating the picture, of entering it and, in some curious way, of unmasking its surface:

Ladies On The Beach

In the picture their high-button shoes
toe the surf that sudses and smoothes
the shallow shoreline; their scarves,
unfurled, shiver out to unveil
the wind's direction. The younger one
on the right inclines her head
towards the older, about to say
something just as a hairpin slips
loosening a few auburn curls.

From their eyes I can tell they sense
my presence, my awe. Suddenly they lift
their skirts, turn back the same way
I imagine they came, and gulls
scatter luminous over glittering water.
Victorian ladies, the older now raises
her parasol, the other holds onto her hat
along the same beach I walk with my mother

97

every summer in our different clothes...
                    If we were these women

around the next bend we would encounter
an inlet surprisingly private. I am
the one on the right who slowly undoes
her gloves, and, like a ceremony,
the buttons tracing the curve
of my spine. Then, the dress drops,
a wrinkled heap, abandoned on the sand.
After I unhook the eyelets of my corset
and step from my shoes, my mother,
always the speaker of good conscience,
will finish whatever it was
she had started to say.

                    —Clare Nagel

One has the sense that the poem was discovered as the poet examined the photograph of a familiar beach taken in an earlier era. The first imaginative leap the poet makes is to imagine that the women in the picture sense the narrator's presence. At that moment, the picture becomes animated and the women begin moving about. Then we are told that it is the same beach the narrator and her mother walk every summer, and a moment later she and her mother have become those two Victorian ladies taking off their clothes on that deserted inlet. The image of the two women stepping from their clothing, the fact that they are proper Victorian ladies, and the description of the narrator's mother as "the speaker of good conscience," set up a complex tension between propriety and intimacy that leaves the reader, once again, with a sense of mystery.

Of course not all photographs these days are still photographs. Here is a poem based on both actual film footage and an imaginary photograph:

The Catch

The film footage wavers
on the gray TV screen:
fistfuls of Marines flung
from a helicopter, a flower
suspended in air
dropping its bloom of pods.
A row of khakied backs, the square-
shouldered shapes of men, knee-deep
in mud and raising rifles
like fishing rods.
There is the bitter smell of powder,
of too much salt, as bodies,

scooped from a trench, are flopped
like fish on a deck.
Here's what is left
of a boy from Maryland, half a face
and his good right arm. The rest,
scattered on a hillside, his pink
testicles split against
the brain-gray rock. In his breast
pocket, a snapshot, his girl
in a bikini, her whole body sprawled
across the hood of a new Camaro.
She's wet from the blue pool, shining,
car keys dangling from her teeth like minnows.

—Dorianne Laux

The distant view of the marines on the flickering TV screen quickly becomes a close-up view, then the narrator—in a radical shift of perspective—unobtrusively enters the action so intimately that she can describe not only minute visual details but even the smells. Then, moving in even closer, now an omniscient observer, she describes the pitifully mutilated remains of a single marine. We have been taken not only from the distant to an ever-closer viewpoint, but also from a general sense of the events to the most specific of descriptions. At first we see only "fistfuls" of marines, but by the end we see the horror of one young man's death and the details of a single photograph in his breast pocket.

The simile that compares the marines raising their rifles to men raising fishing rods is not only an apt visual comparison but one that sets up the underlying theme of the poem—expressing through figurative language what the poem also expresses through its narrative line. This fishing image—an image of both the "good" life of American leisure and a "harmless" sport with unacknowledged deadly consequences for its victims—is extended when the narrator tells us that "bodies, scooped from a trench, are flopped like fish on a deck," and appears again at the poem's conclusion when the girl in the photograph is described mugging for the camera with "car keys dangling from her teeth like minnows." She has been transformed, through this carefully controlled image, into a fish who is "hooked," swallowing the bait. But so too has the marine been "hooked." Are imperialism, colonialism, and exploitation the "catch" in the American dream, the hidden cost of the good life? The basic fish/hooked metaphor of the poem is an example of the rich use of ambiguity—not to confuse readers but to enlarge the conceptual landscape of the poem.

Poem 19: A Family Snapshot

Describe a photograph of some member or members of your family. Look at the photograph long and hard until you are deeply moved. Perhaps the subject of the photo is no longer alive, or it was taken before you were born, or you are there in the picture as a young child. Perhaps behind you stands the house where you grew up and to which you have not returned in many years.

Here are some rules that might appear at first to limit your options, but will actually make the writing easier and the final product richer. Use at least four of the following dozen words in the poem, though not necessarily in their photography-related meaning: *lens, reflex, develop, blow-up, crop, negative, shoot, diaphragm, expose, focus, reel,* and *print.*

Begin the poem by describing the photograph, making three observations about it. Then tell us two or three things that we would not know from the picture. Let those draw you into your past until you discover something that you had never realized or had never articulated—or had never before dared reveal to yourself or others.

Look at how the author of "Mementos, I" creates the emotion that he wishes the reader to feel. How does the author of "The Hat in the Sky" "tell" the reader what to feel about that mysterious photograph taken by his father? What emotion does one feel from "My Wicked Wicked Ways"? How has the author controlled the reader's response?

Work on the poem until the emotions and characterizations develop like one of those Polaroid snapshots that you can watch growing clearer and clearer. Don't call the poem finished until there is the clarity of a striking, revelatory portrait.

Poem 20: A News Photo

Take a news or magazine photo that you find intriguing, haunting or in some way moving. Begin by describing the photograph, but then, somewhere between the fifth and ninth lines, and without the reader being quite aware of what you are doing, animate the characters, setting them in motion. Before the twelfth line, either become one of the characters or tell us an intimate detail or two about that person. Let the poem emerge, as the Clare Nagel poem emerges, somehow of its own volition, without any conscious agenda on your part. This is a poem in which you must trust the process itself, letting the poem take you where it wishes to go.

Experiment and the Tradition

12

Cut-Ups, Cross-Outs, and Ransom Notes

"All poetry is an effort to re-create the language; in other words to abolish current language, that of every day, and to invent a new, private and personal speech, in the last analysis secret."
—Mircea Eliade

It is sometimes said that the collage is the fundamental art form of the twentieth century. Whether accurate or not, it is certainly true that collage, montage, disjunction, fragmentation, non-linear presentation, and the use of disparate elements in the composition of a work are central facets of modern and postmodern art. The cut-up or collage, which in one form or another has been used by many experimental writers of the past century (and, of course, by our leading visual artists), is a particularly useful creative tool. The novels of William Burroughs utilize the method, often with spectacularly effective results. Burroughs claims that his friend Brion Gysin invented the specific technique which has since become known through Burroughs' work as the cut-up method.

Although the cut-up poem is produced by a technique that would probably be familiar to most contemporary visual artists, it might fly in the face of writers who compose with a theme or subject uppermost in their minds. Nonetheless, it can produce striking results and open a poet up to fresh and imaginative ways of using the language.

The cut-up is a technique that permits you to suspend your critical censor and your need for sequential, logical development. It allows the poem to emerge out of sources inaccessible to the conscious mind. It will also allow you to concentrate on the music of the words and phrases you are using without having to worry about the poem's subject matter or significance.

Beware: you will not be producing the kind of clear, relatively straightforward poem we have, until this point, been talking about. The poem will be composed in a strange language.

Poem 21: The Cut-Up

To begin, take two pages from different sections of a daily newspaper. Then tear out (or open to) two pages from two different magazines or catalogues—preferably ones vastly different in nature: *Newsweek* and *Sports Illustrated*, for example; or *Soldier of Fortune* and *Good Housekeeping*; or *Motorcycle World* and *Young Bride*; or *Muscle and Fitness* and *Better Homes and Gardens*.

With a pencil or pen, begin circling phrases or random groups of words from any one of the newspaper pages in front of you. Circle whatever strikes you without spending any time hunting around for "interesting" words or unusual phrases. Just let your eye glance over a few lines and circle something there, then move on.

Let this part of the process be utterly uncensored and altogether non-critical. If you are stopping to make considered judgments about what to circle, you are letting your cognitive faculties get in the way. You might certainly want to circle phrases that seem oddball or interesting, curious or intriguing, but ultimately it doesn't matter what you circle; just keep doing it in a playful, nonjudgmental manner. For example, using the phrases in the previous sentence, you might have circled: "phrases that seem oddball," or "just keep doing it," or "it doesn't matter what." Do not focus on the meaning of the phrases you are circling so much as on their sounds, so that they become an abstract language, their meanings fading and their music becoming increasingly apparent.

When you have circled twenty or thirty items on one of your sheets, move on to one of the other three pages you have chosen. By the time you have finished circling the two newspaper and two magazine pages, you might have about a hundred items circled. Then take this book— the one that's in your hand right now—and copy down at random three phrases gleaned from different poems.

Now you're ready to compose the first draft of the poem by connecting the words and phrases you have circled, adding, where necessary, your own connective and transitional words and phrases. Give

103

yourself the liberty to change parts of speech wherever you need to in order to turn those phrases into what looks, syntactically, at any rate, like real English sentences.

For example, you can connect "churches having every right" and "it will be out in the open" to form "churches will have every right to be out in the open." Or perhaps, "Churches will be open on the right."

Don't feel obliged to use all the phrases you've circled, and if there are uncircled phrases that pop out at you while you're composing, certainly feel free to use them, too. Hopefully, most of the sentences you make up won't mean much of anything, for your task is to work not for meaning but for intriguing combinations of words and phrases and a playful assemblage of sounds. It is as if you are writing in a beautiful new language that utilizes English vocabulary and syntax but is not quite decipherable to an ordinary speaker of the language. If your assemblage starts making a good deal of literal sense, resist that urge! You are trying for a magical language here, not the ordinary one. On the other hand, don't be surprised if some sense creeps into the poem. Once the words are arranged in conventional English syntax, the phrases and sentences so constructed tend to become interpretable, meaningful.

For example, from the previous three paragraphs we might construct the following:

Connecting the Words

When the literal speaker has moved
the assemblage of random sheets,
changing—wherever necessary—
into the vicinity of decipherable
conventions, you will then
have uncircled the urge of this book
—yes, this book, with its strange liberty
of intriguing churches and open hands.

If you look back over the previous three paragraphs, you will see that almost all the words are contained there, but, of course, in a completely different order and context. The word "you" and a few connectives have been added, and the form of some words has been changed. Note that our cut-up sounds like a perfectly good English sentence and a fairly eloquent, gracefully made poem. It is just this sort of writing that you should be trying for in your cut-up. Note too that our little cut-up comes from only one source and from only three paragraphs in that source. I have suggested using five sources for this first cut-up in order to give you lots of material to work with—but, as you can see, all those texts aren't always necessary if your ears are open to the possibilities.

Make sure that you do not simply connect your fragments together into separate phrases that seem to have nothing to do with each other. Remember, you are free to plug in connective words and phrases and may change word forms. The word *moving* might need to be changed to *moved* or *had moved* or *moves*. Try to make your sentences rich and complete, so that no sense of fragmentation occurs for your reader. Imagine that you are trying to convince your readers that what they are reading is real English, a poem that is intriguing, thickly textured, complex, and elusive.

Here is the first draft of a cut-up made from the newspaper and magazine pages reproduced on the following page:

> There are men in this world that lacking
> any personal history only two
> people know that nectarines and peaches
> were right through summer's misguided attitudes
> It's the fuchsia infection of those fresh
> little pots of her credibility.
> They were disfigured leaves where real people
> lurk in the shadows of misguided societal attitudes,
> and pounce, with their gorgeous shadows
> in the first flush of spring.
> Consider this gem: the lily-white brilliance.
> You wouldn't want to go a step further
> than the nectarines of misguided and warm rains
> of winter though it looks like an under-reported crime.

That's not a bad first draft; there are some imaginative connections and interesting phrases. But overall it seems a bit choppy and unwieldy. For example, the phrase "There are men in this world that lacking any personal history only two people know," is decidedly awkward. The verb "were" in line four seems weak. A more active verb would certainly help. For example, "nectarines and peaches wept/ bloomed/ sweetened/ rode, through summer's..." would be far stronger. On the other hand, "The fuchsia infection of those fresh little pots of her credibility" is good. "Disfigured leaves," "gorgeous shadows," and "lily-white brilliance" are fairly imaginative and crisp as well.

In a second and third draft, the author has pulled out most of the weak phrases and lines and gone back to the circled text to come up with the poem at the top of page 107.

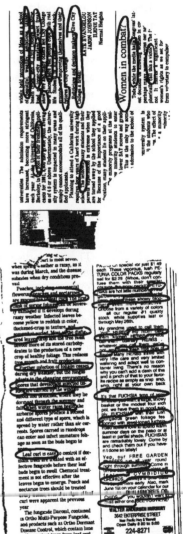

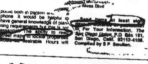

Drumroll: Imperial Justice

Nectarines! Dark insolent peaches! First
heroic versions of crime! those fresh
little pots of credibility's
fuchsia infection.
Consider this: the lily-white brilliance
of misguided leaves
where the woven scarf
of the hangman's hands
lurks in the shadows
and summer's imperial history
buzzes—disfigured branches and shoots
in the first flush of warm rain.
You—fully conscious, head high—
wouldn't want to go a step further,
wouldn't—festooned with that jewel
of bleak courage—

want to miss either one.

By concentrating on the sounds, on the quality of the verbal music, and
the strangeness of the juxtapositions rather than on the "meaning," one
often comes closer to the secret language of the unconscious. Is a
meaning beginning to impose itself on this draft? Do you see it lurking
beneath the odd combination of phrases? If, on the third or fourth
draft, you wish to move the poem in that direction, do so—but not at
the expense of the magical texture that you have created. On the other
hand, your impulse might be to move even further in the direction of
strangeness, of an indeterminate language that refuses all attempts at
interpretation.

Here is a cut-up, by an experienced poet, that seems surprisingly
coherent:

Imagining Red

In our room, a picture of farmland—
    blue inside white groves of almonds.
        Through the tops of trees,

Fluttering like a cotton sash over our heads,
    hundreds of butterflies,
            gold wings folded like cloth.

Under the flames, someone is trimming a hedge
        as the sun, amber wheel, sparks the orchard
            drops stars on jagged trunks—

Beneath the frame, this man I cannot get over
   is combing my hair, burning rope tangled
      beside me, turning to copper—

he is humming to himself
   lost in the soft mud of this room,
      that kind of weightlessness,
         just before going to bed together.

He has carried me upstairs
   like a sleeping child, spread me like warm
      linen on the forest floor—

The red hood of his sweatshirt
   propped under my head, as if protected
      from the rough earth.

           —Deborah Harding

The fact that this richly evocative love poem emerged from a cut-up would surely surprise any reader.

Poem 22: The Cross-Out and White-Out

Here's another kind of cut-up poem, the ransom note. For this one you'll need a newspaper, a pair of scissors, some glue-stick, a sheet of paper—and your most playful visual and literary creativity:

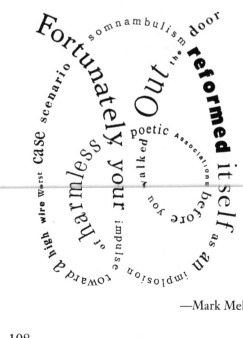

           —Mark Melnicove

Another text-generated poem is the cross-out. The method is simplicity itself. All you need is a newspaper column (or other text), and a nice, dark felt-tip pen. Here's a sample by Mark Melnicove, a poet who's been writing such poems for many years. The author, aware of both the visual and literary aspects of this sort of concrete poem, often designs his cross-outs playfully for visual appeal, presenting them in their original form so that the reader can see not only the poem that emerges from the text, but the background text itself. This piece is called "Living Standards."

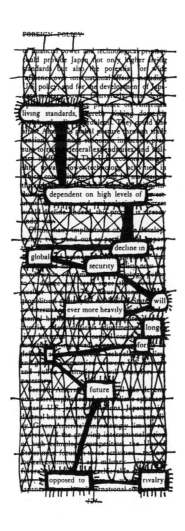

A nifty variation is the white-out poem in which the author erases with white-out ink, instead of black ink, everything that is not the poem. Here's what one looks like:

Each		soul
Is a glowing spark of		
	light	
learning to		
		pulsate
On the wings of		the
		unequivocal
		mother

—Mark Melnicove

Ransom notes, cross-outs, and white-outs are tailor-made for poets with a good visual eye who delight in the interface between the literary and visual arts.

Poem 23: More Cut-Ups, Cross-Outs, White-Outs, and Ransom Notes

For your next cut-up, make at least one sentence an exclamation, make another two sentences questions, and repeat one phrase three times. For another, follow the procedure of "Imagining Red": allow subsequent drafts to become increasingly coherent, even if it means imposing more of your own language on the poem, so that no reader will suspect the process by which it was written. Nonetheless, make certain it retains its mysterious and oddly phrased aspects.

For cut-ups, cross-outs, white-outs, and ransom notes try using all sorts of texts—dictionaries, recipe books, technical books, specialized magazines. Some might be generated by old letters from friends or by the junk mail that awaits you every afternoon in your mailbox. Use photocopies when you don't want to destroy the originals.

110

13

The House of Language

Whenever contemplating the position of the serious writer in this maelstrom of coin and pulp, I grow delirious and speak glibly in extinct tongues.
—Bern Porter

Stanza XV

I have not come to mean
I mean I mean
Or if not I do not know
If not I know or know
This which if they did go
Not only now but as much so
As if when they did which
If not when they did which they know
Which if they go this as they go
They will go which if they did know
Not which if they which if they do go
As much as if they go
I do not think a change.
I do think they will change.
But will I change
If I change
I can change.
Yes certainly if I can change.
It is very foolish to go on
Oh yes you are.
How could one extricate oneself from where one is
One is to be one is to extricate whichever
They can be not for this any for an occasion
Of which they are remarkable as a remembrance.

—Gertrude Stein (from "Stanzas in Meditation")

Have you ever said a word over and over until it lost all significance and became a series of odd, alien, and magical sounds? At such a moment we see language functioning at another level, functioning more as primal sound disassociated from its conventional referents. Children, of course, play with language in this way all the time: they repeat words again and again for the sheer pleasure of it. They love rhyme, they love sounds.

Many poets have attempted to write a poetry liberated from subject matter and theme in order to invest themselves in the medium of language itself. In the past century, visual artists have recognized that beyond subject matter their ultimate concerns were with color, paint, line, form, and relationships among those elements. In a similar manner, poets too have sometimes attempted to use the language without conscious reference to the world outside language.

To what degree this impulse lies behind the above poem is difficult to say. A friend and patron of the great innovative visual artists of the early twentieth century, Gertrude Stein, America's most relentlessly experimental writer, was influenced by the cubist experiments of her painter friends—and wished to investigate the objects of her attention simultaneously from numerous angles. Through a series of continual permutations on a few ordinary phrases, wrenching the common syntax of English from its moorings, she shaped language into new configurations. If there is often a sense that her poems represent language at pure play, at times there is also a sense that a complex meaning is being elucidated through an hermetic language that has become hypnotic and seductive in its continual repetition and variation. Stein did not believe her poems were "abstract" in the sense that they did not refer to the material world outside of language itself. She once wrote, "I took individual words and thought about them until I got their weight and volume complete and put them next to another word and at this same time I found very soon that there is no such thing as putting them together without sense."

E.E. Cummings has commented that "Gertrude Stein subordinates the meaning of words to the beauty of the words themselves...words becom[ing] autonomous objects...rather than symbols of something else." Kenneth Rexroth has commented that "Gertrude Stein showed, among other things, that if you focus your attention on 'please pass the butter,' and put it through enough permutations and combinations, it begins to take on a kind of glow, the splendor of what is called an 'aesthetic object.'"

The Concrete Poem Another interesting species of linguistic invention is the visual or concrete poem. These are pieces that combine visual art with language art. We have already seen two such poems in Mark Melnicove's "Living Standards" and ransom note. Here is another, titled "#," made up of an interface between the visual and literary—a poem that one might say spans the gamut from A to Z:

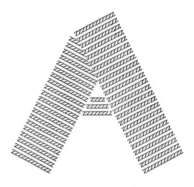

—Norman Henry Pritchard II

A *concrete* or *conceptual poem* of this sort can be composed by computer using a desktop publishing or graphics program. Or you could design a conceptual poem by cutting out and pasting up texts to suit yourself.

The Found Poem Sometimes one comes across a passage in a letter or a newspaper or some other printed material that is—with little or no editing—a perfect poem. Perhaps it's a segment of an instruction manual on tattooing or a droll news clipping, or a list of supplies needed for shrinking heads. Here's a grimly humorous found poem that was culled from the *Dictionary of Occupational Titles*. The author has abridged the description somewhat and broken it into poetic lines.

Embalmer (a found poem)

Washes bodies using germicidal soap
and towels, or hot air dryer.
Inserts convex celluloid or cotton
between eyeball and eyelid.
Presses diaphragm to evacuate air

113

from lungs. May join lips
using needle and thread or wire.
Packs body orifices with cotton
saturated with embalming fluid
to prevent escape of gases
or waste matter. Inserts tubes
into artery. Starts pump
that drains blood from circulatory
system and replaces blood
with embalming fluid.
Reconstructs disfigured or maimed bodies,
using clay, cotton, plaster of paris
and wax. Applies cosmetics
to impart lifelike appearance.
Dresses body and places body in casket.
May maintain records
such as itemized list of clothing
or valuables delivered with body
and names of persons embalmed.

—Cordelia McGuire

Aleatory Poetry The cut-up, cross-out, and white-out poems that we looked at in the previous chapter depended for their composition on chance elements—words and phrases that emerged from other sources. Here is a poem that was composed by a "nonintentional" method, an *aleatory* poem, by Jackson Mac Low, a poet who has been writing such poetry for many years. It is from a sequence called "5 Poems for & from Louis Zukofsky 1 May 1963."

Z 3

GETS DOWN FOR A MOMENT ON ONE KNEE.
WHAT'S TROUBLING YOU?
AREN'T YOU DEAD?

LISTEN.

WE WERE GOING SOMEWHERE,
STEPPING OFF SOMEWHERE.

REMEMBER? FROM ANOTHER WORLD
SAD RECOGNITION.
WE'RE GOING TO A WEDDING.
AFTER THE DREAM CURTAIN FALLS.

—Jackson Mac Low

Mac Low composed this poem by drawing sentence elements from five poems by the poet Louis Zukofsky. He often uses what he calls a "diastic reading-thru text-selection method." He reads through a text, finds words and other linguistic units that have the letters of a seed word, name, or phrase, and constructs his poem out of those words and phrases. In this manner he composes poems in any of a variety of imaginative methods that can be described as "nonintentional."

The following *sound poem*, though charming and comically pointed when read quietly to oneself, was probably written with an eye to its performance aloud. Keep in mind that this is poetry as performance art, sound as music. Its intention is to be not just satire but an act of visual and auditory pleasure:

The Card Index Song for the Filing Sisters

A Aa Ali Ame Ardo Az
Ba Bamo Biom Boyl Bra Btm Bs
Cep Chi Clm Cmno Cpr Cqs Ct Cye Cx

D Dag Dimh
Ele Epe
Fri Fro Frm Frp
Gh Ghi Gr
H Heq Hrf Hst Huz Hy
Ip Iq
J
Kia Kpm
Lim Lin Liq
Megi Megg Midi Mie Mye Mysm
Nih Nylq
Op Ope Opa Oq
Pel Pda Pik Prl Prp Psn
Qt Qu Qy
Rik Riln
Sby Sca Shu Si Sja Sk
T Tn Tqa
Um Uop
V
W Whi Wj
X Xx
Ym Yn Yo Yp Yq
Zz

—Bern Porter

Translitics A translitic is a poem "translated" from a foreign language by paying attention not to the meaning of the words but to their sounds. The poet uses as a guide whatever homonymic associations come to mind. So a line like "Garni vers un plus immortel" (from a poem by Jules Laforgue) might vaguely sound like "Garnish worst of plush immortals" or "Carnivore's impulsion or tells" or "Carny verse unplugs the mortals." Needless to say, it is easier to use a poem in a language you don't know. You can stick close to your first reading or, in later drafts, simply use what you have as a springboard and go as far afield of the original as you wish, making the final poem entirely your own. Here is a poem by Charles Baudelaire:

Bien Loin D'ici

C'est ici la case sacrée
Où cette fille très-parée,
Tranquille et toujours préparée,

D'une main éventant ses seins,
Et son coude dans les coussins,
Écoute pleurer les bassins:

C'est la chambre de Dorothée.
—La brise et l'eau chantent au loin
Leur chanson de sanglots heurtée
Pour bercer cette enfant gâtée.

De haut en bas, avec grand soin,
Sa peau délicate est frottée
D'huile odorante et de benjoin.
—Des fleurs se pâment dans un coin.

> —Charles Baudelaire

And here is how one person rendered it into English. Bear in mind that this is the author's fourth draft, each subsequent attempt moving further from the original, though still, as you can see, maintaining some relationship to the sounds of the French phrases:

Frost at the open window, wind chills the casement,
the drapery heaves, waiting & ready.

That night during the main feature
a boy dances with his cousin,
the basins acute with pleasure.

Ah, it's Dorothy's room!
The breeze tugs at her loins, as
lewd songs tease from the painful vacant lot, the
tiny gate banging berserk,

thumping to the hot bass. The huge swan, victorious,
rubs his delicate feathers
on the scented wheel of the bench, the
glittering floor paved with coins.

> —Mary Petrangelo

The word "ici," which the author rendered as "icy" in her first draft, has been transformed into "frost" in this later one. Here is another writer's translitic of that same Baudelaire poem. In order to show something of the freedom which the poet allowed herself, take a look at her first "literal" version:

Good Indication of Icy Loins

It's a case of sacred ice.
Oh, such fillies, three pairs,
tranquil, always prepared.

The main event of six rivers,
a cloudy son without his cousins,
execute pleasure in basins.

It's Dorothy's bedroom.
The breeze smells contented at loin.
Learn song of sang hearty.
Pour drinks set infant goatees

of fashion behind, with big sun.
Say peace delicate is frosty,
the wheel deodorant of good joy.
—The flowers pavement without a dime.

—Cherry Vasconcellos

If you look at the final version below, it will be clear at once that the author used that first draft as a springboard, feeling perfectly free to transform that raw material into her own poem. Here's the poem she ended up with, four rewrites later:

Six Rivers

A girl on a horse,
both of them
young and ready to ride
six rivers
around the sun.
Pleasure is a valley
of dreams in the girl's eyes.
She's singing
as they ride.
Joy spins the sun.

—Cherry Vasconcellos

Perhaps the most interesting and impressive series of translitics in contemporary poetry is a collection of translations of the Latin poet Catullus done by the American poet Louis Zukofsky, who tried to duplicate the sounds of the original while at the same time attempting to render the poems' meanings into English.

Poem 24: A Language-Centered Poem

Write a poem in which you try to play with language, ignoring the issue of sense or communication. Begin it with "I have not come to...." Then repeat whatever word you use after "come to," in various contexts several times in the next several lines, using that word as a musical pulse to thrust the poem forward. Try permutations on one or two phrases as well, in the manner of Gertrude Stein. If there is some underlying or hidden meaning, or if some impulse toward meaning arises in you as you work, that's fine. But don't consciously try to impose meaning on the words.

Poem 25: A Found Poem

Keep your eyes open for a found poem: it could be a fragment from a grocery list, instructions for starting a new wristwatch, a section of synonyms from a thesaurus. You might look through the personal ads in your local newspaper and parse odd fragments together. Or try a foreign language phrase book. It is sometimes a matter of simply calling attention to the most ordinary fragments of language by shaping them into a poem. Abridge it if necessary, break what you use into lines that emphasize the musical nature of the language, and then give your poem a title. If the idea of found poems delights you, do a series of them.

Poem 26: A Chance Poem

Write a poem by selecting words or phrases from a dictionary in conformity with the numbers in your birth date. If you were born on May 7, '62 (5/7/62), choose the first word as well as the closing word from pages 5, 7, 6, and 2, then from page 57, 62, 576, and 762. Use other permutations of those numbers if you like. In the *American Heritage College Dictionary*, the first word on page 57 is "fastened," while the final word on that page is "something." Write a poem of a line length determined by the sum of those single digit numbers (in this case 5+7+6+2 = a 20-line poem), making sure that you use all the words from your list.

Write another chance poem using a phrase book from a foreign language. Invent a chance method of choosing English phrases from the book. Make sure the system requires that at least three phrases be in the other language.

A similar "game" can be played generating texts by rolling dice, throwing cards, etc. If you are using this book in a class and/or with a group of poet-friends, each participant might want to invent a set of intricate rules to be used for the creation of a poem by another group member or by the entire group.

A poem that contains a slight aleatory element is an *acrostic*. Write a poem in which the first letter of each line, reading down the page, spells out your name. If your name is Deidre Amsterlin, for example, the first letter of the first line would be a *d*, the first of the second line would be an *e*, the first letter of the third line an *i*, and so on. Make it an autobiographical poem.

Poem 27: A Translitic

Using a poem in a foreign language, create a translitic. Keep the first draft as close to the original in sound as possible. Then, when a first draft is completed, go over it a second time, smoothing out whatever you wish, changing whatever you like, so that you end up with a poem—a musical composition in real English (or something approximating real English). For your third version, feel free to shift things around as much as you wish, adding and deleting whatever you want to. You may wish to remain somewhat close to the original or, like the model by Cherry Vasconcellos, you may prefer to cut loose from the original and discover the poem that is hiding in the translitic.

If you are interested in doing such a poem immediately but don't have a foreign language poem handy, try your hand at the following poem by Paul Verlaine:

Clair de Lune

Votre âme est un paysage choisi
Que vont charmants masques et bergamasques,
Jouant du luth et dansant et quasi
Tristes sous leurs déguisements fantasques.

Tout en chantant sur le mode mineur
L'amour vainqueur et la vie opportune,
Ils n'ont pas l'air de croire à leur bonheur
Et leur chanson se mêle au clair de lune,

Au calme clair de lune triste et beau,
Qui fait rêver les oiseaux dans les arbres
Et sangloter d'extase les jets d'eau,
Les grands jets d'eau sveltes parmi les marbres.

—Paul Verlaine

Remember, once you have done an initial draft or two, consider it your own poem and go with it where you will. Your only obligation is to make it as interesting and evocative as you can.

14

Flying Into Oneself:
Dream Work and the Magical Image

Hair Poem

Hair is heaven's water flowing eerily over us
Often a woman drifts off down her long hair and is lost
—Bill Knott

In 1900, Sigmund Freud published *The Interpretation of Dreams*, a study in which he attempted to "demonstrate that there is a psychological technique which makes it possible to interpret dreams, and that on the application of this technique every dream will reveal itself as a psychological structure, full of significance."

In that work, which was to become a highly influential text for Western culture, Freud postulates a symbolic language of the unconscious, a language of suppressed desires that speaks to us most dramatically and vividly in the dream state. It is a language of visual and auditory images, as well as one of puns and linguistic ambiguities. In the dream life, time and space are malleable, objects fuse seamlessly into one another, and the logic of our commonplace reality is transformed into the hallucinatory and seductive logic of symbolic fantasy. Dreaming that a goblet of champagne has shattered on the floor of a gymnasium crowded with pillows might be the acknowledgement of one's desire that the newly launched business of an acquaintance fail, or of the dreamer's suppressed envy at the acquaintance's reputation as a sexual athlete. At another level it might suggest anxiety that the dreamer, who fears that he cannot hold his liquor, will have his world shattered by the revelation of his drinking problem. At yet another level it might indicate that the dreamer, dissatisfied with his unrewarding job, would rather relax than jump through hoops. There are, of course, any number of private meanings that dropped champagne or pillows on a gymnasium floor might have—meanings that only the dreamer, or someone listening closely to the dreamer's musings about the dream, will be able to decipher .

Influenced in part by Freud's ideas, a group of brilliant poets and painters in the early decades of the century conceived a program to create an art that would celebrate and explore the powerful reality of the unconscious—the turbulent river of thought that streams beneath the surface of consciousness, with its odd associative laws and subterranean flow of emotions—an art that would follow the laws of the pre-rational, meta-logical, and super-real. Out of that impulse to explore and transform our reality by giving voice to the strange language of the unconscious, the Surrealist movement was born. Surrealist paintings by Jean Arp, Salvador Dali, Max Ernst, Marcel Duchamp, and Rene Magritte have made *surrealism*, at least as a visual art, a concept familiar to the general public, though the movement was first and foremost a literary one. In both arts, however, the influence of surrealism, long after the original "movement" had ended, exerts a viable force on Western art. Its liberating philosophy and methodologies have entered the mainstream of world art, and almost every writer and visual artist of our age has to one degree or another been influenced by its tenets.

One method of releasing those deep, unconscious images is to suspend the impulse to *impose* meaning and connections, trusting that the images that flow out of the unconscious stream will be those most highly charged with significance. You have done something of the sort in the poems that you wrote for the previous two chapters.

"Hair Poem" by Bill Knott violates the logic of realistic description. Comparing long hair to heaven's water is odd and striking, but the idea of a woman drifting off in the "flood" created by her hair is more curious yet. Nonetheless, the logic of the images is fairly easy to understand on the intuitive level. Since the woman's hair might be long and wavy, its similarity to water isn't, after all, so far-fetched. And, of course, if it were the hair of a woman he loved, the relationship to "heaven's water" would make sense as well. That her hair, on some symbolic level, dominates her life, at least for brief stretches, is again not terribly far-fetched. Since hair often suggests sexuality, the idea of a woman losing herself, during lovemaking, in the flood of her sexuality, would again make sense. The image as a whole seems more discovered than invented: a strange, disconcerting bit of "fantastic" imagery that is not soon forgotten.

122

Here is another "dreamlike" poem that makes sense on an intuitive level:

The Room

With crayons and pieces of paper, I entered the empty room.
I sat on the floor and drew pictures all day.
One day I held a picture against the bare wall:
it was a window. Climbing through,

I stood in a sloping field
at dusk. As I began walking, night settled.
Far ahead in the valley, I saw the lights
of a village, and always at my back, I felt
the white room swallowing what was passed.

—Gregory Orr

"The Room" makes an observation about the nature of reality and the imagination, the world of real-time and the world of art, and the movement from one to the other. But exactly what that connection is remains elusive. In the real world, one cannot climb through a picture of a window—and yet how accurately that image describes the way we "escape" into the imaginary world of the mind. Notice how clear every image is in this poem. And yet it is all disconcertingly strange: the sloping field at dusk, the lights of a distant village, that white room that the narrator feels behind him.

Here is a poem of a similar sort:

Year's End

Now the seasons are closing their files
on each of us, the heavy drawers
full of certificates rolling back
into the tree trunks, a few old papers
flocking away. Someone we loved
has fallen from our thoughts,
making a little, glittering splash
like a bicycle pushed by a breeze.
Otherwise, not much has happened;
we fell in love again, finding
that one red feather on the wind.

—Ted Kooser

To think of the "splash" someone makes falling from our thoughts is striking and novel, but to compare that splash to the sound a bicycle might make being pushed by the breeze is even more interesting and

123

imaginative. It is an unanalyzable image and yet somehow right, somehow accurate and poignant, just as it seems appropriate to think of falling in love again as "finding that one red feather on the wind." Logically, the image cannot be justified, though one might say that "red" is traditionally a color that expresses passion and that a feather is the lightest of objects and calls up images of flight—images which are apt to connote blissfulness ("I was flying high in those days"). Freud has argued that dream images of flight represent male sexual arousal. Whether or not such "explanations" seem far-fetched, the image feels right.

Here is a poem that is, at first, perfectly reasonable and realistic—and then slides into the surreal:

The Bagel

I stopped to pick up the bagel
rolling away in the wind,
annoyed with myself
for having dropped it
as it were a portent.
Faster and faster it rolled,
with me running after it
bent low, gritting my teeth,
and I found myself doubled over
and rolling down the street
head over heels, one complete somersault
after another like a bagel
and strangely happy with myself.

—David Ignatow

There is both pleasure and humor in this poem's tone, though it shares with the others in this chapter a kind of quiet, otherworldly tranquility. There is more stillness than action, as if one were describing a dream landscape rather than a human event. As with the other poems we have been looking at, the emotions seem to be contained within the images themselves and there is a sense that there is something of the flattened affect and dissociative feeling of dreams—as though the emotions seething below the surface were cloaked in a blanket of drugged calm.

It is not unlikely that "The Bagel" was an imaginative extension of an actual experience. Perhaps the author had dropped a bagel or some other small item on a windy street as he was returning home with groceries, and found himself chasing after it, at first annoyed, but suddenly, finding himself running in the wind, feeling a surge of childlike cxuberance—as if he, like the object of his chase, were tumbling helter-skelter through the street. Whether that was the germinating experience or not, the poem seems a celebration of just that sort of moment.

Here is a little dream-like poem that is perhaps still more difficult to analyze in any logical way. And yet how magical and touching it is:

Practical Concerns

From a distance, I watch
a man digging a hole with a machine.
I go closer.
The hole is deep and narrow.
At the bottom is a bird.

I ask the ditchdigger if I may climb down
and ask the bird a question.
He says, why sure.

It's nice and cool in the ditch.
The bird and I talk about singing.
Very little about technique.

                    —William J. Harris

In the bird's song one might say there is no technique; there is just singing. We do not walk down the street by using some "technique" for engaging the muscles of the legs, but simply by walking. If a poem such as this cannot be analyzed in any simple, straighforward manner, so much the worse for analysis! The meaning of a poem cannot always be pinned down neatly. The poem is an experience, a story, a piece of music, a set of images, and not simply a tidy symbolic equation in which every element "represents" something else.

Poem 28:
A Short Magic-Landscape Poem

To try your hand at one of these strange, disquieting poems, begin by creating a series of vivid dreamlike landscape images with no particular purpose in mind. Put things together that in the real world are not found together. Color objects in ways that nature does not. Let the images conform to the endless possibilities of dream, rather than to the laws of nature. This means allowing your intuitive sense of language to take over from the more "rational" and sequential aspect of your mind. It means letting the writing flow—at least for the initial draft—without stopping to decide what your images mean. For some

125

this will be second nature, the way genuine poetic composition has always come. For others, those used to a more cognitive method of composition, it will be a strange journey. The poems you wrote in the previous two chapters should, however, help make this sort of intuitive poetic composition easier.

Perhaps in your poem there will be some object melted by the moon, or a silver fish thin as leaves swimming through the palm of someone's hand, or cherry-colored birds leaping through a canopy of dark trees. Perhaps in your poem there will be house keys, the stub of a plane ticket, the white moons of someone's fingernails, the brass knob of a door, a doe standing against a white rock, an engine purring across a frozen lake. Whatever the images are that come to you, keep them spare and enticing.

Create several of these fantastical images; do not worry about what they might mean, but simply jot them all down. Get as visual and colorful as you can, but remember to include the other senses as well: the sounds and smells and tactile sensations of this gorgeous and dreamlike landscape that is being created out of the depth of your unconscious mind. Simply allow these images to flow out of you, and accept whatever is given. Do not censor anything that comes up. There will always be opportunity for that in later drafts, when you are selecting and editing.

Once you have several images that you feel happy with, try to juxtapose one against the next, as if they all belonged logically together. You will probably have to juggle with the syntax, putting in connective words and phrases and altering things here and there. Do not struggle to fit everything neatly into a rational and "coherent" whole. If the poem gets written in something akin to a trance state, that's fine!

Keep your pictures simple and clear, just as they are in the model poems we've been looking at. And stick with real objects—not flying saucers or intergalactic telecommunication devices. You are not writing science fiction or space opera. Try to duplicate both the simple vocabulary and the quiet tone of the model poems.

Your task in revision and polishing is to get rid of any line, image, or phrase that does not add to the power of the whole poem, using that same intuitive faculty to guide you. If you can sense what the poem is trying to say in its own symbolic language, fine—let it lead you further in that direction.

Poem 29: The Dream Poem

In Chapter 9 it was suggested that you write a poem based on a real dream, a dream that you could sense was a metaphor for some charged element in your life. Several of the model poems in that chapter, the ones made up of strange, fantastic stories, would also be called surrealistic, though their symbolic significance is perhaps clearer and more straightforward than that of the poems in this chapter. Write another poem based on an actual dream. But this time, concentrate on the images rather than the narrative.

Usually dream records have to be transcribed immediately upon waking, for dreams have the mysterious quality of evaporating quickly in the light of waking consciousness. Keep your notebook beside your bed and spend a few minutes in the morning jotting down whatever images, feelings, and thoughts you remember from your dreams. Then, when you have more time, start shaping those images into a poem. You are probably better off not telling the reader that the poem is the transcription of a dream or worrying too much about the specific meaning of the dream. Rather, concentrate on the intriguing images. Let it remain a poem that is not obviously about one thing or another. Feel free to let the poem veer as far from the actual dream as you like. You might wish to read some of the many dream books that are on the market. These books will give you lots of ideas—many fanciful and far-fetched—about interpreting your dreams. Unlike many of his other books, which are technical and written for fellow doctors, Freud's *The Interpretation of Dreams* was written for the lay reader and remains an exciting and provocative text. Any fair-sized library will have a copy.

Poem 30: Bending Reality

In our discussion of "The Bagel" we have suggested the poem's possible genesis in an actual event. In similar fashion, briefly describe an activity of your own—stooping to tie your shoe, searching for your car key, brushing your teeth, dropping a coin into a beggar's cup, leaping over a puddle after a rain, being pulled along by an open umbrella, trying to unfold a newspaper in a wind, discovering that a particular song has been running through your head all morning—and then transform that experience, staying as realistic as possible in your descriptions, into a fantastic action that somehow becomes a fanciful analogue for your state of mind. Like David Ignatow, begin with a realistic description and then let the poem move quietly into the fantastic. "The Farewell" by Edward Field in Chapter 9, and "Ladies at the Beach" by Clare Nagel in Chapter 11 also work this way.

15

Deranging the Senses:
Automatic Writing and Ecstatic Poetics

Dancing before him!
To whirl and to spin!
Charming his artistic passions,
testing old urges—
O Dark One, beloved, I fasten my anklets,
true love is drunk.
Worldly shame! family decorum!
who needs such virtues?
Not for an instant, one eyeblink,
do I forget him—
he has seized me and stained me,
that Dark One.

> —Mirabai
> (*Translated by Andrew Schelling*)

Mirabai, a fifteenth-century Indian princess and devotee of Krishna, composed ecstatic songs that are still sung throughout India. As in many other religious traditions, the central metaphor of the union with God is the erotic union with an earthly lover. In such songs as these we see poetry most nakedly for what it is—a transcendent intoxicant.

In 1871, the young French poetic genius Arthur Rimbaud wrote the most famous of his "visionary letters," in which he explains to his friend Paul Demeny the dangerous psychic journey upon which he has embarked in order to transform himself into a visionary poet. In that letter Rimbaud wrote:

The Poet makes of himself a visionary through a long, extravagant and deliberate derangement of all the senses. Every form of love, of anguish, of madness; he searches himself, swallowing every poison so that he may retain their quintessence. Unspeakable torment that will require an absolute faith, a superhuman strength—that he become the supreme sufferer, the great criminal, the unholiest damned,—and the supreme savant! For he reaches the unknown! Because—fecund to begin with above all others—he has cultivated his soul. He reaches the unknown—and even if, driven to madness, he should end up having lost all understanding of his visions, nevertheless he has seen them! Though he die while soaring among those ineffable and unnameable things, other frightful workers will follow; they will begin at the horizons where he succumbed.

—Arthur Rimbaud
(Translated by H.S. Matthews)

Not surprisingly, Rimbaud's poems tend to be intoxicated evocations of encounters and landscapes, filled with an explosive excess of passion and image. Ecstatic and hallucinatory, they are full of motion, color, excitation. They are, as he says, "phantoms of nocturnal extravagance." Here is one of the hallucinatory prose poems in his collection *Illuminations*:

Mornings of Drunkenness

Oh my Good! Oh my Beautiful! Terrible fanfare where I am not undone! Enchanted torture rack! Hurrah for the dazzling works and for the marvelous body, for the first time! All began to the laughter of children and with that laughter will end. This poison will remain in our veins even when, fanfare turning, we'll be returned to ancient disharmony. And now may we, so deserving of these tortures, with ardor act upon this superhuman promise to our created souls and bodies: this promise, this madness! Elegance, silence, violence! We've been promised the burial in darkness of the tree of good and evil, the deporting of tyrannical propriety, that we might carry out our purest love. That love began with some disgust and ends—since we cannot in an instant seize this eternity—ends in a riot of perfumes.

Laughter of children, discretion of slaves, austerity of virgins, horror of the faces and objects here, may you all be made holy by the memory of this vigil. See how what began in all vulgarity ends with angels of flame and of ice.

Little vigil of drunkenness, holy! if only for the mask

you've granted us. We affirm you, method! We do not forget that yesterday you glorified each one of our ages. We have faith in this poison. We know how to give each day our entire life.

Now is the time of the Assassins.

—Arthur Rimbaud
(Translated by Joan Lindgren)

Rimbaud abandoned literature when he was nineteen and disappeared into North Africa. When he returned to Paris at the age of thirty-seven, dying of syphilis, his poetry was already well known, his life already a legend.

Henry Miller is an American writer who resembles Rimbaud in the hallucinatory and ecstatic fervor of his language and the ability to unhinge all logic in order to find an idiom closer to the miraculous intensity of the world. Here is a brief passage from one of his autobiographical novels, *Tropic of Capricorn*:

> We lived glued to the ceiling, the hot rancid fumes of the everyday life steaming up and suffocating us. We lived at marble heat, the ascending glow of human flesh warming the snakelike coils in which we were locked. We lived riveted to the nethermost depths, our skins smoked to the color of a gray cigar by the fumes of worldly passion. Like two heads carried on the pikes of our executioners we circled slowly and fixedly over the heads and shoulders of the world below. What was life on the solid earth to us who were decapitated and forever joined at the genitals? We were the twin snakes of Paradise, lucid in heat and cool as chaos itself.

—Henry Miller

Here is a richly textured poem of ecstatic consciousness full of images that are at once wildly inventive and luminously coherent:

Forced Entry
With its foot in the door of your head
With its drop of light
With its bunch of flowers   of grass   of sea-spray
With its oil of sexual fish
With its beginnings of corruption   with shameless laughter
With its blast of desire
With its taste for your salt-lipped beauty
With its silence
With its window that says *Casa*
With its buds opening like Chinese flowers
                                        around ancient cities
With its vibration of an African drum

131

With its blackbird flown to Vera Cruz
With its lion cub roped to a tree
With its clipped wings
With its valise full of travel posters
With its hatred of metals
With its cutting edge
With its submarine of survivors
With its flagpole that has run down all flags
With its shape of a grave-digger's shovel
With its vein of ore
With its speed of a runner who leaves no tracks

I jab into your mouth, this poem, this tongue.

—Jack Marshall

In a series of stunning, expressionistic metaphors, the poet has described the kind of poetry he writes—his own aesthetic tastes and predilections.

No less ecstatically passionate is the brilliant Martinique poet Aimé Césaire. Césaire, a seminal figure in the Negritude movement, and one of the major figures of twentieth-century poetry, is also one of surrealism's greatest exemplars. Here is a brief excerpt from one of his major long poems, "Notes on a Return to the Native Land," a poem that moves restlessly between prose-poetry and verse. Written in French, it is here translated by Ellen Conroy Kennedy:

I would retrieve the secret of great combustions and great communications. I would say storm. I would say river. Tornado I would say. I would say leaf. I would say tree. I would be watered by all rains, dampened by all dews. I would rumble onward like frenetic blood on the slow stream of the eye my words like wild horses like radiant children like clots like curfew-bells in temple ruins like precious stones so distant as to discourage miners. He who would not understand me would not understand the roaring of the tiger either....

—Aimé Césaire

By "ecstasy" we usually mean overwhelming bliss, but for our purposes think of it simply as overwhelming passion. It can be joyful or filled with grief. Poets can express this heightened level of feeling through their imagery or music or pacing or vision—or through a combination of all those elements. The most renowned of American ecstatic poets was, of course, Walt Whitman—a man utterly intoxicated with life. Here is part of the second section of his masterpiece, "Song of Myself":

The atmosphere is not a perfume, it has no taste of the
    distillation, it is odorless,
It is for my mouth forever, I am in love with it,
I will go to the bank by the wood and become undisguised
    and naked,
I am mad for it to be in contact with me.
The smoke of my own breath,
Echoes, ripples, buzz'd whispers, love-root, silk-thread,
    crotch and vine,
My respiration and inspiration, the beating of my heart,
    the passing of blood and air through my lungs,
The sniff of green leaves and dry leaves, and of the shore
    and dark-color'd sea-rocks, and of hay in the barn,
The sound of the belch'd words of my voice loos'd to the
    eddies of the wind,
A few light kisses, a few embraces, a reaching around of
    arms...

—Walt Whitman

To be in love with the very air, with one's own breath, the rocks and
hay, the scent of leaves and dry grass—that is to be enraptured with life
indeed! America's best-known contemporary ecstatic poet is Allen
Ginsberg. The opening half-dozen lines from his long poem "Howl"
will give some sense of the wonderful fecundity and power of his
hallucinatory imagery. The poem is at once a joyful exultation and a
rhapsodic inventory of destruction and despair:

I saw the best minds of my generation destroyed by madness,
    starving hysterical naked,
dragging themselves through the negro streets at dawn look-
    ing for an angry fix,
angelheaded hipsters burning for the ancient heavenly con-
    nection to the starry dynamo in the machinery of night,
who poverty and tatters and hollow-eyed and high sat up
    smoking in the supernatural darkness of cold-water flats
    floating across the tops of cities contemplating jazz,
who bared their brains to Heaven under the El and saw
    Mohammedan angels staggering on tenement roofs
    illuminated,
who passed through universities with radiant cool eyes hallu-
    cinating Arkansas and Blake-light tragedy among the
    scholars of war...

—Allen Ginsberg

An Exercise in Automatic Writing

A method of composition much favored by the French surrealists was automatic writing, a technique of composition by a kind of trance-induced free association which permits the unconscious free play without being inhibited by our rational censor.

The method of automatic writing is simplicity itself—if you're willing to let go of the cognitive, "rational" faculty of the mind. The poems you wrote in the previous three chapters should make this adventure relatively simple for you. Pick up a pen (or sit before the keyboard if you can type with facility and speed), and start writing—anything! Even if it's absolute gibberish. But don't lift your pen from the page. Just keep writing. Don't bother to put what you write in verse form if that's inhibiting—stick with prose. To get started, you might want to write "about" something, but let yourself drift away from that subject as your mind or pen wishes to. Don't worry about what you're writing. Just write whatever comes to your mind, however idiotic, banal, repetitive, strange, nonsensical.

Do not censor, judge, look over your work, correct mistakes, revise, or do anything else that might slow you down. If you go blank, begin the next sentence with the two or three words with which you ended the sentence before it. Or open a book or newspaper and find a phrase that catches your eye and use it to begin your next sentence. Inevitably you will start flowing again. If you write ten or twenty lines of gibberish—that is to say, in a language that invents itself on the spot—that is perfectly appropriate. Write a dozen more!

Although at first you might find yourself writing stiffly and self-consciously, by the time you are at the end of the first page, or somewhere in the middle of the second or third page, your hand will probably be writing without any "inner critic" inhibiting the flow. Language should just be pouring out of you. You will be writing as feverishly, dissociatively, and freely as you can. Allow the mood to be an ecstatic one, a "deranged" and non-rational one. If the mood is anger, let it be a wild anger; if it's descriptive, let the language run free and make the description as unpredictable and supercharged as possible. Let the mountains be bruise-red and the sunset intestinal green and the trees shooting out of the ground like missiles out of subterranean silos. Allow the most far-fetched "illogical" images to pour forth. Play with the language as crazily as you wish. Give vent to emotions you've dared not express, opinions you don't understand, secrets you've never told anyone (including yourself). Lie by all means. Invent. Pretend. Fantasize. Confess to unthinkable crimes and aspirations. Let your vocabulary be exotic, far-fetched, as strange as it can be. Give expression to your wildest dreams, greatest hopes, most embracing visions, most secret fantasies, angers, fears, and joys. Let the poem be at once the most intimate confession and the most wild cacophony of ideas, images, phrases, hiccups, what have you. Let feelings burst forth with uninhibited intensity!

If, at last, exhausted and emotionally disoriented, you end up weeping or giggling while you write, so much the better. If you can write five or six pages this way, that's terrific. If twenty, better yet!

Inducing Ecstasy

Allen Ginsberg begins his rhapsodic long poem "Kaddish" by giving the reader a clear idea of the trance-like state in which he is writing. He tells the reader that he's been up all night reading the Kaddish (a Hebrew prayer for the dead) aloud, listening to Ray Charles on the phonograph, reading the last triumphant stanzas of "Adonais" (Shelley's ecstatic elegy for Keats), and talking. It's a fine recipe for altering one's state of consciousness!

Driving across the state to visit someone you haven't seen in a long time, or walking alone along the beach, or strolling out at dawn to watch the world awaken, or visiting the grave of someone you love are also apt to open the emotional center and unleash psychic and verbal energies that do not ordinarily find expression. At five in the morning, after visiting friends, partying, listening to rapturous music, walking the beaches or streets, too wired and ecstatic to sleep, one is likely to be vulnerable and open. Those are fruitful occasions for doing some "automatic" writing.

There are, of course, any number of ways to shift one's consciousness into this Dionysian mode. Alcohol has traditionally been used for such purposes, but it is not to be recommended, since its ultimate effect is to deaden the senses. Better to sit up talking with old friends; dance around your room until you're filled with energy; read ecstatic poetry aloud (try Keats, Smart, Mirabai, or Rumi), while you play the music that you most love; look at old photos of family and friends or an old address book until you are overwhelmed with emotion; read old love letters; drive past a house where you once lived; do something adventurous, different, chancy. It is when the doors to our emotions are open that we are most likely to be able to write full-throttled, dangerous, naked poetry that shimmers with intensity.

Poem 31: An Ecstatic Poem

After you're done with your bout of automatic writing—burnt-out and exhausted—give yourself a rest (you'll need one!) and then, perhaps the following day, start underlining passages that, in your more rational self, continue to excite you. When you've come up with a page or two of material, start putting it together. Don't worry about ordinary logic or obvious connections or traditional notions of continuity. All you are doing is removing the writing that you find uninteresting and shaping the rest into a musical composition. Let the poem leap wherever it wishes to leap. Just trust your ear to put the pieces together into a whole, so that you end up with a piece of impassioned writing—the writing of a wild gaiety.

If you are not inclined to set it in verse, don't. As you have already seen, much great poetry is written as prose. And don't discard the rest of that material if it looks like there's more usable writing there. Often the germ of several poems will be discovered in a piece of automatic writing.

16

Coils of Hardened Copper:
The Modernist Revolution

Song

When I am dead, my dearest,
   Sing no sad songs for me;
Plant thou no roses at my head,
   Nor shady cypress tree:
Be the green grass above me
   With showers and dewdrops wet;
And if thou wilt, remember,
   And if thou wilt, forget.

I shall not see the shadows,
   I shall not feel the rain;
I shall not hear the nightingale
   Sing on, as if in pain:
And dreaming through the twilight
   That doth not rise nor set,
Haply I may remember,
   And haply may forget.

       —Christina Rossetti

This graceful poem by Christina Rossetti, who died a few years before the beginning of the twentieth century, exemplifies the charm and poise one so often finds in traditional English verse.

If you count the syllables you will discover that the comparable lines in each stanza have the same number: the first line in each stanza has seven syllables, the next six, the next eight, the next six, the next seven, the next six (if one elides *showers* into a single syllable), the next seven and the last six.

137

The *rhythmic structure* is discernible if you read the poem aloud, exaggerating the syllables upon which the natural accents fall. If you speak any two- or three-syllable word aloud, you will notice that one of the syllables is expressed more loudly and energetically. If you begin with the second stanza, which is a bit more regular, you will probably hear the pattern. We'll notate it for the moment by putting the accented (emphasized) syllables in bold capital letters:

> i **SHALL** not **SEE** the **SHAD**ows
> i **SHALL** not **FEEL** the **RAIN**;
> i **SHALL** not **HEAR** the **NIGHT**in**GALE**
> sing **ON**, as **IF** in **PAIN**

One way to describe this pattern of accented and unaccented syllables is to say that they alternate, with the accents falling on the even-numbered syllables. If we arbitrarily divide them into pairs we can say that the rhythmic unit is a *metrical foot* of two syllables with the accent falling on the second one: da**DA**. *Meter* in English poetry designates any pattern of stressed and unstressed syllables found within a poem. This particular two-syllable pattern, with the second being emphasized (da**DA**), is called *iambic meter*. Iambic verse is the most common metrical verse in English. All sonnets, all blank verse, the plays of Shakespeare, and the vast bulk of *metrical* verse in the language are written in *iambs*—a pattern in which each alternate syllable is stressed: da**DA** da**DA** da**DA** da**DA** da**DA**, etc.

Rhymed metrical verse is familiar to anyone who reads English. Along with other poets of his time, Geoffrey Chaucer, who died in 1400, broke with the older conventions of Anglo-Saxon poetry, based largely on alliteration, and established rhyme and meter as the basis of his poetry. Those innovations, copied from French and Italian poetry, quickly took root, and almost all poets in the language after Chaucer wrote metrical, rhymed verse. Those conventions remained essential aspects of English-language poetry until the beginning of the twentieth century.

Although the English poets Christopher Smart (1722–1771) and William Blake (1757–1827) and the American Walt Whitman (1819–1892) had made successful experiments with *non-metrical* poetry, poetry in which there was no discernible pattern of stressed and unstressed syllables, it was not until the twentieth century that the mainstream of English-language poets began abandoning those time-honored conventions. American poets, those in the forefront of the modernist revolution, became infatuated with the experiments of the late nineteenth-century French poets Arthur Rimbaud, Stephen Mallarmé, and Jules LaForgue and began experimenting with non-metrical poetry, as well as with a poetry that functioned in ways radically different from ordinary prose.

By the early decades of the twentieth century, poets had been shaken out of their faith in rational, sequential narrative development. The ideas of Sigmund Freud concerning the symbolic language of dreams and the flow of a subconscious life helped generate lyrical experiments with extravagant verbal imagery and elusive connections, a poetry that valorized image over idea and which delighted in complexity and ambiguity. Modern poetry became increasingly difficult, private, elusive, fragmentary, and experimental.

Freed of its formal conventions, poetry in English today permits the greatest possible freedom. Some poets work at a complexly textured, multi-voiced poetry that is not simply difficult but indeterminate. Just as the non-objective "abstract" painters abandoned subject matter, so have many contemporary poets. If some poets want nothing to do with subject matter, others want little to do with traditional *prosody* (the study of versification) and write in a style that seems to the untrained ear more prose than verse, while others write a poetry that shifts tone, subject, level of diction, and linguistic direction with dizzying rapidity. As you have seen in the preceding chapters, there are poets who write according to chance operations, and there are poets who insist that the only real subject matter of poetry is language itself. At this point, the only rule that a poet must follow would seem to be—in the words of the Chilean poet Nicanor Parra—"to improve on the blank page."

To give us some idea of the poetic revolution of our own time it might be worthwhile to compare another poem of Christina Rossetti's with a contemporary American poem that is based on it. Here is Rossetti's poem:

Who Has Seen the Wind

Who has seen the wind?
  Neither I nor you.
But when the leaves hang trembling
  The wind is passing through.

Who has seen the wind?
  Neither you nor I.
But when the trees bow down their heads,
  The wind is passing by.

                —Christina Rossetti

The poem is built of two *quatrains* (a quatrain is a stanza of four lines), and it has a rhyme scheme *abcb adcd*. That is to say, the second and fourth lines in each stanza rhyme (the "b" and "d" rhymes), while the first and third in each stanza do not, although the first line in each stanza is identical. Though the rhythm is varied with *metrical substitutions* (variations from the dominant metrical pattern), it is basically written in the iambic *measure* that we saw in her other poem; that is, every alternate syllable is stressed, beginning with the second syllable of each line:

> but **WHEN** the **TREES** hang **DOWN** their **HEADS**
> the **WIND** is **PAS**sing **BY**

As with Rossetti's poem "Song," enough variation of this pattern is permitted so that the poem's expressive music is enriched and not in danger of becoming monotonous or sing-songy.

Now here is another poem with the same title, very possibly a direct response to Rossetti's poem, by the contemporary American poet Bob Kaufman:

Who Has Seen the Wind

> A Spanish sculptor named Cherino
> Has seen the wind.
> He says it is shaped like a coil of hardened copper
> And spirals into itself and out again,
> That it is very heavy
> And can break your toe if it falls on your foot.
> Be careful when you are moving the wind,
> It can put you in the hospital!
>
> —Bob Kaufman

Reversing the central perception of Rossetti's poem by suggesting in the opening lines that someone has indeed seen the wind, Kaufman establishes a surprising, humorous, and provocative premise. Before very long the reader understands that the sculptor Cherino has created a sculpture of the wind, and the shock of the initial assertion becomes both a clever joke and an intriguing perception about the nature of art and its ability to make the abstract and invisible become concrete and tangible. The two final lines, giving the reader good common-sense advice about moving the wind, nicely completes the droll assertion of the piece.

But what of the poem's music? What is it that would induce someone to call it a poem in the first place? It has no rhyme, no discernible rhythmic pattern, and is written in a manner that approximates conversational American speech. Nonetheless, a close reading will show that however colloquial the effect, the words and phrases have been carefully chosen for their musical values as well as for their meanings, and the whole poem has been artfully composed.

Alliteration plays a significant role in this poem. Notice, for example, the string of *s* sounds in the first sentence, including the *ch* variation of that sound in the name of the sculptor. Those *s* sounds continue into the third line with the phrase "spirals into itself." If you say the phrase "shaped like a coil of hardened copper" several times to yourself, you will feel how gracefully the words trip off your tongue. The *l* sounds in *like* and *coiled* are responsible for some of that grace; so is the repetition of the *c* sound in *coiled, copper,* and *like.* But the slightly different *o* sounds in those two words also have something to do with the music of that phrase. The alliterative use of the *f* in the phrase, "if it falls on your foot" is another obvious example of the conscious use of alliteration for musical effect.

Notice also the use of internal rhymes. *Shaped* in line three echoes the sound of *break* in line six, and *foot* in line six rhymes with *put* in line eight.

Iambs and Anapests Surprisingly, if one were to look at the rhythmic pattern of Bob Kaufman's poem, one would find a great deal of traditional English meter. The first two lines, for example, are made up, in the main, of alternating stressed and unstressed syllables. Throughout the poem, one finds a stressed syllable preceded by either one or two unstressed ones. If we capitalize the stressed (accented) syllables, the third line of the poem reads like this:

He **SAYS** it is **SHAPED** like a **COIL** of **HARD**ened **COP**per.

One sees at a glance that the accents fall on the second, fifth, eighth, tenth, and twelfth syllables, and that there are either one or two unaccented syllables preceding each accented one. This is, with a few exceptions, the metrical pattern throughout the entire poem—a combination of the two most common metrical feet in English poetry: the iamb, which we have already discussed, and the *anapest,* which denotes two unaccented syllables followed by an accented one (dada**DA**). Rossetti's poem also employs this combination in the second line of each of her stanzas.

The metrical pattern of the Bob Kaufman poem, far less apparent to the reader than the more patently rhythmic verse of Rossetti, should alert you to the fact that contemporary poets, no matter how "free" their verse may appear, need to be just as conscious as their predecessors of the patterns of sound created by their choice of syllables. However, the Kaufman poem, like much contemporary poetry, is written in so disarmingly conversational a tone that the careful patterning of sounds is not apparent.

One needn't choose between Christina Rossetti's poem and Bob Kaufman's contemporary response to it. Nor is it necessary to abandon rhyme and meter to become a powerful contemporary poet. If you love rhyme and meter, you are in good company: so do many of our finest poets.

The Difficulty of Modern Poetry   Many years ago, the American poet and critic Randall Jarrell wrote an essay called "The Obscurity of the Poet," in which he suggested that people who claimed not to read modern poetry because it was difficult, generally did not read poetry at all—poetry of any period. Jarrell is right in suggesting that not just the poetry of our own age but the poetry of all periods tends to be "difficult." But anyone who has tried to read twentieth-century poetry knows that much of it is not only difficult but utterly opaque—poetry characterized in large measure by incoherent discourse and indecipherable imagery.

Of course, in any age there are poets who are more and others who are less difficult. Longfellow is probably easier to understand than Emily Dickinson, but that does not mean he is the better poet—the one who will yield most pleasure to a serious reader. Greeting card verse is surely simple to understand, but that does not make us wish to read more of it. If you have read the previous four chapters and written some of the poems suggested, you can probably understand what might excite a poet about writing poetry that does not communicate in any conventional, sequential, or obvious way.

There are a number of reasons why so much poetry—and particularly modern poetry—is difficult. For one thing, poetry tends to use language as concisely as possible; because of that, it is likely to contain fewer cues to meaning than one is likely to find in essays or stories. A second reason for the difficulty is that poets delight in using language in fresh ways, rather than being content to utilize the common phrases whose meanings we understand at a glance. Another reason for the difficulty is that poets are apt to use phrases with less regard for their clarity than for their sound. Then, too, poets are often allusive and scholarly; they are likely to refer to myths, history, the arts and sciences, and the works of other writers. These references can be daunting. Yet another reason is that just as dreams work through symbols that are often as mysterious to the dreamer as to anyone else, so poets—especially modern poets—often permit their poems to emerge out of that same mysterious source.

Poets are often trying to say things that are elusive, difficult, all but impossible to articulate in words. Poems often begin as sensations and feelings, stray images that won't leave the poet in peace, the fragment of a recollection or emotion that tantalizes and is finally given shape. It is in the realm of the unexpressed or the inexpressible that poetry resides. Often poets are not themselves sure what their poem is getting at. Perhaps this has always been true of poetry to some degree; now, however, poets often cultivate that non-rational, intuitive impulse.

Many experimental poets—taking their cue from non-objective painting—wish for a non-objective poetry, a poetry in which language is the true subject. Such poets are not concerned with ordinary notions of coherence. For others, the "meaning" of a poem has little to do with the sort of conventional assertions in ordinary syntax that we usually designate as significant or meaningful. The fact that prose has become the dominant literary form of the culture has induced poets to stake out a territory distinct from its more straightforward and "factual" language. T.S. Eliot once suggested that the "meaning" of many poems is simply there to satisfy an expectation of the reader and as such is relatively unimportant. He compared the poet to a burglar who might throw a bit of meat—the "meaning" of the poem—to the house dog while he's robbing the house. Eliot suggests that there are other poets (and implies his own sympathies are with that company) who have become impatient with such ruses and wish to get rid of meaning altogether.

Perhaps much poetry is also difficult because it deals with intensely personal material. If images well up to reveal traumatic events and powerful feelings, the psyche, at the same time, will often do its best to camouflage them and keep them hidden.

There are other causes for the obscurity of poetry, causes that are decidedly more questionable. For one, the current intellectual climate simply favors difficult poetry. In a seminal essay on the seventeenth-century Metaphysical poets, T.S. Eliot asserted that poets in our civilization must be difficult. Given the complexity of our culture, the poet was bound to become more allusive and indirect, in order to "dislocate...language into his meaning." Whether or not Eliot's logic is flawed, the fashion for difficult poetry became one of the hallmarks of "serious" poetry. Anyone using the early "masters" of twentieth-century modernism as models for their own work—Eliot, Stevens,

Crane, Pound, H.D., or the like—will come away with a sense that to be a modernist, one simply must be difficult.

A motive for writing abstruse poetry that is even less justifiable than the fact that it is fashionable is that by writing obscurely one is likely to impress people—and one should never underestimate the seductive power of impressing people. Young intellectuals are particularly prone to this disease. A closely related "virtue" of willful obscurity is that when readers can't understand what's being said, the poet is in little danger of being seen as dull, predictable, or sentimental. How much better to be thought erudite than commonplace! In our culture, with its deep reverence for the intellect and its distrust of the feeling center, many writers dread nothing so much as having written simply enough to be understood by one's mother. An even deeper fear is emotionality. Among contemporary poets and critics, it is far more acceptable to be incoherent, which is often considered something of a virtue, than to be gushingly emotional.

Finally, much poetry is obscure because it's awfully hard to write with clarity in verse even when one's meaning is not elusive. Many poets, whether journeymen or novices, imagine their latest poem is perfectly clear, when in fact it is clear only to themselves. Any poetry-writing workshop will convince one of that fact rather quickly.

Poem 32: A Response

Write a poem in eight to fourteen lines of unmetered verse responding to Rossetti's "Song" in much the same way that Kaufman responds to "Who Has Seen the Wind." Refute the premise of the poem by giving altogether different instructions to your beloved than the ones Rossetti gives. Perhaps you would like your love to pine for you to the very end of his or her life, or you want your beloved to tend your grave assiduously, or you'd like to be quick-frozen.

Begin the poem with "When I am dead, my dearest." The rest of your poem will be written in a colloquial American idiom, in your true language (though it might be fun to have another phrase from her poem find its way unobtrusively into yours). Make the poem genuine and poignant. You are, after all, talking about your own death. And of course make it beautiful and memorable, though not in any obvious or conventional way.

Poem 33: A Difficult Poem

Write a poem that is ultra-modernist: its diction sophisticated, its imagery dense, its high seriousness evident—and its meaning totally incomprehensible! Use some of the techniques of the preceding chapters to assist you. Although Ezra Pound's *Cantos* are the perfect model to imitate, just about any anthology of twentieth-century poetry will give you plenty of models to choose from. Though the task sounds silly and might be approached as a lighthearted game, you are likely to find the process of writing such a poem becoming increasingly intriguing. Your job is to write a poem that is musical, interesting, and appealing, despite the fact that its "meaning" is—at least on the conscious level—nonexistent.

17

Playing With Meter:
The Measure of a Poem

Remember

Remember me when I am gone away,
  Gone far away into the silent land;
  When you can no more hold me by the hand,
Nor I half turn to go yet turning stay.
Remember me when no more day by day
  You tell me of our future that you planned:
  Only remember me; you understand
It will be late to counsel then or pray.
Yet if you should forget me for a while
  And afterwards remember, do not grieve:
  For if the darkness and corruption leave
  A vestige of the thoughts that once I had,
Better by far you should forget and smile
  Than that you should remember and be sad.

                    —Christina Rossetti

The Sonnet The sonnet is a fourteen-line rhymed poem written in the same iambic meter which we discussed in the previous chapter when we looked at the Christina Rossetti poem "Who Has Seen the Wind." The iamb, as you will recall, consists of two syllables, the second of which is accented. If you read aloud the line "Remember me when I am gone away," you will notice that it can easily be read so that the emphasized syllables fall on the second, fourth, sixth, eighth, and final syllable. If we put those in bold-face capital letters and you read the line emphasizing those syllables, you will see that, however exaggeratedly, you are reading the line with its natural emphasis:

reMEMber ME when I am GONE aWAY

To avoid confusion it is useful to keep in mind that different syllables and words in a sentence are emphasized to different degrees, and that any sentence can be read in different ways. The sentence above, for example, can be read without strongly accenting the words *me* or *gone*. We can read it without torturing normal English pronunciation like this:

reMEMber me when I am gone aWAY

But if you read three or four lines of Rossetti's poem, you will see that the emphasis in general tends to fall on those even-numbered syllables. This pattern that establishes itself across several lines, and which the poet obviously imposed on the poem as a rhythmic structure, is the meter of the poem. If you read the poem in as natural a manner as you can, emphasizing only those syllables that you would in ordinary speech, you will be less likely to hear the meter, the underlying iambic pattern.

In a metrical poem, the meter is usually rather easy to discern, once you have a little experience. If you read this poem aloud, emphasizing every even syllable, you will see that you do not have to pronounce very many words artificially. This will produce a reading of the poem that emphasizes the iambic meter. Since an *iambic foot* consists of two syllables, the first unaccented and the second accented, we can say that most lines of this poem are made up of five iambic feet. There are a few notable exceptions. Although we can pronounce in**TO** as two words, with the accent on *to*, it is more usual to pronounce that word with the accent on the first syllable. Therefore, the second line of Rossetti's poem, which takes an accent on the fifth syllable, cannot be said to be made up exclusively of iambic feet. Line seven begins with two syllables that again do not fall into an iambic foot. The word **ON**ly normally takes its emphasis on the first syllable. The word **BET**ter, which begins the next to the last line, also takes its accent on the first rather than the second syllable, so that line also has one foot that is not iambic.

A line with five metrical feet or five stressed syllables is said to be written in *pentameter*; therefore, we can say that this poem is written in *iambic pentameter* (despite the three non-iambic feet that we have pointed out).

One way of notating the pattern of stressed and unstressed syllables is by placing a *breve* (˘) over the unaccented syllables and an *ictus* (/) over the accented ones. An iamb then would be designated as ˘/ and a line of iambic pentameter would have five of those. It would be notated as ˘/ ˘/ ˘/ ˘/ ˘/ . Taking the poem's fourth line, we would notate it like this:

˘ / ˘ / ˘ / ˘ / ˘ /

When you can no more hold me by the hand,

This is the meter of that line. It points up the iambic metrical pattern. If one were to *scan* the line the way one might speak it in conversation, one might notate it like this:

˘ / ˘ ˘ ˘ / ˘ ˘ ˘ /

When you can no more hold me by the hand

Or, alternately, one might read it emphasizing the words *no, more,* and *hold* along with the final word, *hand.* We would then scan it:

˘ ˘ ˘ / / / ˘ ˘ ˘ /

When you can no more hold me by the hand

In short, different people can read the line in different ways. But if you read the line in a sing-songy, exaggerated way, emphasizing the daDA daDA pattern of it, you will at once hear the underlying metrical pattern. Though at first this process of finding the metrical pattern might seem strange and artificial, after a while you will be able to pick out a traditional poem's meter with little trouble. Of course, a good poet does not want you to read his or her poem in a silly, sing-songy way. The metrical pattern is meant to help give musical shape to the poem— not straightjacket it into greeting card inanity.

Meter and Ordinary Language Don't get confused and think that metrical feet only exist in poetry. We're talking about the rhythms of our own language as it's actually spoken. Can you scan the following sentence for its accentual pattern? "If you don't understand what we've said, read this section again and again." One common reading of the sentence would view it as a series of six anapests:

˘ ˘ / ˘ ˘ / ˘ ˘ /

If you **DON'T** under**STAND** what we've **SAID,**

˘ ˘ / ˘ ˘ / ˘ ˘ /

read this **SEC**tion a**GAIN** and a**GAIN.**

Remember that in a particular spoken context the emphasis could be different. Perhaps, for example, the speaker wished to emphasize the word *you*. The line would then read: if **YOU** don't under**STAND** what we've **SAID**....

Metrical Substitutions As we have already seen, although the basic measure in "Remember" is iambic, the poet has made three metrical substitutions, rather than holding rigidly to the iambic measure throughout. Good poets writing in meter tend to vary their measures now and again by substituting a different meter for the one that predominates in the poem. In the notational system employing the breve and ictus, the line "Only remember me; you understand" looks like this: /ˇ ˇ/ ˇ/ ˇ/ ˇ/ . That first metrical foot—the opposite of an iamb—is called a *trochee*. We can now say that that line consists of an initial *trochaic* foot followed by four iambs.

Caesuras Poets writing in strict meters tend to vary their *caesuras*, the internal pauses within the lines. In line seven of the sonnet by Christina Rossetti, you will find a semicolon and within line ten a comma, indicating natural pauses in the speaking voice. These *caesuras* are easy to hear. Less obvious internal pauses not demarcated by punctuation can be experienced by reading the poem aloud. In the line "It will be late to counsel then or pray," you're probably going to hear a brief pause after the word *then*. We call this slight, all-but-unnoticed pause a *weak caesura*. Good poets tend to vary their caesuras within a metrical poem as another way of gaining variety and flexibility within the regularity of strict meter. It gives the poet the ability to make the poem sound more natural and less rigidly patterned.

Here is a contemporary sonnet by an American poet:

Therapy

My brother's in the house. I close my door.
He's in the kitchen. Bottles, knives. He breaks the lock,
drags me by one arm across the floor.
A small bird thrums its wings inside the clock:
now it's coming out, it's keeping track
of each indignity: that helpless day,
my father's drinking, Christ, the whole black
drama of my childhood's on display
like a document in a museum. And you
sit listening, and nodding, like those toys
I've seen, their heads on springs. It's too

ridiculous, this ordering the noise
the past makes into music. What's it for?
Time's up. You're in the house. I'm through the door.

—Kim Addonizio

Just as we compared Rossetti's graceful nineteenth-century poem "Who Has Seen the Wind" with Bob Kaufman's modern poem of the same title, we can see the striking difference between Rossetti's sonnet and Addonizio's. "Therapy" has contemporary subject matter: a woman sitting in her therapist's office (or home, as the final line suggests), remembering—and recounting—a painful episode from her childhood. The world the poet paints is a harsh one, containing bottles, knives, alcoholism, and violence. And the narrator isn't even sure that telling all this makes any sense. (She seems to suggest in those last two lines that she's uneasy about telling her story, both in therapy and in poetry.)

Notice how much more internal punctuation there is—how abrupt and "anti-lyrical" the feel of this poem is. It is far more irregular than Rossetti's poem, with a great many metrical substitutions. Line two has six metrical feet instead of five, and line eleven has only four metrical feet.

Octave and Sestet Sonnets are traditionally broken up, in terms of thematic movement, into the first eight lines, called the *octave*, and the final six, called the *sestet*. The ninth line of "Remember" begins with the word *Yet*, signaling a *turn* in the thought, the beginning of a new idea. But "Therapy" violates this convention; the poem turns at the final two syllables of the ninth line, when the narrator's attention shifts to the therapist listening and nodding and her own uncertainty about whether she should be telling her story at all.

Like most contemporary poets, Addonizio feels no compulsion to follow all the formal rules of the sonnet, but is comfortable in adapting the traditional structure to her own purpose. It is decidedly a sonnet, nonetheless: a fourteen-line poem with a distinctly iambic pentameter pattern.

An Exercise in Recognizing Syllables

Do not feel self-conscious or foolish if you have trouble counting the number of syllables in a word. You are probably among those who were never taught to identify syllables in the early grades.

With a bit of concentrated practice, you should be able to recognize the number of syllables in any word without difficulty.

First, check to see that you are sure how many syllables are in the following words: *green, repeat, deliver, institution, refrigeration, unsubstantiated*. You should be able to divide these words easily into their separate syllables. If you can't, repeat those words very slowly, pausing for two or three seconds wherever it is logically possible do so. You will find that you can only pause logically between syllables, each of which makes an unambiguously discrete sound: *un...sub...stan...ti...a...ted*. On the one-syllable word *green*, you can't do it at all.

A syllable can also be determined by counting each separate vowel or *diphthong*. A diphthong is made of two or more vowels coming together in a word, creating a single sound, as the *ea* sound in *smear*. Each such vowel or diphthong is part of a single syllable. Each syllable, therefore, contains a single vowel or diphthong along with either a consonant or group of consonants before it, after it, or both. In the word *repeat*, the sound that includes the first *e* will make one syllable: *re*. The vowels *ea* will be part of a separate syllable: *peat*. In *deliver* there are three such vowel sounds, and indeed the word has three syllables: *de-liv-er*. Each of these three can be spoken separately, pausing between them, without in any way distorting the individual sounds. Jot down a list of twenty-five words, some long and some short, and then write down next to each the number of syllables.

If you are still a bit shaky about recognizing syllables, practice until you are clear, checking your answers against a dictionary, which will separate the word for you, usually with a dot between each syllable. Practice the concept until it is second nature. Once you get it, you will find it simple.

An Exercise in Recognizing Accents

Once you know how many syllables are in those twenty-five words that you wrote down, establish for yourself where the accents fall. *Jennifer* is a three-syllable name with the accent falling on the first syllable (**JEN**-ni-fer). *Rebecca* is a three-syllable name with the accent falling on the second syllable (re-**BEC**-ca). *Angelica* is a four-syllable name with the accent falling on the second syllable (An-**GEL**-i-ca). Once you can recognize syllables and can recognize where accents fall, you can understand how meter works in English. If this concept is not already clear to you, use the two-, three-, and four-syllable words on this page for practice. You can check your work with a dictionary. It will usually distinguish the accented syllable with an ictus (an accent mark) above it. In long words, there are apt to be two accented syllables, a major one and a minor one. The dictionary usually uses a bold-faced ictus for the major accent and a lighter ictus to designate the syllable that is accented less strongly.

Once you recognize accents with 100% success, try your hand at finding the accented syllables in phrases—and then in entire lines of poetry.

An Exercise in Recognizing Meter

If you are still confused, reread the material in both this chapter and the previous one, making sure that you do not go past any words that you don't understand. The material in Chapters 18 and 20 should clean up any remaining confusion.

Now return to the Emily Dickinson poem that begins "There is a pain—so utter—" in Chapter 7, and put an ictus over every syllable that seems accented and a breve over every unaccented one. Notice the pattern that emerges. Now go to the poem "Lot's Wife" that begins Chapter 10, and do the same thing.

An Exercise in Using Meter

Once you are clear about meter, begin practicing by writing a line of iambic pentameter. Then write three more. It should get easier and easier. If you're finding it hard and you feel confused, clear up any misunderstandings by rereading the pertinent material in this and the preceding chapter and doing the relevant exercises. Being able to recognize meter might be easier at this stage than trying to write in it. Test yourself by reading your metrical lines aloud, accenting in an exaggerated way the even-numbered syllables. If the line can be read that way without having to pronounce anything artificially, you have probably got it right. When you have confidence that you can write such a line any time you wish, you are on your way.

Now try writing a line of *iambic tetrameter* (four beats to the line instead of five). Then try a line of *iambic hexameter* (six beats to the line). Then write some lines alternating pentameter and tetrameter.

Once you can write a line of iambic verse, try your hand at a quatrain (a stanza of four lines) in iambic pentameter. Rhyme it *abab*. Make sure the quatrain makes perfect sense and doesn't sound artificial. If that's successful, try another, but this time make one metrical substitution: start a line with a trochaic rather than an iambic foot. That means the line will begin with an accented syllable followed by an unaccented one. Make the rest of the quatrain iambic.

18

A Lighthearted Look at Formal Structure:
Limericks and Double-Dactyls:

A poor working stiff named McGuire
consigned to the Stygian Fire
sent a fax to the Devil:
Are you on the level?
This is not where I'd planned to retire.
                    —Anonymous

Lots of people know what a limerick is—which makes it a perfect tool for continuing our study of rhyme and meter. Can you extrapolate from this limerick to the formal rules of all limericks? That is to say, can you explain what makes a limerick a limerick?

Limericks often start by introducing a character—sometimes by name and sometimes by location ("There was a young woman from Leeds..."), the tone is almost always lighthearted, the story is usually funny and far-fetched, and—at its best—it is a clever little tale with a catchy punchline. But beyond those qualities, limericks are characterized by a definite rhythmic and rhyme pattern.

The Rhyme Scheme In a limerick the first, second, and fifth lines rhyme with each other, and the second line rhymes with the third. *McGuire*, *Fire*, and *retire* all rhyme; so, too, do *Devil* and *level*. The rhyme scheme of a limerick is *aabba*.

The Meter of Limericks Limericks are made up of iambs ($\breve{}$ /) and anapests ($\breve{}\breve{}$ /), which can be used interchangeably. There are three metrical feet in the first, second, and fifth lines, and two metrical feet in the second and third lines.

If we mark the whole poem in our notational system you will be able to see the patterns more clearly:

> A poor working stiff named McGuire   ˘/ ˘˘/ ˘˘/
> consigned to the Stygian Fire   ˘/ ˘˘/ ˘˘/
> sent a fax to the Devil: ˘˘/ ˘˘/ ˘
> Are you on the level?   ˘/ ˘˘/ ˘
> This is not where I'd planned to retire.   ˘˘/ ˘˘/ ˘˘/

Note that lines three and four end with an extra, unaccented syllable. This addition of an extra unaccented syllable to any traditional metrical foot (in this case it's an anapest with an extra unstressed syllable ˘ ˘/ ˘) is called a *hypermetric* or *hypercatalexic* foot, though a metrical foot of this configuration (˘ ˘/˘) can also be called a *third paeonic*. You will be relieved to know that these three technical terms are rarely used and should be memorized only if you want to impress your friends! On the other hand, the terms *iambic* and *anapest* are important, commonly used terms in metrical composition and discussions.

Here's a limerick that comments cleverly on one of our perennial controversies—and on man's incorrigible arrogance:

> A monkey sprang down from a tree
> And angrily cursed Charles D.
> "I hold with the Bible,"
> He cried. "It's a libel
> That man is descended from me!"
>
> —Laurence Perrine

And here's one that uses a series of interesting rhymes—*immutable, irrefutable,* and *inscrutable*—to make another droll comment on the vagaries of theological speculation:

> Our God, some contend, is immutable,
> And their faith is, indeed, irrefutable:
> When He does what He should,
> It's because "He is good,"
> When he doesn't, "His ways are inscrutable."
>
> —Laurence Perrine

Since limerick writers are likely to be people who love to play with words, it's not surprising that many of them love puns and clever ambiguities:

> A collector of clocks, Mr. Reiking,
> Had a wife very much to my liking.

155

"I'll come again soon,"
I informed him one noon;
"Everything that you have here is striking."

—Laurence Perrine

Poem 34: A Limerick

Now write your own limerick. Remember to stay true to the form: five lines with an *aabba* rhyme scheme, the *a* lines being iambic and/or anapestic *trimeter* (three accents) and the *b* lines being iambic and/or anapestic *dimeter* (two accents). To put that another way—to those who are still a bit shaky about these matters—make certain that every accented syllable is preceded by either one or two unaccented syllables and that lines one, two, and five have three accented syllables and the other lines have two. Since the off-color limerick—bawdy, scatological, downright obscene—is a time-honored part of the limerick tradition, you might (when no one is looking, of course), try your hand at one of them!

Here are some suggested first lines to start you off:

There was an old Man name of Moe...
A boy from the town of Bombay...
A lady who lived in a shoe...
A chap with a seven-foot nose...

Be warned: For certain kinds of demonic personalities, the limerick is highly addictive. Once started on this course, there is no turning back!

Higgledy-Piggledy: The Double-Dactyl

A few decades ago, the American poet Anthony Hecht and his friend Paul Pascal invented a wonderfully silly and challenging little verse form that they called "the double-dactyl." Many of Hecht's efforts and those of his friends and correspondents are published in a charming little book called *Jiggery Pokery* published by Athenaeum Press in 1966.

Here's a sample of the form—this one, a pointed comment on T.S. Eliot's poems that often seem to be bemoaning the vulgarity of our century and reminding us of the grandeur of the past. "Miniver Cheevy," by the way, is a poem by E.A. Robinson that pokes fun at just such a character:

Helliot Smelliot
Thomas Stearns Eliot
says that the 20th
century sucks.

Miniver Cheevy's frayed
psychopathology
cloaked in propriety's
top hat and tux.

—Anonymous

Here is another double-dactyl so that you can get a sense of the form that both poems share:

Torridy Lorridy
Moral Majority,
scourge of debauchery's
priapic zoo,

plague of all nympho- and
gynecomaniacs'
endless libidinous
hullabaloo.

—Anonymous

A double-dactyl is made up of two quatrains (four-line stanzas), the first three lines of which are made up of two *dactyls*. A *dactylic* foot is one that contains an accented syllable followed by two unaccented ones. The word *higgledy* is a dactyl. **DA**dada. *Higgledy-piggledy* is a double dactyl (/˘˘ /˘˘). A line made up of two dactyls has six syllables, the accents falling on the first and fourth. The final line of each stanza is, however, a single dactyl followed by a single accented syllable: **DA**dada**DA** (/˘˘/).

The first line of a higgledy-piggledy is a nonsense phrase—which can easily be rhymed with the second line. You can make that one up to suit yourself. The second line, however, must be a proper name, or at least a proper noun. Even more challenging is the second line of the second stanza, which must be made up of a single word. That means you have to find a six-syllable word that is accented on the first and fourth syllables! The final rule is that the last line of each stanza must rhyme.

Here is one more higgledy-piggledy, this one dedicated to all cat fanciers:

> Hestimus-festimus
> *Felix Domesticus*
> Regal as princes and
> lazy as bums.
>
> Partial to canned food and
> ultra-magnanimous
> folks who have got those op-
> posable thumbs.
>
> —Anonymous

Poem 35: A Double-Dactyl

Well, we certainly wouldn't have gone to all this trouble explaining what a double-dactyl is unless we wanted you to write one. But in case you're having trouble coming up with double-dactyl words that would pass muster for line six, here are a few possibilities: antediluvian, bisexuality, extraterrestrial, multidimensional, phantasmagorical, permeability, uncomplimentary, and veterinarian.

And if you're having trouble coming up with proper nouns for line two, you might want to consider the following double-dactyls: Bank of America, Blind Lemon Jefferson, Eleanor Roosevelt, Hans Christian Andersen, Jacqueline Kennedy, Statue of Liberty, and Tess of the D'Urbervilles.

On the other hand, you may want to find your own proper noun for line two and your own six-syllable word for line six—words that don't come from our crib sheet. There are lots of others to choose from—once you put your mind to finding them.

19

More Pleasures of Form and Rhyme:
Sonnets and Villanelles

How Annandale Went Out

"They called it Annandale—and I was there
To flourish, to find words, and to attend:
Liar, physician, hypocrite, and friend,
I watched him; and the sight was not so fair
As one or two that I had seen elsewhere:
An apparatus not for me to mend—
A wreck, with hell between him and the end,
Remained of Annandale; and I was there.
I knew the ruin as I knew the man;
So put the two together, if you can,
Remembering the worst you know of me.
Now view yourself as I was, on the spot—
With a slight kind of engine. Do you see?
Like this....You wouldn't hang me? I thought not."

—E. A. Robinson

This sonnet by Edwin Arlington Robinson is a *dramatic monologue*, a poem in which the narrator is clearly not the poet and is addressing not the reader but some specific individual. The speaker, a physician who is explaining why he euthanized his friend, might be addressing a judge, a police officer, or a prosecuting attorney.

Rhyme Schemes The rhyme scheme of this sonnet is *abbaabbaccdede*. This rhyme scheme characterizes Robinson's poem as an *Italian sonnet* (sometimes called a *Petrarchian sonnet*), a sonnet characterized by an *abbaabba* rhyme scheme for the octave and any rhyme scheme for the sestet, as long as it is based on three rhyme pairs and avoids a final rhymed couplet (two successive lines that rhyme). It is a rather difficult rhyme scheme in English because the first eight lines are limited to only two rhymes. "Remember," the sonnet by Christina Rossetti that begins Chapter 7, is also an Italian sonnet. Its octave has the same rhyme scheme. Its sestet also contains three sets of rhymes, though in a slightly different configuration. "Therapy," the sonnet by Kim Addonizio, is an *English sonnet* (sometimes called a *Shakespearean sonnet*) which is characterized by an *abab cdcd efef gg* rhyme scheme.

End-Stopped and Enjambed Lines When a line of poetry ends at the end of a phrase or sentence, so that it comes to a natural pause, we say that the line is *end-stopped*. All but the fourth line of "How Annandale Went Out" is end-stopped. Almost all of the lines end with a piece of punctuation, a clear signal that it is the end of either a phrase, clause, or sentence. One naturally pauses at the end of each end-stopped line as one does at the end of any phrase unit or sentence. In E.A. Robinson's poem the fourth line is *enjambed*. "The sight was not so fair/as one or two that I had seen elsewhere" is all one phrase so that one pauses only briefly—if at all—at the word *fair* which ends the fourth line.

Enjambment is a useful tool for muting the regularity of metered verse. Allowing a phrase to run over into the next line helps give a rigid metrical form flexibility and keeps it from sounding monotonously repetitive. Also, since rhyme is less noticeable if it falls in the middle of a phrase than at the end, because that syllable or word will be given less emphasis, enjambment helps mute the rhyme. In "Therapy," line five and lines seven through twelve are all enjambed.

The Rhetorical Structure of Sonnets As we have already noted, sonnets are often divided thematically into the octave, the first eight lines, which state the premise; and the sestet, the final six lines, which turn the poem by commenting on the situation or idea presented in the first eight. Robinson has broken this poem into the octave, in which the narrator describes his friend Annandale, and the sestet, in which the first three lines are an implicit confession that he euthanized his friend, and the last three a plea that he not be hung for that crime.

Masculine and Feminine Rhyme Robinson has chosen relatively simple rhymes for his poem. They are all *perfect rhymes*, each *rhyme-mate* sharing the same final vowel and consonant sound. Most rhymes that we see in poetry are *masculine rhymes*. These are rhymes that take their rhyme-sound on the final syllable of the rhyme word. Often such words are found in one-syllable words. All the rhymes in "How Annandale Went Out" are masculine rhymes. So, too, are all the rhymes in the sonnets we've looked at by Christina Rossetti and Kim Addonizio. *Feminine rhymes* are rhymes that take their rhyme-sound on the next to the last syllable of a word or phrase—an accented syllable that is followed by a final unaccented one. To rhyme the word *better* with *letter* would be to employ feminine rhyme, since each of those two words rhymes its next to the last syllable, its accented one. The final syllables are identical in both words. In the poem by W. D. Snodgrass, "Mementos, I" that we looked at earlier, we find the rhyme *carried* and *married*. That too is an example of feminine rhyme. *Immutable, irrefutable*, and *inscrutable* in Laurence Perrine's clever limerick in the previous chapter are *double feminine rhymes*—rhymes that take their rhyme sound on an accented third-from-final syllable. The final two syllables in each word are identical to the final two syllables in the other two words. If you look back at that wonderfully silly Ogden Nash poem "Very Like a Whale," you will see several examples of ingenious rhymes. The first two lines rhyme *better for* with *metaphor*. This is another example of double feminine rhyme. That is, the rhyme-sound is on an accented syllable of a word that contains two more syllables, the two following syllables being identical sounds—or nearly identical sounds—rather than rhyme sounds. Double and triple feminine rhymes are often simply called feminine rhymes.

In the final two lines of Ogden Nash's poem we have the word *dimly* rhymed with *simile*. *Dimly* would be a feminine rhyme with *simile*, which is a double feminine rhyme-mate because it has two additional syllables after the rhyming one. *Longevity* and *brevity* are double feminine rhymes as well. So too is that wonderfully silly and imaginative rhyme *Tennyson* and *venison*. These ingenious rhymes are, of course, not the least of that poem's pleasures.

The Pleasures and Pitfalls of Rhyme As we can see from our models, when rhyme is well used it has great charm. But for the poet in the act of composition, rhyme has an additional virtue: the search for a rhyme-word forces the mind out of its familiar track and onto more adventurous and unfamiliar paths. To find a rhyme for "friend," Robinson must have had a string of possibilities run through his mind—possibilities that led in a variety of directions. End-rhyme, then, is not only a delight to the ear of the reader when used well, but a spur to the imagination of the writer.

But there is also a downside that must not be ignored. The problems of end-rhyme are two-fold: The first is the danger of coming up with a line that is tortured in diction or syntax in order to get in a rhyming word at the end. The second danger, prevalent among even accomplished poets, is the possibility of being seduced into writing a line that one really doesn't believe, mean, feel committed to—but which fulfills the formal rhyming requirement. Many a respectworthy poet, under the pressure of finding a rhyme-word, has ended up with a line that was clever, elegant, interesting, or novel, rather than a line that was felt and believed.

The Villanelle Just as rhyme forces the mind into unfamiliar paths, so too does any formal structure. The following somewhat lighthearted poem is an example of a *villanelle*, a form that, though considerably more limited than the sonnet in its range of possibilities, is one that contemporary poets have found attractive:

The Grammar Lesson

for D.

A noun's a thing. A verb's the thing it does.
An adjective is what describes the noun.
In "The can of beets is filled with purple fuzz"

of and *with* are prepositions. *The*'s
an article, a *can*'s a noun,
a noun's a thing. A verb's the thing it does.

A can *can* roll—or not. What isn't was
or might be, *might* meaning not yet known.
"Our can of beets *is* filled with purple fuzz"

is present tense. While words like *our* and *us*
are pronouns—i.e., *it* is moldy, *they* are icky brown.
A noun's a thing; a verb's the thing it does.

Is is a helping verb. It helps because
filled isn't a full verb. *Can*'s what *our* owns
in "*Our* can of beets is filled with purple fuzz."

See? There's almost nothing to it. Just
memorize these simple rules...or write them down:
a noun's a thing; a verb's the thing it does.
"The can of beets is filled with purple fuzz."

—Steve Kowit

The villanelle contains not only a strict rhyme scheme but *refrains*, entire lines repeated at specific intervals. A poem of nineteen lines, the

162

first is repeated as the sixth, the twelfth, and the eighteenth. The third line is repeated as the ninth, the fifteenth, and the nineteenth. The first and third lines rhyme, and that rhyme is repeated in the first and third lines of the next four stanzas. If we designate A^1 and A^2 as the refrains, the rhyme scheme of the poem is A^1bA^2 abA^1 abA^2 abA^1 abA^2 abA^1A^2. Although villanelles needn't be written in iambic pentameter, they often are.

Notice that full consonance is used instead of an exact rhyme in *noun/known* and that *known* is then used as a rhyme with *owns*. Notice, too, the use of caesuras in various places within the lines to break up the iambic rhythm and get it to sound more like colloquial speech.

An Exercise in Rhyme

1. Find as many perfect one-syllable rhymes with *ball* as you can (*fall, tall, hall*, etc.). You should be able to come up with at least fifteen.
2. Find one-, two-, and three-syllable rhymes for *hand* (such as *bland, demand, countermand*, etc.). You should be able to find more than fifteen.
3. Find as many words that create rich consonance with *ball* as you can. You should be able to find at least five.
4. Find as many feminine rhymes with *wearing* as you can. Many of these will have a rhyme-mate for the sound *wear* and end with the same "*ing*" ending.
5. Find as many perfect rhymes with *shoot* as you can (*boot, coot*). Now try for off-rhymes. These can be examples of assonance (*tune, reputed*), of which you should be able to find a great number, or rich consonance (*mate*).

Poem 36: The Sonnet

At this point you should be ready to try a sonnet. To make it more challenging, try your hand at one that's also a dramatic monologue. Your narrator is a fictional character revealing a secret to someone. Perhaps the narrator is the wife of an alcoholic or of a sexually promiscuous minister; or it's a teenager about to commit suicide over an unhappy relationship or family problem; or an elderly woman living in a run-down nursing home; or an airline stewardess who knows something the passengers don't; or a local sheriff; or a.... Well, you get the idea. You will also have to decide whom your narrator is addressing, and, of course, what it is he or she is revealing.

Choose either an English sonnet (rhymed *abab cdcd efef gg*) or an Italian sonnet (rhymed *abbaabba* for the octave and either *cdecde* or *cdcdcd* or *ccdede* for the sestet). Enjamb at least two lines. Try for perfect rhymes rather than off-rhymes, and see if you can use feminine rhyme at least once. Make at least three but no more than six metrical substitutions in the poem. Also, have internal punctuation within at least four lines—commas, semicolons, dashes, periods, what you will. Be certain, of course, to maintain five beats in each line.

Remember, the trick is to get your meters and rhymes right without sacrificing other elements of the poem. Do not torture your syntax in order to get your rhythms or rhymes. The poem must flow naturally. If any of it sounds tortured and artificial, keep working until it does not —and until you have a real poem. And keep your language contemporary: just because the sonnet is a traditional form doesn't mean it has to sound like an old-fashioned poem.

Needless to say, this is a challenging poem to write, but working on it with energy should give you valuable experience with metrical verse.

Poem 37: The Villanelle

Try your hand at a villanelle. Contemporary poets sometimes play with the refrains, slightly rewording them at each use. Since the entire poem turns on only two rhymes, be sure that both your rhyme words have many available rhyme-mates. The word *ball* would be usable, for example, while the word *sneakier* would probably be a tough one to find several rhymes with—though that sort of difficult rhyme is perfect for a poet trying for comic effects.

Once you have your two rhymes, it would be wise to make a long list of rhyme-mates for each, which you can continually refer to as you hunt around for the next line. You might even extend that list to off-rhymes to give yourself more options.

It is safest not to enjamb lines one and three—the lines that will be used as the refrains, but to end-stop them. If you don't already have an idea for the subject matter, try writing a villanelle that is either a set of simple instructions, as in our model (how to say goodbye, destroy a relationship, ruin an evening, apologize, pretend not to be hurt), or a villanelle that is inspired by a headline in one of those juicy scandal sheets like the *Weekly World News*, a paper filled with space aliens, pigs eating babies, crime victims returning from the dead, sightings of Elvis, and similarly bizarre events.

164

20

A Cribsheet of English Meters

The Most Common Meters The four most common metrical feet in English are iambs, anapests, trochees, and dactyls, with the iamb being the single most common of the four. Also common are the *spondee* (two syllables—both stressed), and the *pyrrhic* foot, (two syllables—unstressed).

Here is a brief list of the most common rhythmic feet in English language poetry:

iambic	˘/	daDA
trochaic	/˘	DAda
anapestic	˘˘/	dadaDA
dactylic	/˘˘	DAdada
spondaic	//	DADA
pyrrhic	˘˘	dada

Notice that the trochee is just the opposite of the iamb, the dactyl the opposite of the anapest, and the spondee the opposite of the pyrrhic foot. Here is an example of trochaic verse:

> Go and catch a falling star,   /˘/˘/˘/
> Get with child a mandrake root,   /˘ /˘ /˘/
> Tell me where all past years are   /˘ /˘ /˘/
> Or who cleft the Devil's foot.   /˘ /˘ /˘/
>
> —John Donne

The last metrical foot in each line is *truncated*, that is to say, a syllable short. Truncated lines are common in trochaic verse. Though one can as easily say that the final syllable is an extra one, or that the third is a *cretic* foot made up of an unaccented syllable flanked by accented ones. Notice too how easily trochaic lines can be turned into iambic ones. All you need do is place one unaccented syllable at the beginning of the line. For example:

> Let's go and catch a falling star ˘/ ˘/ ˘/ ˘/
> Let's get with child a mandrake root. ˘/ ˘/ ˘/ ˘/

Here is an example of anapestic verse. Because there are four anapestic feet in each line we can call this verse anapestic tetrameter:

> ˘ ˘ / ˘ ˘ / ˘ ˘ / ˘ ˘ /
> For the Angel of Death spread his wings on the blast,
> And breathed in the face of the foe as he passed;
> And the eyes of the sleepers waxed deadly and chill,
> And their hearts but once heaved, and forever grew still!
>
> —George Gordon, Lord Byron

The above quatrain is written in rhymed couplets: *aabb*. Did you notice that one of the feet in this quatrain is not anapestic? The first foot in the second line is an iambic substitution:

> . ˘ / ˘ ˘ / ˘ ˘ / ˘ ˘ /
> And breathed in the face of the foe as he passed;

Here is a quatrain of dactylic verse:

> / ˘ ˘ / ˘ ˘ / ˘ ˘
> Lie with me, courage, at night, when the
> Phantoms of darkness and fearfulness
> Savage my dreams. Let the arms that you
> Wrap me with cincture the gashes of Hell.
>
> — H.S. Matthews

Spondaic and Pyrrhic Feet Since a *spondee* consists of two stressed syllables, one is not apt to come across whole lines written in that measure unless they are part of a list of one-syllable words. The first line of this rhymed couplet is spondaic:

> / / / / /
> Cheese, grapes, pears, nuts, beans
> combined in a salad with lots of fresh greens.
>
> —E.D. Jameson

Here is the first line of Coleridge's "Epitaph," which employs two spondaic feet and three iambs:

> / / ˘ / ˘ / / / ˘ /
> Stop, Christian passer-by!—Stop, child of God,

It is impossible to find a whole line of poetry that is made up of *pyrrhic* feet, since one cannot pronounce four syllables in English without finding one of them exhibiting more stress than others. Nonetheless, pyrrhic feet are common in poetry, though we will not always designate them as such, since those syllables are often considered as part of other measures. For example, any line that is anapestic or dactylic will have several examples of two unstressed syllables together. One can call the first line of the following verse a combination of pyrrhic and spondaic feet, though one could also say it's an anapest, a dactyl, and a spondee. One could, in similar manner, call the second line either an anapest and a cretic foot or a pyrrhic, a spondee, and an iamb:

$$\breve{}\ \ \breve{}\ \ /\ \ \ /\ \ \breve{}\ \breve{}\ \ /\ \ \ /$$

On the first hour of my first day

$$\breve{}\ \breve{}\ \ \ /\ \ \ \ /\ \ \ \breve{}\ \ /$$

In the front trench I fell.

—Rudyard Kipling

Other Metrical Feet Here are the names of metrical feet that are less widely used but still useful to know:

amphabrach	$\breve{}/\breve{}$	daDAda
cretic	$/\breve{}/$	DAdaDA
bacchic	$\breve{}//$	daDADA
antibacchic	$//\breve{}$	DADAda
Ionic major	$//\breve{}\breve{}$	DADAdada
Ionic minor	$\breve{}\breve{}//$	dadaDADA
Paeonic	$\breve{}\breve{}/\breve{}$	dadaDAda

In first paeonic, the accented syllable is the first syllable; in second paeonic, it is the second syllable, etc. The one we have listed above ($\breve{}\breve{}/\breve{}$) would be called "third paeonic."

An Exercise in Recognizing Poetic Meter

To see whether you understand this material, answer the following questions. Keep in mind that this chapter does not need to be memorized. It is here so that you may refer to it when you wish. Look over the necessary material in this chapter when answering each question:

167

1. Which of the following two lines is iambic pentameter and which is made up of two anapests followed by two iambs?
   a. When you're sleepy and old and very gray
   b. When you are old and gray and full of sleep

2. Which of the following two lines is a mixture of iambs (˘/) and anapests (˘˘/) and which can be said to begin with a dactyl (/˘˘) followed by a trochee (/˘), an anapest (˘˘/), and an iamb (˘/)?

   c. In the West is the bird who whistles in the night.
   d. West is the Region where I heard her sing.

3. Which one of the following two lines is made up entirely of iambs, and which is made up of an initial trochee followed by a series of iambs?

   e. Come now, this world is wiser than you think.
   f. The morning light doth break upon the hill.

If you are unable to answer the questions above, it means that some of the "technical" terms that we've been using are still not clear. Don't get too upset. It's not easy to learn all about poetic meter in a few minutes. It would be an excellent idea, however, for you to clear up the words in this chapter that you misunderstand. You can check within the chapter (the first usage of any technical word is in italics), or go back to the earlier chapters that dealt with meter. You can also look up any confusing words in an ordinary dictionary. Then come back to our little quiz and take it again.

Poem 38:
A Metrical Poem...With a Vengeance

Wouldn't it be fun to write a poem in which you use all of the meters we've mentioned? That would be sixteen different metrical feet—if you do all four paeonic measures. If you're ambitious and have a quirky sense of humor, such a task should appeal to you. Make the poem sixteen lines long, with three or four feet to each line.

A fine resource for poets interested in meter is *Strong Measures*, by Philip Dacey and David Jauss. The book contains numerous poems in traditional forms by contemporary American poets as well as useful appendices about meter and form.

21

Line Breaks

In traditional metrical poetry, poetry in fixed forms, the question of where one ends a line does not arise. If, for example, the poem is in iambic pentameter—as sonnets traditionally are—then each line will end after the metrical foot containing the fifth accented syllable, that is to say, after the fifth metrical foot.

Sometimes a poet only counts accents per line rather than both accents and syllables. This is called *accentual verse*. Here are some lines from an accentual poem which contains two accents per line despite differing numbers of syllables:

> Everybody's
> had this room
> one time or another
> and never thought
> to sweep. Outside
> the snows stiffen,
> the roofs loosen
> their last teeth
> into the streets.

> —Philip Levine (from "Saturday Sweeping")

Other poems find their formal structure by the number of syllables in each line rather than by the number of accents or metrical feet. Philip Levine, whom we have just quoted, sometimes likes to work in loose *syllabic verse*. In his poem "What Work Is," most of the lines are nine syllables long. Here are the first eleven lines of that poem, all but two of which are that length:

> We stand in the rain in a long line
> waiting at Ford Highland Park. For work.
> You know what work is—if you're

169

old enough to read this you know what
work is, although you may not do it.
Forget you. This is about waiting,
shifting from one foot to another.
Feeling the light rain falling like mist
into your hair, blurring your vision
until you think you see your own brother
ahead of you, maybe ten places.

—Philip Levine (from "What Work Is")

An interesting example of a syllabic poem is Sylvia Plath's "Metaphors." It is a riddle-poem, and the fact that there are nine lines and each line has nine syllables are two of the clues. The title, appropriately, has nine letters. The answer to the riddle will be found near the end of this chapter.

Metaphors

I'm a riddle in nine syllables,
An elephant, a ponderous house,
A melon strolling on two tendrils.
O red fruit, ivory, fine timbers!
This loaf's big with its yeasty rising.
Money's new-minted in this fat purse.
I'm a means, a stage, a cow in calf.
I've eaten a bag of green apples,
Boarded the train there's no getting off.

—Sylvia Plath

But what of verse which is unrhymed and unmetrical and written in conformity with no predetermined pattern whatsoever? Where in that case does one end the verse line?

The truth is that there are no rules—one decides as one goes. Two experienced poets writing the same sentence might well choose to break their lines in different places. Some poets tend to prefer lines that are relatively short, some prefer lines that are somewhat long, and others vary the line length continually. The question of how you want the poem to sound will often determine where you break your lines, for to some extent your line breaks act as part of the poem's musical notation, determining pauses, tension, emphasis, and pace. Here are several common reasons for breaking a verse line at a particular place:

1. It is often logical to stop a line of poetry at the end of a sentence or phrase unit, as in the following poem:

I Advertised for a Part-Time Job

A man called;
said he'd been in an accident,
needed someone to massage his wounds.

I said I was sorry
but wasn't qualified,
neither nurse nor masseuse.

He said he'd teach me;
he'd pay $60.00 an hour!

"WHERE are your wounds?" I asked.

After a slight pause he said,
"You'd have to not be too modest."

I took a job in an office,
$6.00 an hour.

I don't do wounds.

     —Kathleen Iddings

The author has divided this poem into seven stanzas, one for each sentence. Notice in the following poem how each line ends where there would be a natural pause in speaking it. Line three, though it follows this pattern, gives additional emphasis to the phrase, "I've caught her," while expanding upon it in the following line. Notice too that the author plays with stanza breaks, turning this brief six-line poem into four stanzas:

The Freedom Fighters

her mother ranks cleanliness
just a little higher than godliness,

so when my daughter realizes I've caught her
wiping her hands on her jammies in the kitchen,

she winks conspiratorially,

and I wink back.

     —Gerald Locklin

2. Often for pace and/or a sense of unbroken flow, one works against this principle of ending at the end of a natural phrase unit and enjambs the line, ending in the middle of a phrase unit and forcing the reader to either ignore the line end or pause slightly where, had one been

171

reading prose, one would not have thought to. As we have mentioned earlier, in rhymed poetry enjambment helps mute the rhymes, calling less attention to the rhyme word. Letting the meaning constantly run from line to line often increases both the sense of urgency and—as in this case—the illusion of ordinary, nonpoetic conversation. In the following excerpt the brevity of the lines also helps to create this effect:

> he was holding a
> fifth of whiskey
> in his right
> hand.
> he was about
> 30.
> he had a cigar
> in his
> mouth,
> needed a
> shave.
> his hair was
> wild and
> uncombed
> and he was
> barefoot
> in undershirt
> and pants.
> but his eyes
> were
> bright.
> they *blazed*
> with
> brightness...

—Charles Bukowski
(From "The Man with the Beautiful Eyes")

3. You may want to break a line to give special emphasis to a particular word or phrase by putting it at the end of a line, which often calls more attention to it. "Tugging" in the following stanza takes on an ominous ring it might otherwise not have had. Here, too, the poet is working against the natural pauses, enjambing her lines for increased tension. Read the lines aloud and you will hear it:

> Darker now. I put out
> the wet laundry. In the wind
> the pulley creaks and shifts.
> My dresses lift, tugging

at the pins. I go in
to where my daughter sleeps.

　　　　—Kim Addonizio (from "Night Feeding")

4. There are times when a line break can play the part of punctuation, clarifying the syntax and meaning. Since punctuation notates a breath pause as well as a syntactic shift, line breaks are often used so that the reader will know where to pause when reading the poem. As such, they are also a musical notation. Such line breaks are especially useful in poems that have little or no punctuation:

this is the final insult
flat on your back
in the open casket
made up to look
like a harlot
wrinkled face twisted
into a mortician's
idea of bliss...

　　　　—Al Masarik (from "Dirge")

5. Perhaps you have conceived of a poem as somewhat "tight" and minimalist, the thought and emotion emerging with great compression and energy. That effect might be accomplished more effectively with short lines. Note how the following lines seem to spit out of the speaker:

Kiki Diaz spits
just like I used to spit
back when I was growing up
thirty years ago
in Memphis
on Prescott Street.

　　　　—Bobby Byrd (from "Good Field, No Hit")

And here's the same effect in the opening stanza of a poem called "The Vocal Groups":

every block had one
in the halls
in the parks
in the projects
hangin' out on the corner.
o-o-o-o-in' & ah-h-h-in'
& doo-whap-doo-wha-a-a,
false tenors cracking the air
in half

　　　　—Robert Scotellaro (from "The Vocal Groups")

173

6. A large-spirited poem with an embracing vision might seem to require long, inclusive lines. So the lines in the visionary poetry of Whitman, Blake, and Christopher Smart are often extremely long. In twentieth-century American poetry, we see this impulse toward the long, inclusive line in Carl Sandburg, Allen Ginsberg, and Thomas McGrath, among others. Here is a passage from Section 2 of Whitman's "Song of Myself." Notice the kind of sweeping lyricism he achieves with the long line:

> Stop this day and night with me and you shall possess the
>   origin of all poems,
> You shall possess the good of the earth and sun, (there are
>   millions of suns left,)
> You shall no longer take things at second or third hand, nor
>   look through the eyes of the dead, nor feed on the
>   spectres in books,
> You shall not look through my eyes either, nor take things
>   from me,
> You shall listen to all sides and filter them from your self.

When the poetic line extends past the right-hand margin of the page, the convention is to indent the rest of it so that the reader knows it is part of the previous line. Were the paper wide enough, the words would be placed on a single line.

7. Sometimes you may wish to break your line for the surprise or irony that is caused when the first word or phrase of the following line alters the meaning that was established in the previous line. In the following excerpt, note how the fourth line completes the third in a surprising way, changing the idiomatic phrase "carried on" to a different idiomatic expression, "carried on business":

> In the other room, I'd dance
> To the radio with Annie's kids
> While she carried on
>
> Business in her bedroom. She paid me
> Those afternoons by the hour
> To keep her children
>
> Happy and out of the way.
>
>   —Corrine Hales (from "Annie's House")

Here are the opening lines of a poem by Jack Marshall, a poet who tends to use line breaks for irony, surprise, and enrichment of meaning. Notice how the second line seems to have one meaning—until the reader, continuing to the following line, completes the phrase. The same thing, to perhaps a lesser extent, is also true of the following line:

> This is the bodiless night
> when those who've loved no longer can
>
> live as one wearing their flesh
> with easy knowledge that it is common...

> —Jack Marshall (from "This is the Bodiless Night")

8. Poets are often concerned with the visual shape of their poems—perhaps more so than is generally acknowledged—and will often break lines based on how those line lengths make the poem look on the page. Occasionally you may have a particular visual design that you're interested in accomplishing. Here are lines that take advantage of the computer's ability to center lines on a page:

> Imagine Whitman remembering each blade of grass.
> Imagine Stalin phoning Mayakovski.
> Imagine Stalin phoning Frank.
> You can't imagine that?
> Frank phoning Stalin?
> Of course.

> —Andrei Codrescu (from "The Inner Source")

9. Anaphoric verse, that is to say verse that tends to begin with the same word or phrase in each line, is usually end-stopped, the line ending at the end of the sentence or clause. Here is the beginning of a long-lined anaphoric poem by Harold Norse. Each line begins with "In November." At times the poetic lines run on for as many as eight actual lines on the page:

> In November I lost my foodstamps, the computer said I did
> not exist
> In November I lost my best friend who said I did not exist
> In November I lost my manuscripts and felt as if I did not
> exist
> In November I sent 2 postcards to my mother who wrote
> back saying she had not heard from me and DID I
> STILL EXIST?
> In November I paid the telephone bill and received a final
> notice for the non-payment
> In November my girlfriend accused me of unreality and
> infrequence with a tendency to dematerialize on week-
> ends and holidays even Jewish ones and stormed out
> leaving a sinkful of dirty dishes and linen blackened by
> her feet, souvenirs of blood and tobacco burns...

> —Harold Norse (from "In November")

10. Line breaks are often guided by the poet's intuitive sense of what is needed, rather than by any conscious reasoning. Perhaps you simply feel that a line needs to end at a particular word, not for any reason that you can articulate but simply because that line break feels right to you. It might have something to do with musical notation and with emphasis. It is not unlikely that a great many lines in free verse poetry are broken where they are for just this intuitive sense of where the line ought to end.

11. Sometimes a poet will break a line to mask a rhyme—so the rhyme words don't fall at the ends of lines. Addonizio, in the excerpt from "Night Feeding," could have broken lines to create end rhyme with *pins/wind* and *creaks/sleeps* but chose not to, thereby muting those rhymes. By the same token, a poet might wish to end a line on a rhyme word to call attention to it.

12. On occasion, there are special reasons for particular spacing and line breaks. Here is a poem by Paul Blackburn that attempts to be a transcription of the author's last phone conversation with one of his mentors, William Carlos Williams. Williams had suffered a number of strokes and had great difficulty speaking during the last few years of his life. Notice how poignantly Blackburn captures the hesitant, clipped anguish of Williams' voice by his line breaks, odd spacing, and use of punctuation:

Phone Call to Rutherford

"It would be—
             a mercy if
you did not come see me...

"I have dif-fi / culty
             speak-ing, I
cannot count on it, I
am afraid it would be too em-
             ba
             rass-ing
for me   ."

             —Bill, can you still
             answer letters?

"No . my hands
are tongue-tied . You have...made
a record in my heart.
             Goodbye."

        —Paul Blackburn

13. Many modern poets, abandoning the feeling that a new line must start at the left-hand margin, use a more improvisational or open typography to help notate their poems so that the reader has some indication of respective pauses. This isn't, of course, a precise system of time measurement, but if one reads the Blackburn poem with the spaces indicating pauses, one probably comes closer to the author's intention. Why has he separated the periods from the final letter of the sentence? Isn't that a perfect way to give a sense of the tension within a statement by someone for whom each word is agony? It is almost like a silent sigh a second or two after the sentence has been completed. Many contemporary poets do not start their lines at the left margin but vary their line placement the way Blackburn does here.

Here are a few lines written in *tercets* (three-line stanzas) that have a progressively indented margin:

> What interests me
>   is what turns
>   over at the boiling point, peeling
>
>   mass from light
>   letting bone show through.
> Not the pinned down, home
>
> sweet home, but the phantom
>   photon jumping orbit to feed
>   what's given with time back
>
>   into time; flame
>   to be lived, out-
> living flowers still to come...

> —Jack Marshall (from "Chaos Comics")

The author of those lines says that the jagged shape of the tercets—he thinks of them as both analogous to sawblades and to the flow of water—appeals to him for its sense of continuous movement, and that tercets themselves appeal to him—more than quatrains would—because the odd number of lines offers less sense of closure. The form creates a sense of torque in which everything tightens and turns. Given this sense of what he wants his poems to do, one can understand why, for the same reason, he is given to line endings that often set up a surprise—the following line often giving the sense of the bottom dropping out from under the reader.

14. There are times when the line breaks of a poem are an inevitable facet of the poem's logic. This is the beginning of such a poem by Terry Hertzler:

> **A** is for America. It's funny the things we do for love.
>
> **B** is for bombs. B-52s dropped thousands of bombs on Vietnam—they tore up a lot of ground. Bouncing Betties were small, anti-personnel bombs used in ambushes. One blew the legs off a friend of mine.
>
> **C** is for Charlie; the Viet Cong. They thought we were invading their country.
>
> **D** is for dead.
>
> **E** is for E-1, E-2, E-3, etc. Those are Army ranks. The higher the number, the less chance you'd fall under "D".
>
> —Terry Hertzler (from "A Vietnam Alphabet")

The Solution to Plath's Riddle The answer to the riddle poem by Sylvia Plath—and the explanation for her use of a nine-syllable line—is: a pregnant woman. One will rarely have so specific a motive for breaking lines of unmetered poetry at particular places. Your line break decisions will often be guided by one or another of the reasons listed above.

Poem 39: Working with Line Breaks

Write a poem that has lines longer or shorter than the length you're comfortable with and generally use. If you tend to work in very short lines, avoid them in this poem. If you have never used very long lines, experiment with them. Try for at least one line break that generates surprise or irony. Include in this poem the name of someone you haven't seen in several years; a kitchen appliance; an article of clothing; the name of a street, newspaper, song or movie; one line about a town you've never lived in; and any three of the following words: mucus, tongue, sprawling, relaxed, maniacal, wrinkle, and spinach.

Poem 40: An Accentual Poem

Write a poem about a job you once had. Speak in the voice of someone convinced that the reader has probably experienced something similar. Begin with the phrase "Everybody's had this...(boss/problem/job/feeling/notion/experience, etc.)." Alternate between two-beat and three-beat lines. Make sure that they don't fall neatly into iambic feet. Remember that some lines that have three accents might be only five or six syllables long, while others that contain three accents might be ten or twelve syllables long. To decide how many beats there are in each line, you are going to have to trust your ear. Keep reading your poem aloud to see how it sounds, and where the accents fall. See, too, if you can't use at least one striking metaphor in this poem and an instance of rich consonance.

Poem 41: Working with Syllabics

Write a short rhymed poem that contains lines of alter-nately seven and nine syllables. Though you can keep to perfect rhymes where you wish to, try for enough off-rhymes—assonance and partial consonance—to keep it from having too formal and rhymy a feeling. In fact, if the casual reader doesn't notice that it's a rhymed poem, all the better. You may wish, in order to further mute the end-rhymes, to use a more subtle rhyme scheme than *abab*. Perhaps every fourth line will rhyme so that you end up with something like *abcdabcd* or some varia-tion on that pattern. Or perhaps you will opt for a random rhyming pattern in which the only rule is that every line must rhyme with at least one other line.

In this poem reveal at least two of your smaller secrets ("I never go anywhere without dental floss"/ "I read Harlequin Romance novels every chance I get," etc.). Then compare your more innocent foibles with the monstrous crimes of Hitler, Stalin, Attila the Hun, or whoever comes up in your mind. It might be a real person in your life, perhaps your mother's father, or a neighbor who shot his wife, or perhaps it's someone you recently read about in the paper: a man who killed a family of six, or a woman who drowned her two children. Let whatever tone and discourse that emerges out of this situation develop as it will.

Poem 42: Open Field Poetics

Write a poem in which you alter the conventional typogra-phy so that at least a third of your lines do not start at the left margin. Look at the excerpts from Blackburn and Codrescu in this chapter and at the Anne Waldman poem in Chapter 23, and try playing with your typography in a way that seems meaningful for the poem. If you work on a computer you might wish to try centering the poem on the page or justifying the right rather than the left margin.

Make this a *discursive poem*, a poem that explores ideas that are close to your heart. Ideally, you will be investigating these ideas, rather than merely stating them, in the poem. Find oblique ways of making the case—cutting into the discourse fragments of anecdotes, dialogue, information, musings, so that the discursive thread is woven through a constantly surprising texture that is never straightforward and simple. Allow for some confusion on the reader's part. There might be people referred to as if the reader should know who they are, or dialogue that has too little context for its import to be entirely clear. Let the scene shift three or four times, surprising and disorienting the reader. Perhaps the most interesting model of this kind of nonsequential discursive poetry is to be found in the work of T.S. Eliot, but many postmodern poets work this terrain of disorienting collage, and models can be found easily in almost any anthology of contemporary poetry. The cut-ups, translitics, surreal poems, and "experimental poems" that you tried in previous chapters should have given you a feel for this kind of nonsequential writing that is so centrally a facet of modern and postmodern poetics.

The Perennial Themes

Ars Poetica 1974

Poetry
pardon me for having helped you to understand
that you are not made of words alone.
        —Roque Dalton
        (Translated by Richard Schaaf)

22

The Body Politic

Agonies are one of my changes of garments,
I do not ask the wounded person how he feels, I
myself become the wounded person,
My hurts turn livid upon me as I lean on a cane
and observe.
—Walt Whitman

The Burning of the Books

When the Regime ordered that books with dangerous teachings
Should be publicly burnt and everywhere
Oxen were forced to draw carts full of books
To the funeral pyre, an exiled poet,
One of the best, discovered with fury, when he studied the list
Of the burned, that his books
Had been forgotten. He rushed to his writing table
On wings of anger and wrote a letter to those in power.
Burn me, he wrote with hurrying pen, burn me!
Do not treat me in this fashion. Don't leave me out. Have I not
Always spoken the truth in my books? And now
You treat me like a liar! I order you:
Burn me!

—Bertolt Brecht
(Translated by H.R. Hays)

Since it is the job of writers to bear witness to the truth, and the habit of writers to read widely, think deeply, and seek their own counsel rather than adopt the propaganda of their leaders and the self-serving rationalizations of their fellow citizens, it should not be surprising that writers often find themselves in mortal opposition to the state apparatus. Salman Rushdie, an internationally respected writer, lives in hiding because a novel of his offended an orthodox, fundamentalist religious group; Naguib Mahfouz, a Nobel Prize-winning author, was stabbed for his liberal, secular political and religious views. Another Nobel laureate, Wole Soyinka, Nigeria's leading poet-playwright, had to flee for his life because of his support for democracy. Taslima Nasrin, a Bangladesh essayist who wrote in favor of women's rights, was recently forced to flee to Europe under threat of assassination by religious extremists. In the United States, there are well-organized groups in many areas agitating to censor books from school libraries—not pornography or cheap fiction, but serious works of literature by such brilliant authors as Mark Twain, Richard Wright, Alice Walker, Maya Angelou, and J.D. Salinger.

Bertolt Brecht, a German communist and one of the notable playwrights of the twentieth century, is also one of the great moral voices of our age. An outspoken foe of Hitler's regime, and later of the oppressive communist regime in East Germany, Brecht sought refuge first in Finland and then in the United States. In the Third Reich's burning of the books, Brecht's works were surely *not* forgotten.

Brecht's bitter, sharply-honed irony is a perfect vehicle for political warfare. Roque Dalton, a Salvadoran revolutionary poet, also wrote acerbic, in-your-face political poems of stinging irony. In the one below, he explains the fundamental relationship between Latin-American dictatorships and U.S. neocolonialism, a relationship which, in El Salvador, cost the lives of some 200,000 citizens—most of them victims of an oligarchy that was generously supported by the United States government. OAS stands for the Organization of American States, that multi-national Latin-American organization whose policies are often dominated by Washington:

OAS

The President of my country
is called for the moment Colonel Fidel Sánchez Hernández.
But General Somoza, President of Nicaragua,
also is President of my country.
And General Stroessner, President of Paraguay,
is also a little the President of my country, though less
than the President of Honduras, namely
General López Arellano, and more than the President
    of Haiti,

183

Monsieur Duvalier.
And the President of the United States is more President
    of my country
than the President of my country,
that one who, as I said, is for the moment
called Colonel Fidel Sánchez Hernández.

                              —Roque Dalton
                              (Translated by Richard Schaaf)

Dalton's explanation is whimsical, absurd, fiercely hilarious, and, many would suggest, savagely precise.

Here is a quieter, but no less effective way of making comments about the history of extermination:

Fort Robinson

When I visited Fort Robinson,
Where Dull Knife and his Northern Cheyenne
were held captive that terrible winter,
the grounds crew was killing the magpies.

Two men were going from tree to tree
with sticks and ladders, poking the young birds
down from their nests and beating them to death
as they hopped about in the grass.

Under each tree where the men had worked
were twisted clots of matted feathers,
and above each tree a magpie circled,
crazily calling in all her voices.

We didn't get out of the car.
My little boy hid in the back and cried
as we drove away, into those ragged buttes
the Cheyenne climbed that winter, fleeing.

                              —Ted Kooser

Once again we see a poet finding a story to tell that symbolizes a larger, more general idea, a story that *embodies* the author's meaning. The story of the slaughter of the magpies and the horror it evokes in the narrator's son cannot help but remind the reader of the more excruciatingly horrible slaughter of the Cheyenne. Yet the analogy remains implicit, for the author never needs to spell out the connection between the two events. It is a deft and effective device for making that shameful piece of American history real to the reader. At the same time, the extermination of the birds is not minimized, is not simply a symbol for the slaughter of the Cheyenne, but is conveyed to the reader as a

184

terrible event in its own right. Given our growing consciousness of the destruction of whole species, acts that are rapidly denuding the planet of its once immense variety, the killing of the birds themselves is not to be taken lightly. The poem, then, is about the murder of both the birds and the indigenous people—about the thoughtless destruction of others who are, from our limited and egocentric perspective, nothing but "pests."

In the following poem, Ernesto Cardenal has also found a story to tell that works as a controlling metaphor, expressing the plight of the Nicaraguan people through the story of a group of parrots. Like "OAS," the poem is an unambiguous protest against neocolonialism:

The Parrots

My friend Michel is a commanding officer in Somoto,
    near the border with Honduras,
and he told me about finding a shipment of parrots
that were going to be smuggled to the United States
    in order for them to learn to speak English.
There were 186 parrots, and 47 had already died in their
    cages.
And he took them back to the place from where they'd
                  been taken,
and when the truck was getting close to a place
                  called The Plains
near the mountains where those parrots came from
    (the mountains looked immense behind those plains)
the parrots began to get excited and beat their wings
    and press themselves against the walls of their cages.
And when the cages were opened
they all flew like arrows in the same direction
                  to their mountains.
That's just what the Revolution did with us, I think:
it freed us from the cages
    in which we were being carried off to speak English.
It brought us back to the Homeland from which
                we'd been uprooted.
Comrades in fatigues green as parrots
         gave the parrots their green mountains.
But there were 47 dead.

       —Ernesto Cardenal
       (Translated by Jonathan Cohen)

It is interesting to note that Cardenal, a Catholic priest as well as a political revolutionary, was minister of culture in the short-lived revolutionary government that followed the successful revolution against the dictatorship. Cardenal, like Pablo Neruda before him, is both a major political and artistic figure in Latin America.

It is usually not effective to write about the sufferings of people in general terms. To say that millions are desperately poor is likely to touch a reader less powerfully than to sketch in the lives of one or two individuals. The following poem by Muriel Rukeyser simply presents a moment in the life of two adolescents. The restrained dignity of the poem, its reluctance to preach, is paralleled by the quiet yet desperate dignity of the young boy and his sister whose lives we are momentarily permitted to watch:

Boy With His Hair Cut Short

Sunday shuts down on this twentieth-century evening.
The El passes. Twilight and bulb define
the brown room, the overstuffed plum sofa,
the boy, and the girl's thin hands above his head.
A neighbor's radio sings stocks, news, serenade.

He sits at the table, head down, the young clear neck
    exposed,
watching the drugstore sign from the tail of his eye;
tattoo, neon, until the eye blears, while his
solicitous tall sister, simple in blue, bending
behind him, cuts his hair with her cheap shears.

The arrow's electric red always reaches its mark,
successful neon! He coughs, impressed by that precision.
His child's forehead, forever protected by his cap,
is bleached against the lamplight as he turns head
and steadies to let the snippets drop.

Erasing the failure of weeks with level fingers,
she sleeks the fine hair, combing: "You'll look fine tomorrow!
You'll surely find something, they can't keep turning you
    down;
the finest gentleman's not so trim as you!" Smiling, he raises
the adolescent forehead wrinkling ironic now.

He sees his decent suit laid out, new-pressed,
his carfare on the shelf. He lets his head fall, meeting
her earnest hopeless look, seeing the sharp blades splitting,
the darkened room, the impersonal sign, her motion,
the blue vein, bright on her temple, pitifully beating.
                                        —Muriel Rukeyser

How reticent the author is to shout out her pity and indignation. Had she done so, how easily the poem could have turned sentimental. Two impoverished children, alone, without resources: surely a lesser poet would have grown rhetorical, self-righteous, theatrically indignant, milking their plight and overstating a situation that is more effectively presented as Rukeyser presents it, without comment, without explicit emotion. For the children, too, are reticent; they, too, refuse to speak openly of the terror of their plight. The girl's brave reassurances to her brother tell us all we need to about their desperation and poverty.

People who are capable of being anguished by the anguish of others are likely to want to write about the experiences of the beaten-down, the impoverished, the oppressed—poems about bigotry and needless suffering and injustice. But the task of writing poems about the social and political world presents special problems for a poet—and special pitfalls. In such poetry it is doubly useful to hold to particulars. Sweeping generalities and self-righteous rhetoric are likely to have little emotional impact. Simply to say that you hate to see the homeless in the streets, and that you are sick of the stupidity of war, ignorance, and greed, is not likely to engender memorable poems.

One way to avoid political speeches masquerading as poems is to embody those emotions and opinions in a story, the narration of a particular incident. We have already seen how successful that tactic is in the poems we've examined. Brecht's poem is not simply about tyrants burning the books of patriots; it is the story—albeit an apocryphal one—of one such writer who found that his books had not been included in his government's auto-da-fé. Roque Dalton doesn't generalize about colonialism and puppet regimes; he gives us the names of the people about whom he is speaking. Cardenal and Kooser both find incidents that represent a political perception—incidents that illuminate symbolically the histories of oppression and slaughter.

All the poems we have looked at so far in this section have been "realistic" ones—poems about real events—or that might have been about real events. In contrast, the following prose poem is a fable:

The Uninvited

As the heads of state feast with one another, the tables in the gilded hall loaded with caviar, venison, exotic fruits and vegetables and gallons of champagne, there's a tapping on the windows. A child's face, then another, presses against the

187

panes, the eyes in them black as the night the children stand in, their mouths open as if they were howling with the wind.

"Who are they?" ask the guests uneasily. "Where did they come from?"

"Keep them out!" yells the host. "Get Security! Where's Security?"

But the children are so thin, they slip under the doors, around the edges of the windows. Noiselessly. In great numbers. They move forward to the tables. Their fingers grip the edges of the tables. Their eyes gaze upward into the enormous openings and closings of official mouths.

—Virginia R. Terris

How urgently and vividly the author has painted this chilling scene. How disquieting and unnerving are the pictures she makes us see: the children "so thin, they slip under the doors, around the edges of the windows," children with eyes "black as the night they stand in," with mouths "open as if they were howling with the wind." It is, thematically, not far different from "Boy With His Hair Cut Short," a story of impoverished children, but one that is more explicitly political, one that lets the reader see above the children the "openings and closings of official mouths." Imagine if Virginia Terris or Muriel Rukeyser had written explicitly about their indignation rather than creating stories that embody those points of view. How difficult it would have been to keep such a poem from seeming overbearing, pious, and sentimental.

Here is a poem that also speaks in a quiet voice about the most wrenching suffering. It, too, avoids breast-beating generalities, substituting instead the horrific details that speak for themselves. Unlike the previous poems, with which the common reader can vociferously empathize and agree, this poem is more difficult to stomach—because it is not about them but about us! The poem brings to life a horror that is so pervasive in the daily existence of our civilization that many readers will have no recourse but to deny its significance. Like the Cardenal poem, at the end the author comments on what he has seen.

No One Talks About This

They go in different ways.
One hog is stationed at the far end
of the pen to decoy the others,
the hammer knocks the cow
          to his knees,

the sheep goes gentle
                    and unsuspecting.
Then the chain is locked
around the hind leg
and the floor descends
                    from under them.
Head down they hang.
The great drum turns
the helpless objects
and conveys them slowly
to the butcher waiting
at his station.
The sheep is stabbed
behind the ear.

Gentle sheep, I am powerless
to mitigate your sorrow.
Men no longer weep
                    by the rivers of Babylon
but I will speak for you.
If I forget you, may my eyes
lose their Jerusalem.

—Carl Rakosi

If the poem is discomforting, that may be because the savage bru-
tality implicates the reader, for it is surely about nothing if not last
night's dinner.

For our final model, let us return to the technique of political
irony—but rendered here so quietly, with such unassuming but lethal
finesse, that the reader is caught entirely off guard. Who could be more
reasonable than this most reasonable African-American citizen who
wants nothing better than to agree with his white compatriots. Since it
is part of a long poem, "malcolm," the intended irony of this section
might be harder to see. One might, reading just this section, mistake it
for a conciliatory poem of someone who really does feel humble in the
presence of a white civilization. In the context of the full poem, how-
ever, that reading would be difficult to make:

The Beast Section

i don't think it important
to say you murdered malcolm
or that you didn't murder malcolm
i find you vital and powerful
i am aware that you use me
but doesn't everyone

i am comfortable in your house
i am comfortable in your language
i know your mind   i have an interest
in your security. your civilization
compares favorably with any known
your power is incomparable
i understand why you would destroy
the world rather than pass it to lesser
people. i agree completely.
aristotle tells us in the physics
that power and existence are one
all i want is to sit quietly
and read books and earn
my right to exist. come—
i've made you a fantastic dish
you must try it, if not now
very soon.

—Welton Smith

There is something so chillingly seductive and "reasonable" about Smith's tone that we almost buy into the insanity of his agreeable logic. Surely the hint of dark humor at the end (what is the fantastic dish the narrator has in store for those who have treated him as a lesser being?) is the more devastating for being so understated.

A Process for Germinating Poems of Social Consciousness

To prime yourself for writing a poem of social consciousness, do the following:

1. Start clipping articles and photos from your daily newspaper that sadden you, anger you, or in some other way move you. Keep the articles in a folder and the photos where you can see them.
2. List the social issues about which you feel deeply.
3. Recall an incident of mockery directed at someone for being old, infirm, poor fat, disabled, homosexual, socially awkward, or "ugly."
4. Recall someone you knew who had been touched by war.
5. Recall encountering someone who was homeless and/or desperately poor.
6. Recall an injustice that you witnessed.
7. Make a list of other "political" incidents or encounters in your life, things that have either happened to you or that you have witnessed that involved such issues as injustice, intolerance, exploitation, war, or cruelty.

Poem 43: The Photo Poem

"Boy with His Hair Cut Short" has the frozen starkness of a black-and-white Depression-era photograph, and might well have been precipitated by one. Take one of the photographs that moves you deeply: children in a refugee camp, bodies lying in a street in a besieged city, a woman weeping across a barbed wire fence, a photograph of someone being lynched or shot, and write a poem based on it.

Begin the poem by describing the scene without announcing to the reader that you are describing a picture. If you prefer, suppress that information entirely, allowing the reader to sense the immediacy of the situation (which your disclosure might short-circuit). As you write, try to discover where the poem is leading you and what it wants to say about the world—or, if that seems too closed and limiting a way of approaching your poem, ask what questions the poem might want to pose, what issues it could raise, what complexity or ambiguity it might illuminate. You might wish to use the news story that accompanied the photo for details, names, and background, or you might even do some research in history books. Remember to spend little time talking about emotions and a lot of your descriptive talent presenting details that will make your readers feel the scene deeply. Try for a restrained "objective" manner. The genius of such a piece will probably lie in the power of the created details rather than in your commentary. The poems by Rukeyser and Rakosi in this chapter and "The Catch" in Chapter 11, which describes a newsreel that the author evidently saw on TV, would be well worth looking back on as models.

Poem 44: A Poem of Witness

Take the memory that has come to you most vividly from the process for germinating poems of social consciousness, the one that you feel would be most powerful to write about, and start writing down as many details of the incident or encounter as you can remember. Let it all flood back to you as you write. But also write down any generalizations or larger truths that one might extrapolate from the incident. Report this incident in as "objective" a voice as possible, allowing an accurate and graceful description to create a powerful response from the reader, as Rakosi does in "No One Talks About This," or as Rukeyser does in "Boy with His Hair Cut Short." Be careful not to overplay your hand: do not get melodramatic or theatrical. Don't hit

191

the readers over the head, pointing out the significance of what they should have been able to understand from the description itself. Simply let the story enter the reader's heart like a spike.

Poem 45: Political Irony

Select a social issue about which you feel passionately and write an "argument" in the manner of Welton Smith, addressing those who hold beliefs and attitudes you passionately oppose. Assure them that you understand and sympathize. Do not paint their argument with so broad a satiric brush that your opposition to their ideas is apparent. Like Smith, keep your irony so restrained that it cannot be seen. Then, find some way of showing the absurdity or horror of their position without departing from your rational and sympathetic tone. The great model in English literature of the devastating use of this satiric strategy is Jonathan Swift's "A Modest Proposal."

Roque Dalton's irony is based on arguing something that is at once true and patently absurd. If a political situation lends itself to that strategy, try your hand at such a poem.

Poem 46: A Political Fable

Create a little political fable in the manner of "The Uninvited" or in the manner of the poems in the chapter on the controlling metaphor—"The Divorcing Men," "A Very Wet Leavetaking," or "Gretel"—which can also be read as political fables. "The Burning of the Books" and "The Parrots" might have been stories the poets heard from friends, though the Brecht poem might well be a fiction, something he imagined he would do if the Nazi regime refused to include him in their list of banned authors. Because such a poem depends in part on the power of the story told, and its fitness to your purpose, be sure to choose—or invent—the incident wisely. Keep your notebook handy and jot down ideas as they come to you until one of them jells. Once you have an idea that looks promising, even though you're not sure exactly where it's going or what it comes to, you may want to begin the poem, letting its implications work themselves out as you write. On the other hand, if you are more comfortable plotting out the whole tale, getting it airtight before you start writing, by all means do so. Despite current theories and aesthetic fashions about process, the "correct" method of approach is always the one that works for you.

Poem 47: The Political Cut-Up

Try your hand at a cut-up, using two articles that act in ironic counterpoint to one another. For example, an article about religious persecution or bigotry cut in with fragments from the Bible, or an article about starvation cut in with an article about gourmet foods or haute cuisine. A list of current street and military weapons could be interspersed with dialogue from a romance novel to form a nightmarish poem.

Poem 48: A Poem of Political Rage

Use the automatic writing technique to compose several pages of wildly savage political invective. Curse, rant, accuse, threaten, explode! Give vent to all your pent-up political frustration and rage. But do it in a richly imaginative language. This material will, of course, be chaotic, disorganized, frenzied, and perhaps incoherent. But later drafts should let you shape it into a coherent and powerful poem—without dissipating any of its wildness and savagery.

23

As Soon As These Blossoms Open:
The Poetry of Love and Longing

> *I'm caught in this curling energy! Your hair!*
> *Whoever's calm and sensible is insane!*
> —*Rumi*
> *(Translated by John Moyne and*
> *Coleman Barks)*

Aubade

Il n'est mie jors,
Saverose au corps gent,
   Si me consent Dieus
L'aloete nos ment.

It is not daylight,
O sweet one with the gentle body
   So God help me,
The lark lies to us.

        (—Provençal, twelfth or thirteenth century)

The speaker pleads that it is not yet dawn, that the lark is not heralding the morning. May the night never end! In four lines of great tenderness, this unknown Provençal poet has epitomized the exquisite passion of erotic love.

An *aubade* is a morning song, a poem which usually expresses the regret of lovers that dawn has come so soon and that they must part. One of the most famous examples of this motif in English poetry is the

194

scene in *Romeo and Juliet* in which the young lovers awaken from the only night they will ever spend together. Romeo must leave at once for exile in Mantua. The setting is Juliet's chamber, overlooking the garden:

> Juliet: Wilt thou be gone? It is not yet near day:
> It was the nightingale and not the lark,
> That pierced the fearful hollow of thine ear;
> Nightly she sings on yon pomegranate tree:
> believe me, love, it was the nightingale.
>
> Romeo: It was the lark, the herald of the morn,
> No nightingale: look, love, what envious streaks
> Do lace the severing clouds in yonder east:
> Night's candles are burnt out, and jocund day
> Stands tiptoe on the misty mountain tops.
> I must be gone and live, or stay and die.
>
> Juliet: Yon light is not daylight, I know it, I:
> It is some meteor that the sun exhales,
> To be to thee this night a torch-bearer,
> And light thee on thy way to Mantua:
> Therefore stay yet, thou need'st not to be gone.
>
> Romeo: Let me be ta'en, let me be put to death;
> I am content, so thou wilt have it so.
> I'll say yon grey is not the morning's eye.
> Tis but the pale reflex of Cynthia's brow:
> Nor that is not the lark whose notes do beat
> The vaulty heaven so high above our heads:
> I have more care to stay than will to go.—
> Come, death, and welcome! Juliet wills it so.—
> How is't my soul? let's talk,— it is not day.
>
> Juliet: It is, it is,—hie hence, be gone away!
> It is the lark that sings so out of tune,
> Straining harsh discords and unpleasing sharps.
> Some say the lark makes sweet division:
> This doth not so, for she divideth us:
> Some say the lark and loathed toad change eyes;
> O, now I would they had changed voices too!
> Since arm from arm that voice doth us affray,
> Hunting thee hence with hunt's up to the day.
> O, now be gone; more light and light it grows.
>
> Romeo: More light and light,—more dark and dark our woes!

(Act III, Scene V)

The scene is written in *blank verse*—unrhymed iambic pentameter, though it contains occasional end rhyme and two rhymed couplets to end off the passage. There is a great deal of alliteration, assonance, and repetend, creating a lovely internal music. There is also a great deal of syntactic balance, eloquent phrasing, and effective figurative language. The wit of the speeches, the speakers' evident passion, and the tenderness and grief of the human emotions behind the language make this brief scene—like so much of Shakespeare—memorable and moving.

Carpe diem—seize the day! Here is how Izumi Shikibu, an eleventh-century Japanese poet, pleads with her beloved. In five short and exquisite lines—only a handful of syllables—she manages to express the intensity of her longing and her sense of life's brevity:

Come quickly—as soon as
these blossoms open,
they fall.
This world exists
as a sheen of dew on flowers.

—Izumi Shikibu
(Translated by Jane Hirshfield with Mariko Aratani)

The image of the "sheen of dew on flowers" as an expression of impermanence, a central theme in Buddhist thought, loses little of its evocative power in the translation.

How to speak of one's love, one's infatuation, one's obsession, and passion? This charming love poem—at once oblique and perfectly clear—is only three lines long. In its English version (the original is in Greek), it is a mere eighteen words—but speaks volumes! Ritsos, one of the important poets of our time, wrote many three-line poems:

You forgot your comb on the dresser.
The stars are my witness,
I will not give it back.

—Yannis Ritsos
(Translated by Minas Savvas)

And here's another brief love poem, a very American poem inspired by the Greek poet Sappho:

(after Sappho)

O

everyone
                quit hounding me!
I'm no good at my duties

            demands   invitations

leave me cold

Blame Jack
He introduced us

& now I'm wild & crazy
with love of the boy

—Anne Waldman

The poet takes great freedom with her typography, laying out the words and phrases on the page both as a substitute for punctuation and—perhaps it comes to the same thing—as a notation for the performer. But the line and spacing decisions are not only meant to act as a kind of musical notation; they are also an indication, visually, of the poem's field of energy—giving the reader some intuitive sense of the poem's passion and "wildness." Here's another jaunty poem that plays with the joyful insanity of infatuation:

I Think You're Wonderful

I think you're wonderful.
I'm driving my car
and your name is on every mailbox.
I'm kissing you
and my shoes crawl away
in darkness, sweet gadgets
sing in my wrists, the life
I dumped into the river years ago
is reported found in the Philippines....
Why do I tell you this?
Because your lingerie
is burning, because a lone drop
of rain is falling somewhere
above the Sahara, because
I think you're wonderful.

—Thomas Lux

There is a crazy kind of logic to the poem that communicates its passion and pleasure without ever getting literal or solemn, the surreal images nicely conveying the narrator's slaphappy feelings. Whether or not we can rationally "analyze" each of its images, we should be able to "get" the poem immediately—understanding his sense of wonder and renewal. Nonetheless, if you stop to consider the images closely, you will find that they do make a kind of screwball sense. Perhaps if you visualize the poem as a series of animated cartoons, you will see the logic of the images more clearly.

197

Spewing from the speakers of millions of radios and CD players all over America are paeans to and laments about love: soppy country ballads and rhythm and blues and hard-edged rock lyrics praising one's latest love, or anguishing over his cheatin' heart, promising eternal faithfulness if only she'll come back, or moaning over one's inconsolable loss. So the challenge for the love poet is to make it new. If it's the pop singer's role to croon about the last night we spent together, it's for a poet like Ritsos to swear by the stars that he won't return your comb. The Grand Ol' Opry star can sing that he sees his sweetie just everywhere he goes, but it's for a real poet like Lux to turn it into the droll assertion that your name is on every mailbox. Here's what a torch song sounds like when it's been transformed by a gifted poet—a poem that's breathlessly romantic, lyrical, and passionate, yet manages to avoid the conventional props and predictable sentiments of romantic ballads:

Reunion

*Just as he changes himself, in the end
eternity changes him.*

—*Mallarmé*

On the phonograph, the voice
of a woman already dead for three
decades, singing of a man
who could make her do anything.
On the table, two fragile
glasses of black wine,
a bottle wrapped in its towel.
It is that room, the one
we took in every city, it is
as I remember: the bed, a block
of moonlight and pillows.
My fingernails, pecks of light
on your thighs.
The stink of the fire escape.
The wet butts of cigarettes
you crushed one after another.
How I watched the morning come
as you slept, more my son
than a man ten years older.
How my breasts feel, years
later, the tongues swishing
in my dress, some yours, some
left by other men.
Since then, I have always

wakened first, I have learned
to leave a bed without being
seen and have stood
at the washbasins, wiping oil
and salt from my skin,
staring at the cupped water
in my two hands.
I have kept everything
you whispered to me then.
I can remember it now as I see you
again, how much tenderness we could
wedge between a stairwell
and a police lock, or as it was,
as it still is, in the voice
of a woman singing of a man
who could make her do anything.

     —Carolyn Forché

The poet has chosen to counterpoint the romantic passion of the scene with gritty, anti-romantic details—police locks, wet butts of cigarettes, the stink of a fire escape—mixed with some of the traditional images associated with a romantic tryst: a bottle of wine wrapped in a towel, a torch song on the phonograph, a block of moonlight. But she avoids any hint of the obvious, the sentimental, the predictable.

The poet's line breaks are particularly effective, as you will see if you read the poem aloud, pausing ever so slightly at those enjambed line endings. The poem is highly assonant and alliterative. Look, for example, at lines thirty-two through thirty-six and note those *e* sounds in *kept, everything, then, remember, again, tenderness,* and *wedge,* a sound echoed finally in the poem's final word, *anything.* If you start from the beginning, you will find numerous other examples of that sound running through the poem. There are several other examples of assonant rhyme and a great deal of well used alliteration.

But, of course, there are more subtle and less easily analyzable qualities of sound combinations that contribute to a poem's grace and music. There are harsh sounds and softer ones, phrases that seem quick and emphatic, and others that are slower, more meditative and relaxed. Good poets are adept at placing their syllables just where they need one or another sound—though this is likely to be done without any analytic or fully conscious intention. Two phrases may mean the same thing denotatively, but generate different tones, different pace, different shades of expressive meaning. Had a novice poet, concentrating on end-rhyme, written:

> Two glasses of liquid, fragile and black,
> stand on the table next to a bottle, towel-wrapped

we would feel how static and forced the lines sound, and we would probably lose that "suspension of disbelief" that allows us to fully enter the world of the poem. How awful and stiff and downright silly those lines sound next to Forché's simple, swift and natural phrasing:

> On the table, two fragile
> glasses of black wine,
> a bottle wrapped in its towel.

The poems we have been looking at deal with love from the inside, from the point of view of a passionate participant. Here is a poem from the point of view of an older, wiser friend watching with amused, cautionary, and tender sympathy as a frantic adolescent goes through the throes of first love. But it is also a love poem by virtue of being written from the perspective of a loving parent or grandparent:

A Sunday Morning After a Saturday Night

She's so happy, this girl,
she's sending out sparks like a brush fire,
so lit with life
her eyes could beam airplanes through fog,
so warm with his loving
we could blacken our toast
on her forehead.

The phone rings
and she whispers to it
"I love you."
The cord uncoils
and leaps to tell him
she said it,
the receiver melts in her hand
as if done by Dali,
the whole room crackles

and we at the breakfast table
smile
but at safe distance
having learned by living
that love so without insulation
can immolate more than the toast.

—LoVerne Brown

A good deal of the charm of this poem is in the wit of the metaphors, a wit created in part by hyperbole, conscious exaggeration, which is often used for just such comic effect. It is a love, we are told, "so without insulation" that the receiver of the phone melts and the young girl could blacken toast on her forehead. What a clever way of speaking of adolescent infatuation! The final line, which drolly asserts that such love "can immolate more than the toast," extends the metaphor to an incisive final perception—to which the whole poem has been leading.

And here is a poem about another kind of love:

Love in the Classroom
—for my students

Afternoon. Across the garden, in Green Hall,
someone begins playing the old piano—
a spontaneous piece, amateurish and alive,
full of a simple, joyful melody.
The music floats among us in the classroom.

I stand in front of my students
telling them about sentence fragments.
I ask them to find the ten fragments
in the twenty-one-sentence paragraph on page forty-five.
They've come from all parts
of the world—Iran, Micronesia, Africa,
Japan, China, even Los Angeles—and they're still
eager to please me. It's less than half
way through the quarter.

They bend over their books and begin.
Hamid's lips move as he follows
the tortuous labyrinth of English syntax.
Yoshie sits erect, perfect in her pale make-up,
legs crossed, quick pulse minutely
jerking her right foot. Tony
sprawls limp in his desk, relaxed
as only someone can be who's
from an island in the South Pacific.

The melody floats around and through us
in the room, broken here and there, fragmented,
re-started. It feels mideastern, but
it could be jazz, or the blues—it could be
anything from anywhere.
I sit down on my desk to wait,
and it hits me from nowhere—a sudden
sweet, almost painful love for my students.

"Nevermind," I want to cry out.
"It doesn't matter about fragments.
Finding them or not. Everything's
a fragment and everything's not a fragment.
Listen to the music, how fragmented,
how whole, how we can't separate the music
from the sun falling on its knees on all the greenness,
from this moment, how this moment
contains all the fragments of yesterday
and everything we'll ever know of tomorrow!"

Instead, I keep a coward's silence.
The music stops abruptly;
they finish their work,
and we go through the right answers,
which is to say
we separate the fragments from the whole.

—Al Zolynas

Though the poem is about the narrator's love for his students, it is through two other elements—the fragments of music drifting into the room and the lesson on sentence fragments—that the poet is able to create that cosmic sense of wholeness in which the intense moment of the poem occurs.

Notice how Zolynas sets up that epiphanic moment with his simple description of the music, and how simply and clearly he announces it: "and it hits me from nowhere—a sudden sweet, almost painful love for my students." It is worth noting at this point that poetry can be absolutely straightforward and direct, that there are times when the poet simply says precisely and simply what he or she means. This explicit admission of love for his students is immediately followed by the excitation of his inner dialogue, his wish to cry out to them so that they too will see that "Everything's a fragment and everything's not a fragment." But of course he keeps "a coward's silence," and the moment passes.

What is most noteworthy here is the psychological accuracy. One is waiting and silent in one's ordinary consciousness, and then something—in this case strains of unidentifiable music—catalyzes the moment. Inexplicably it becomes a moment of vision, of transcendence. One's consciousness alters, and there is a period of intense excitation. And then that too passes. Because he has caught the dynamics so accurately, the poem is—unlike many lesser poems that attempt to record an epiphanic moment—entirely believable. If you read the other poems by Al Zolynas in this book, you will have a further appreciation of this poet's ability to capture such transcendent moments with the kind of psychological accuracy that makes them perfectly credible.

Finally, to complete our model poems about love, here is a tender poem by a contemporary Chinese poet, a poem of love and longing for her mother:

> Mother, if you see a tiny white paper boat in your sleep,
> Do not wonder how it has entered your dream.
> It was folded by your loving daughter, with tears in her eyes,
> Who begs it to carry home her love and sorrow, over the
> endless mountains and waters.
>
> —Ping Hsin

Poem 49: An Aubade

Try your hand at an aubade—a short poem about the pain of leaving someone you love after spending a night together. This poem needn't be true to your personal experience—any more than the poetry of *Romeo and Juliet* is true to Shakespeare's. Feel free to invent. Avoid the nightingale/lark motif. Rather, keep it contemporary—in your own idiom and about your own world. Make it jaunty or silly, if you want—but be sure not to fall into the most common of pitfalls: writing commonplace sentiments in commonplace language. You must find some angle of approach that makes the poem crisp and memorable. Think of what, in your poem, will fool—or attempt to fool—your lover into believing that it's not yet dawn, or that it's not a workday, or that the clock is an hour fast, or that it would be a good idea to call in sick and spend the day in bed.

Poem 50: A Poem of Longing

The poems by Izumi Shikibu and Ping Hsin are poems of intense longing. The first uses the image of blossoms opening only to fall and this world being nothing but a sheen of dew on flowers; the other creates a metaphor of a paper boat floating into her mother's dream. Try writing such a poem of longing, holding it to no more than seven or eight lines, creating, as those poets do, a striking image with which to represent your love or state of longing. Address the poem directly to the person who is its subject, as those poets do, making the poem an invitation for that person to visit you—or to come back into your life. It doesn't matter if the subject is long gone or is long dead. Make sure it is gracefully said and that the reader can feel the intensity of your longing.

Poem 51: A Goofy Love Poem

Think of the powerful, joyous—if somewhat obsessive and anxiety-ridden—emotion of being in love. Recall, if you are not desperately in love at the moment, a time when you were, and jot down four oddball, surreal images of the sort that Thomas Lux uses in "I Think You're Wonderful." Their "formula" might be something like: "I adore(d) you so much that ..." or, "Because I love you the world is ..." or, "Just thinking about you, I begin to...." Once you have four or five such lines, start putting the poem together with the idea that you want to find another four or five such oddball, hyperbolic, *objective correlatives* for your emotions. "Objective correlative" is a term introduced by T.S. Eliot to imply a set of objects, a situation, a chain of events which stand for, represent, are the formula for a particular emotion, and whose presence in a work of literature evokes that emotion.

Try to include in your poem at least one household object and one reference to either a constellation, a continent, an ocean, or an historic event. Be careful to avoid the obvious, the pedestrian, the predictable; they can make this poem as awful as one of those moronic "Love is" verses that one finds occasionally as space-fillers in daily newspapers. Make sure the poem stays fun and doesn't take itself too seriously— which is not to say that you shouldn't take the poem seriously enough to polish it to perfection!

Poem 52: A Passionate Love Poem

Try your hand at a love poem that deals with a passionate romance from your past. Do not tell the story in a strictly narrative way but use the details to evoke the situation, much as Forché does. Try for pace in your language, the sense of excitement, passion, breathlessness. Again, be sure to avoid the pedestrian: If there is a moon and crashing waves, make certain they're not the generic moon and crashing waves of a million other romantic poems and songs. Try to choose details from the real world, working against the impulse to idealize and romanticize. Make the poem richly assonant so that it has a striking internal music.

Poem 53: The Other Love Poem

Write a poem of love addressed to a friend, a child, or a member of your family. Don't spend more than a line telling the reader how much you love that person. Just find a moment or situation to describe that shows us your love. For models, look back at Dorianne Laux's "Girl in the Doorway" or Linda Pastan's "To a Daughter Leaving Home," both of which are love poems by mothers to their teenage daughters. "The Tooth Fairy" by Dorianne Laux is, among other things, a poem of love for the poet's mother, while "L.A. Morning," which you will find in Chapter 27, is, implicitly, a love poem to the poet's wife and son.

24

Bodies Flaring in the Moonlight:
The Poetry of Desire

After Tsang Chih

I was brought up in a small town in the Mohave Desert.
The boys wouldn't touch me who was dying to be touched,
    because I was too quote
Smart. Which the truck-drivers didn't think as they
    looked and waved
On their way through town, on the way to my World.
                                        —Alice Notley

In the previous chapter, we saw a poem by Anne Waldman based on poetry written centuries earlier by Sappho. This one seems, from its title, to have been inspired by an ancient Chinese poet. Many poets write poems "after" other poets—adaptations that utilize ancient themes in a contemporary idiom. It is a way for poets writing in our own time to take inspiration from and enter into a reverent dialogue with their earlier contemporaries. This poem by Alice Notley about an adolescent girl's longing for the future takes part of its power from the narrator's honest admission of both her adolescent sexual longing and of her longing to escape into a world far beyond the reaches of her provincial little desert town. But part of its grace comes through the repetition of linguistic elements and through subtle syntactic parallels between its phrases. In line two, the phrase "touch me" is echoed in the phrase "be touched," just as in line four, "On their way through town," finds its parallel and completion in "on the way to my World." The juxtaposition of "town" with "my World" nicely points up the narrator's thematic opposition—her wish to exchange her little town for the exciting world.

Poems about sex face the same problems that other poems do. How, for example, does one remain honest, avoiding the platitudes and stock responses that come from what we are told we are supposed to feel? And how does one talk about sex newly and freshly? In addition, such poems face the problem of the culture's sexual unease that makes all explicit writing about that central subject in our lives suspect and forbidden. Here is a poem by Sharon Olds that manages to find a new and engaging way to talk about erotic ecstasy:

First Sex

(for J.)

I knew little, and what I knew
I did not believe—they had lied to me
so many times, so I just took it as it
came, his naked body on the sheet,
the tiny hairs curling on his legs like
fine, gold shells, his sex
harder and harder under my palm
and yet not hard as a rock his face cocked
back as if in terror, the sweat
jumping out of his pores like sudden
trails from the tiny snails when his knees
locked with little clicks and under my
hand he gathered and shook and the actual
flood like milk came out of his body, I
saw it glow on his belly, all they had
said and more, I rubbed it into my
hands like lotion, I signed on for the duration.

—Sharon Olds

This poem is so detailed, honest, and observant that it transcends anything that might be considered vulgar or lewd. The passion here is for experience, and the poet's aim—the very opposite of pornographic writing—is to bear true witness to her experience. It is, paradoxically, a poem of pure innocence. There is nothing here of the fantasy sex of Hollywood, or even of the eroticism we associate with sexually explicit literature. Has anyone ever described sex so passionately, innocently, and clinically at once? It is really only the last phrase of the poem—comic in its unexpectedness—that lets us know her absolute delight in the occasion. It is a sensuous poem without prurience or guilt—a thoroughly subversive poem of pure pleasure.

207

In the following poem, the sensuality emerges out of the simplest and most innocent of domestic occasions:

Baseball in the Living Room

Through the yellow roses on the coffee table
I peer at the ball game, tired of Whitman, tired
of wanting to be great.

"Holy cow," roars the announcer,
"walk him walk him," Dad hollers,
my parents planted in their twin recliners, suited up
in silk pajamas—and when it's Miller time Dad
limps to the kitchen with his bad hip, there's the chink
of spoon and glass as he mixes the nightly dose of meta-
    mucil—
Mom turns to me with that sigh of surrender:
"since the surgery," she says,
"all he wants to do is watch baseball."

Five to three. Top of the eighth.
Leary pitching.
"Who do you think our pin-up boy's gonna be this year?"
jokes one of the guys—and I stare at these beauties,
the hard butts, the kind
you want to sink your nails into, and
the cocks, I bet they're hung like stallions.

The first baseman slides one hand
over his hip, wets his bottom lip—
I think he wants me
then the black one leans over the plate
ready to swing—he means business, that look
you want to see when a man's
on top of you—these men in their prime,
I'd take any one of them
right now on this couch—Dad snoring,
I should go to bed, finish The Body Electric, sleep...

Gonzales fouls one,
spits a stream of tobacco, a thick gold chain ribs
his neck like a rein, wild eyes
dark as river stone—

Mom's drifting now, her head makes little bobs
before she catches it
somewhere in a field of consciousness.

Berryhill slams it to third, the crowd
leaps to their feet—everyone's going nuts,
the full moon, my bare legs, the ball low and outside.

                         —Deborah Harding

It is an amusing poem about a simple lust, the lust for figures on a TV screen. But it is also a poem about the aging of one's parents and the lust for a vitality that the author, sitting in her parents' living room, longs to feel. And it is also about another kind of lust, the lust to be a great poet, and the struggle between the narrator's erotic fantasies and that desire for greatness.

In the following homoerotic poem, the celebration of lust is open and somewhat lighthearted. But the poem is also about aging and the anguish of physical decay:

You Must Have Been A Sensational Baby

1
I love your eyebrows, said one.
the distribution of your bodyhair
is sensational. what teeth, said two.
your mouth is like cocaine, said three.
your lips, said four, look like sexual organs.
they are, I said.
as I got older features thickened.
the body grew flabby. then
thin in the wrong places. they
all shut up or spoke about life.

2
a pair of muscular calves
drove me crazy today.
I studied their size, their shape,
their suntanned hairiness. I spoke
to the owner of them. are you
a dancer? I asked. oh no,
I was born with them, he said.
You must have been a sensational baby,
I said. he went back to his newspaper,
I went back to his calves.
he displayed them mercilessly.
he was absolutely heartless.
men stole secret looks at them.
women pretended he was a table.
they all had a pained expression.
he went on reading the Sports Page.
his thighs were even more cruel
thrust brutally from denim shorts.
the whole place trembled with lust.

San Francisco, 1973
—Harold Norse

Norse uses a series of clipped sentences to give the poem a distinct pace and rhythm and uses dialogue to excellent effect. The first section, which is about others admiring his body, is self-disparaging in a bitter-sweet way, and the second, about his admiration of someone else's body, is openly, unashamedly—and somewhat comically—erotic.

Here's another uninhibited celebration of lust, a comic and silly fantasy—just the sort that would make someone's sweetheart burst out laughing with pleasure:

The Other Night

the other brandysweetened
night, eye dreamed we
was kissing so hard & good, you
sucked my tongue right on out
my trembling mouth
& eye had to sew it back in
in order to tell you about it

—Quincy Troupe

The seven lines of this poem are all one sentence. The idiomatic, slangy speech constructions that the poet uses add significantly to the poem's high-spirited feel. Troupe turns the word "I" into "eye" in many of his poems, the narrational "I" becoming literally the "eye" behind the poems. Here's another somewhat comic poem about lust—one that is, at the same time, elegantly lyrical:

New Hampshire Marble

I called Sue the week I moved back from Rome.
She was getting married on Sunday she said,
but would drive over after lunch to say goodbye.
Later, in the tall grass between some homes,
we were searching around in the torn dirt,
frantic and laughing. Trying to find
the huge diamond engagement ring.
Our bodies flaring in the winter moonlight.

—Jack Gilbert

Gilbert doesn't go into any details about the erotic encounter itself. Instead of showing us the couple embracing, we see them laughing as they look around for her huge engagement ring in the tall grass. The reader is led to understand the situation from those two details. Then the poet surprises us with a stunning last line that pulls us back from the sweet lust of the situation to two figures "flaring" in the winter moonlight—an image of classical poise and beauty, almost as if the figures, which he had described with such good-humored animation, were now figures carved in marble. It is a line that transforms the poem into something larger than itself—one of those turns in a poem that shifts our perspective, in this case calling attention to the poem as an aesthetic object, an object of silence and grace. The brevity with which Notley, Troupe, and Gilbert accomplish their poems is a reminder that in telling a story one is usually well advised to edit it down to its quintessential details.

Lest you get the impression that lust must be mixed with comedy to be effective, here's a poem of unadulterated passion:

This Close

In the room where we lie, light
stains the drawn shades yellow.
We sweat and pull at each other, climb
with our fingers the slippery ladders of rib.
Wherever our bodies touch, the flesh
comes alive. Heat and need, like invisible
animals, gnaw at my breasts, the soft
insides of your thighs. What I want
I simply reach out and take, no delicacy now,
the dark human bread I eat handful
by greedy handful. Eyes, fingers, mouths,
sweet leeches of desire. Crazy woman,
her brain full of bees, see how her palms curl
into fists and beat the pillow senseless.
And when my body finally gives in to it
then pulls itself away, salt-laced
and arched with its final ache, I am
so grateful I would give you anything, anything.
If I loved you, being this close would kill me.

—Dorianne Laux

The last line comes as something of a shock and deepens the psychological complexity of the moment, for the narrator is confessing that the occasion is one of ecstatic sexual gratification and not emotional love. It is surely not easy to write so openly erotic a poem, avoiding all the predictable gestures and emotions of such poetry. But here, in Laux's poem, nothing is predictable. To speak of heat and need gnawing at her breasts like invisible animals, or of eyes, fingers and mouths as sweet leeches of desire, or to describe her brain as full of bees, is to discover a metaphoric language startlingly original and right, to deepen our perceptions, to thrill the reader with intensity and freshness and to bring the reader, without platitude or prurience, into the throes of sexual ecstasy.

Needless to say, not all longing is sexual. There is the lust for warmth, peace, friendship, the past, the longing to be young again, the lust to see one's long dead husband or wife. The poet Nazim Hikmet, a militant communist agitator for human rights in Turkey, spent many years in prison, an experience which made him appreciate all the more acutely the simple pleasures of this world, pleasures symbolized in this poem by—of all things—a single cucumber:

The Cucumber
for Ekber Babayev

The snow is knee-deep in the courtyard
and still coming down hard:
it hasn't let up all morning.
We're in the kitchen.
On the table, on the oilcloth, spring—
on the table there's a very tender young cucumber,
                    pebbly and fresh as a daisy.
We're sitting around the table staring at it.
It softly lights up our faces,
and the very air smells fresh.
We're sitting around the table staring at it,
amazed
        thoughtful
                optimistic.
We're as if in a dream.
On the table, on the oilcloth, hope—
on the table, beautiful days,
a cloud seeded with a green sun,
an emerald crowd impatient and on its way,
loves blooming openly—
on the table, there on the oilcloth, a very tender young
                                cucumber,
                    pebbly and fresh as a daisy.
The snow is knee-deep in the courtyard
and coming down hard.
It hasn't let up all morning.

March 1960, Moscow
—Nazim Hikmet
(Translated by Randy Blasing and Mutlu Konuk)

Poem 54: A Poem of Erotic Longing

In "Baseball in the Living Room" and "You Must Have Been a Sensational Baby," the object of the poet's erotic longing is divorced from the possibility of an actual sexual encounter; we know that nothing will come of the narrator's sexual hunger. Write a poem that takes place in an environment where you tend to feel lascivious. Perhaps it will take place at a sports arena or on the beach or in a restaurant or walking along a particular boulevard or through a shopping center.

You should be trying for both a real sense of the erotic and perhaps, if it seems appropriate to you, a certain celebratory and perhaps slightly humorous flavor in this poem, so that the reader gets some sense of the silliness of the situation, as well as the pleasure of it. Describe the object(s) of your lust in a way that is both erotic and tasteful. Vulgarity in a poem such as this can only be destructive. Give yourself permission to celebrate this sort of innocent lust with unadulterated fun. Such poetry, needless to say, is not for the genteel, the puritanical, or the sanctimonious. Such people are embarrassed to admit that they have such emotions!

Poem 55: First Kiss

To write about the erotic it is hardly necessary to write about an experience of sexual consummation. Instead, write a poem about your first kiss, or first date, an occasion of necking in the back of a car, or of touching someone's arm or face. On the surface, it might entail no more than a conversation over coffee fraught with erotic invitation, eyes meeting across a table. Make sure your descriptions are full of accurate sensory details, and see if you can get in some of the wonderful, almost clinical precision of detail that Sharon Olds is able to get in her poem. Be sure not to fall into the trap of saying things in the way they have been said a million times before.

Poem 56: A Comic Love Poem

"The Other Night" is as much a love poem as it is a poem of lust. Write a comically erotic poem to someone you love, utilizing a fantasy—or dream—just as Troupe does. Perhaps you dreamed you were hugging that person so hard or watching them with such pleasure

213

that——. Make it the sort of poem that would delight the person it's written about. If the spirit moves you, replace the element of lust with friendship or familial affection—the sort of poem one might write to a kid sister, a grandchild, or even a pet German shepherd! Keep it short and playful.

Poem 57: An "After"

Both Anne Waldman and Alice Notley have written poems "after" ancient poets. Go to the library or your favorite literary bookstore and get an anthology of ancient poetry—perhaps it will be ancient Chinese poems or Sanskrit love poetry or poems from ancient Greece or an anthology of traditional Native American or Eskimo poetry. Then find a poem whose theme appeals to you and write a poem in your own idiom that replays that theme. Yours might turn out much shorter or longer and so different from the original that no one would guess that the poem is based on another. Or you might find yourself sticking rather closely to the original (in that case, you are doing a retranslation or version rather than an adaptation, the line between the two being somewhat slippery). Make sure, however, that it is no longer a Chinese or Sanskrit poem, but one that is very much your own, one that has a contemporary feel to it. Subtitle it "After ——," so that the reader will have a sense of your poem's genesis.

Poem 58: Another Kind of Desire

Now write a poem about a lust that is not erotic. Is there an item of food that you find sinfully delicious, a certain fresh spring smell or sight, a piece of music that moves you rapturously every time you hear it? Perhaps it is a lust to lie quietly in a hammock in the courtyard of a house you haven't seen for years, or for a cold glass of fresh water late at night, or a lust to hear the voice of your aging mother over the phone.

Begin this poem with a phrase "stolen" from another poem in this chapter. For example, you might select "All they had said..." or "Somewhere in a field..." or "When my body finally gives in to...." Use that as a jumping-off point. Do not preconceive this poem, but let it find its own direction as the writing proceeds.

25

Flower Burning in the Day:
Poems of Loss

Coats

I saw him leaving the hospital
with a woman's coat over his arm.
Clearly she would not need it.
The sunglasses he wore could not
conceal his wet face, his bafflement.

As if in mockery the day was fair,
and the air mild for December. All the same
he had zipped his own coat and tied
the hood under his chin, preparing
for irremediable cold.

—Jane Kenyon

How quietly the poet has captured this moment of wrenching loss. A lesser poet would probably have milked the emotion and ruined the poem with bathos. But Jane Kenyon touches the moment lightly. She attends to the details, choosing them with care. Perhaps, had the subject been herself or a friend, rather than a stranger, she would have been less able to maintain that sense of quiet detachment and objectivity.

Note how potently the author has used those two coats to tell her story. In the first stanza, it is the coat which he holds that lets us know of the woman's fate. The second coat, zipped and hooded despite the mildness of the weather, presents us with a perfect emblem of the man's irremediable grief. It is both visually strong and psychologically accurate. As we have seen before, writers often find some specific event or

215

object, an objective correlative, to help them make the meaning of an event or moment concrete for the reader. Without those two coats we would be left with the author simply *telling* us that a man was leaving the hospital after his wife had just died, or after realizing that her death was imminent, and that he was numbed with shock, dimly understanding that his life would be less joyful henceforth. But you can see at once that such a statement is abstract and lifeless. It needs to be embodied in a specific scene, a specific moment in time, grounded in a real place and made vivid with sensory details, allowing the reader to both see and feel it.

In the following poem the author has also used a common object to excellent effect. Like the two coats in the previous poem, the acacias in the following one are all but irrelevant to the real story being told, yet they serve an essential narrative function. Just as Jane Kenyon's poem might have been abstract and lifeless without the device of the coats (or some similarly concrete representation of the man's loss and grief), the following poem might have lost an essential element of its drama and poignance without the acacias:

Acacias

Strolling many years ago
Down a street taken over by acacias in bloom
I found out from a friend who knows everything
That you had just gotten married.
I told him that I really
Had nothing to do with it.
I never loved you
—You know that better than I do—
Yet each time the acacias bloom
—Can you believe it?—
I get the very same feeling I had
When they hit me point-blank
With the heartbreaking news
That you had married someone else.

—Nicanor Parra
(Translated by David Unger)

Both the narrator's pretense at indifference and his insistence that "I never loved you" effectively tell us what he cannot bring himself to admit openly. Parra, who has always avoided "poetic" language and the obvious sort of lyricism in which poets tend to indulge, manages here to be both highly colloquial and lyrical at once. Only in the second to last line, in the single word "heartbreaking" (*desoladora* in the original

Spanish), does the narrator own up to his real emotion.

The following poem manages, in a mere four lines, to record the disorienting anguish of separation:

Divorce

Woke up suddenly thinking I heard crying.
Rushed through the dark house.
Stopped, remembering. Stood looking
out at the bright moonlight on concrete.

—Jack Gilbert

How much Gilbert manages to convey in those four lines! The first two are all frenzied action, a rush of excitation and panic. Then the narrator remembers: she is no longer here. In the last line, the moonlight, conventionally the most romantic of images, is seen not in the night sky or reflected on the water as it might be in romantic poetry, but rather reflected on concrete—the hard reality of the world, just as the narrator suddenly faces the hard reality that his love is gone. The omission of the pronoun "I" at the beginning of all four of his sentences quickens the pace of the telling, lending his words a sense of urgency. That final image is a perfect imagistic representation—what we have called an objective correlative—of the narrator's abrupt realization of his misery. And all this accomplished in a mere thirty-three syllables.

Many of the world's most moving and memorable poems are elegies, poems in memory of the dead. "Michiko Dead," the poem by Jack Gilbert that we used in Chapter 9, was an elegy describing how he managed to survive despite the weight of his grief. Here is a contemporary American elegy about the death of—among others—the poet George Oppen:

A Gift

For a long time now I have not been able to listen
to Dinu Lipatti's slender, ascetic fingertips
pressing ever so firmly gentle on the piano keys

in his last recorded transcription of Bach's Cantata
"Jesus bleibet meine Freude" given to me
by George Oppen the year he died.

It is too sad to hear
that severe, geometrically measured stroll of the soul
healthily light-stepping into heaven,

and has become sadder with each loved one's death:
the slow, spare, stately pace wrenching the heart
with its graceful ascendancy over grief,

and staring as if straight into the face of God
which is either everywhere or nowhere, leaving us
nothing to say, nothing to hear as luminous

and meltingly tender as the air
fills with silence, and the heart floods with loss.

—Jack Marshall

The rich music of this meditative poem, its own "slow, spare, stately pace," makes it a memorable and moving elegy, one that, like the Bach cantata, the poem's putative subject, is capable of wrenching the heart. Like "Coats" and "Acacias," the poem doesn't attack its subject directly, but finds an object—in this case a musical composition—to evoke the grief. Loosely speaking, one might say that the two coats of the Jane Kenyon poem "represent" the tragedy she is indirectly witnessing, that for the narrator of "Acacias," those flowers represent his loss, and that for Jack Marshall the Bach Cantata *"Jesus bleibet meine Freude"* represents his grief over the death of his friends.

One of the best known and most ambitious of contemporary American elegies is Allen Ginsberg's "Kaddish," written in memory of the poet's mother. A book-length poem, it is far too long to excerpt in a way that does justice to its enormous innovative power. Here are its opening lines:

Strange now to think of you, gone without corsets & eyes,
      while I walk on the sunny pavement of Greenwich Village.
downtown Manhattan, clear winter noon, and I've been up all
      night, talking, talking, reading the Kaddish aloud, listening
      to Ray Charles blues shout blind on the phonograph
the rhythm the rhythm—and your memory in my head three
      years after—And read Adonais' last triumphant stanzas
      aloud—wept, realizing how we suffer—
And how Death is that remedy all singers dream of, sing,
      remember, prophesy as in the Hebrew Anthem, or the Bud-
      dhist Book of Answers—and my own imagination of a with-
      ered leaf—at dawn—
Dreaming back thru life, Your time—and mine accelerating
      toward Apocalypse,
the final moment—the flower burning in the Day—and what
      comes after...

Ginsberg creates a sweeping, rhapsodic music in these long lines.

In striking contrast, here is an adaptation of a Japanese poem epigrammatic in its brevity, a poem that is no more than a single heartbreaking image. In the original it is a tanka, a traditional Japanese verse form in thirty-one syllables. It was written by the eleventh-century Japanese poet Izumi Shikibu upon the death of her daughter. Another poem of hers—also a tanka—can be found in Chapter 23.

At the Temple Ceremony for Her Departed Daughter

Unendurable grief.
For not so brief an instant
as that between the notes
of the monk's bell
will I forget you.

—Izumi Shikibu

Another species of poem contemplates the poet's own mortality. The author of the following poem comments in the first stanza on some of the traditional reminders of death, then gives us a simple and ingenious emblem of it in the second stanza, and then, in the last two, creates a splendidly imaginative and singular image of his fancied funeral, an image that is at once comical, striking, and oddly touching:

Memento Mori

There is no need for me to keep a skull on my desk,
to stand with one foot up on the ruins of Rome,
or wear a locket with the sliver of a saint's bone.

It is enough to realize that every common object
in this sunny little room will outlive me—
the carpet, radio, bookstand and rocker.

Not one of these things will attend my burial,
not even this dented goosenecked lamp
with its steady benediction of light,

though I could put worse things in my mind
than the image of it waddling across the cemetery
like an old servant, dragging the tail of its cord,
the small circle of mourners parting to make room.

—Billy Collins

Turning a goosenecked lamp into a bent old servant with a long tail is just the sort of tranformation that contemporary sculptors delight in assembling. And who more fit to be at the poet's funeral than that loyal servant with "its steady benediction of light"? Does that tail hint that it is a diabolical old companion—that his old writing lamp helped lead him astray? That anyone who would encourage him to waste his life in so foolish an enterprise as the writing of poetry must surely be old Beelzebub himself?

Our trepidation at the knowledge of our own mortality, of the mortality of all living creatures, has caused every one of us at one time or another to inveigh against death itself. Surely death is the object of our greatest distress, our greatest fear. In the following poem, the author, in mourning the death of a small creature killed on the highway, expresses his anger at the inexorable law that will take us all:

Behaving Like a Jew

When I got there the dead opossum looked like
an enormous baby sleeping on the road.
It took me only a few seconds—just
seeing him there—with the hole in his back
and the wind blowing through his hair
to get back again into my animal sorrow.
I am sick of the country, the bloodstained
bumpers, the stiff hairs sticking out of the grilles,
the slimy highways, the heavy birds
refusing to move;
I am sick of the spirit of Lindbergh over everything,
that joy in death, that philosophical
understanding of carnage, that
concentration on the species.
—I am going to be unappeased at the opossum's death.
I am going to behave like a Jew
and touch his face, and stare into his eyes,
and pull him off the road.
I am not going to stand in a wet ditch
with the Toyotas and the Chevies passing over me
at sixty miles an hour
and praise the beauty and the balance
and lose myself in the immortal lifestream
when my hands are still a little shaky
from his stiffness and his bulk
and my eyes are still weak and misty
from his round belly and his curved fingers
and his black whiskers and his little dancing feet.

—Gerald Stern

Stern does not want to "understand" death, to come to peace with it, to "praise the beauty and the balance" of it, but prefers in his anguish to remain unappeased. This is the rage we are all likely to feel when we are encountering the death of a loved one. How sharply the details are seen—both of the opossum with the hole in his back, and of the "bloodstained bumpers" and "slimy highways." Beyond being a tender elegy, the poem is a philippic against modern, technological culture. Reread the poem and notice how the author establishes our empathy for the opossum—beginning with that first startling simile that compares the opossum to an "enormous baby sleeping in the road," and ending with that evocative series of details in the poem's concluding lines: "his round belly and his curved fingers and his black whiskers and his little dancing feet." Words like *belly*, *fingers*, *whiskers*, and *feet* cannot help but remind us of the opossum's similarity to ourselves.

Note that Stern's attitude in this poem is not the conventional one we might expect. Just as good poets avoid predictable language they avoid predictable sentiments, those conventional and respectable ones that tend to cover our true feelings.

For our last model, here is a quiet, poignantly elegiac love poem:

Your Birthday in the California Mountains

A broken moon on the cold water,
And wild geese crying high overhead,
The smoke of the campfire rises
Toward the geometry of heaven—
Points of light in the infinite blackness.
I watch across the narrow inlet
Your dark figure comes and goes before the fire.
A loon cries out on the night bound lake.
Then all the world is silent with the
Silence of autumn waiting for
The coming of winter. I enter
The ring of firelight, bringing to you
A string of trout for our dinner.
As we eat by the whispering lake,
I say, "Many years from now we will
Remember this night and talk of it."
Many years have gone by since then, and
Many years again. I remember
That night as though it was last night,
But you have been dead for thirty years.

—Kenneth Rexroth

Kenneth Rexroth—a poet who often meditated on the sublime beauty of the natural world and whose writing was often permeated by the elegiac mood—was not only one of our great poets but also one of our great translators from the Chinese and Japanese. He was profoundly influenced by the quiet, imagistic precision and emotional restraint of Oriental verse, a restraint that serves to deepen the emotional power of poems such as this. The narrative strategy of the poem is an interesting one. He recalls one splendid occasion, the two of them sitting about a campfire by a lake on the night of the woman's birthday. They remark that "Many years from now we will/Remember this night and talk of it"—as indeed the poet does, surprising us at the end with the revelation that the woman to whom he is speaking in the poem has been dead for thirty years.

Poem 59: A Short Poem of Parting

Try your hand at a short poem about the pain of leaving or being left by someone you loved—a poem of final parting. Look back at the poems by Jack Gilbert and Izumi Shikibu. Both have a sensory image at their heart: Shikibu's poem is built around the brevity of the interval between rings of the temple bell; Gilbert uses the half-heard sound of crying, an empty house, and the moon shining on concrete. In both cases the poets have grounded their feelings in real places and objects. Make sure you do not write a generalized poem about your sorrow, but find an event, a physical locale, and concrete objects around which to shape your poem. Either keep the poem to a single sentence or use the sort of short, quick sentences that Gilbert employs.

Poem 60: A Poem of Denial

Compose a poem of loss in which you pretend not to care, as Parra's narrator pretends not to care in "Acacias." This is a perfect strategy for writing about a relationship that went sour. If even now that person's memory burns in you, though you would be loath to admit it, the writing is likely to be emotionally charged and the resultant poem an intense one. Try your hand at the sort of irony Parra employs. Be sure to protest that you did not feel whatever it is that you want the reader to understand that you did indeed feel. Part of the task of plotting out this poem is to find a specific moment or occasion to write about—perhaps the last time you saw that person or heard news of him or her. Or choose a moment in more current time, when that person's memory suddenly comes into your mind. If you can, hang the poem on one central image, as Parra hangs his on the acacias blooming. Try for a similarly colloquial and casual feel in your poem so that the reader senses a genuine human voice and personality beneath it. This poem might take some courage—and humility—to write.

Poem 61: Memento Mori

Every now and then we are stopped in our tracks by a reminder of our own mortality. It could be the corpse of a small animal on a country highway, or an obituary notice in the daily paper, or the recollection that a piece of furniture we use daily was given to us by a friend now deceased, and we think, "Ah, someday I too...." Write a poem in which you are reminded that you too will one day die. The poem might start with a line as simple and straightforward as: "Whenever I look at ——, I think about the fact that I'll be gone, too, one of these days." It is probably a better idea to spend your time talking about the object or objects that call forth your feelings than to spend it talking directly about your death. Collins' goosenecked lamp is a good model. If the subject of your own death is too painful or grim to consider, try doing it, as he does, with a little humor, keeping the tone offhanded and finding some fanciful image about your own death or funeral that's comic. But don't let humor—if you decide to use some— overshadow the honest pathos of the poem's emotion. It is easy for humor, if forced or otherwise ill-used, to become sophomoric. Your job is to find a way to make the poem poignant.

Poem 62: An Unexpected Elegy

Write an elegy that misleads us in the way that Rexroth's elegy does. Address the poem to the person who died, but in such a way that the reader is misled into believing the person is still alive, only near the end letting us know the truth. Do not get grandiose or theatrical with your language. Keep it simple, clear, straightforward, and honest. Try for the same kind of quiet and restrained lyricism that suffuses "Your Birthday in the California Mountains." You will probably want to find a single incident to focus on. Like Rexroth, you might wish to choose an incident that sets the person reverently in the natural world. Let your love for the poem's subject emerge through your tone, without your having to announce it.

Poem 63: An Object that Brings Back a Loss

Find an image to represent your loss, some object or detail or event that embodies it, as Jack Marshall does with the record given to him by his friend. Describe that object as a way of talking about your grief. Perhaps it's the view from the window of a restaurant where you used to sit drinking coffee, or a frayed scarf that your friend had given you and that now hangs in your closet, unused. Perhaps, if it was someone who intimately shared your life, it is a door that needs fixing. "That door you never got around to fixing is harder than ever to open" might be a way to begin such a poem. Or perhaps it's an object long gone that you'd like to hold again, touch again. In imitation of "Mementos, I" by W.D. Snodgrass that opens Chapter 11, it might begin: "I awoke this morning thinking of turning that old tennis racket in my hand. Your racket. The one you...." Use that object to explore the relationship it symbolizes—and whatever feelings emerge as the poem finds its way from line to line. Like Rexroth, Marshall, and Snodgrass, try for a tone of quiet formality and dignity.

Poem 64: A Philippic Against Death

Write an angry denunciation of death. The poem might be set in motion by something as "trivial" as the sight of a dead fly on the windowsill or a leaf fallen to the ground or a chance remark overheard or a TV commercial or newspaper article. Just as Gerald Stern's use of the dead opossum sets off his angry tirade, allow this poem to widen into a meditation on death itself. But be sure to ground it in a real occasion, a real place, so that it doesn't become an airy abstraction. Try to get your actual feelings (or your real feelings of the moment) onto the page. Tell us, as Gerald Stern does, of some things you are sick of and assert strongly how you are and are not going to behave. If what you are feeling are "inappropriate" or surprising emotions, give yourself permission to express them. It is important when writing poetry to remember that the reader does not want echoes of a thousand other poets expressing predictable sentiments but the expression of your genuine feelings—however contradictory, odd, unexplainable, or unrespectable they might be. Be sure to let the anger—and anguish—emerge.

26

Into the Dazzling Void:
Writing About the Natural World

Praising Spring

The day is taken by each thing and grows complete.
I go out and come in and go out again,
confused by a beauty that knows nothing of delay,
rushing like fire. All things move faster
than time and make a stillness thereby. My mind
leans back and smiles, having nothing to say.
Even at night I go out with a light and look
at the growing. I kneel and look at one thing
at a time. A white spider on a peony bud.
I have nothing to give, and make a poor servant,
but I can praise the spring. Praise this wildness
that does not heed the hour. The doe that does not
stop at dark but continues to grow all night long.
The beauty in every degree of flourishing. Violets
lift to the rain and the brook gets louder than ever.
The old German farmer is asleep and the flowers go on
opening. There are stars. Mint grows high. Leaves
bend in the sunlight as the rain continues to fall.

—Linda Gregg

In the moment of true experiencing there are no words: there is just the experiencing itself. It is the central paradox of the language of poetry that it is often trying to get beyond language to the sheer suchness of the world—that inexpressible experiencing whose verbal emblem is closer to a sigh or a shudder than to a phrase.

This lovely poem by Linda Gregg is about letting the natural world overwhelm one's spirit so that the "mind leans back and smiles, having nothing to say." The narrator of "Praising Spring" is astonished by the unending motion and impermanence of this world and at the same time, paradoxically, by its continual growth and blooming, its perfection at each moment. The narrator keeps going outside, unable to get enough of the world—confused, delighted, in awe. Even at night she goes out with a light to "kneel and look"—in this world of ceaseless motion and change—"at one thing at a time." The paradox is made explicit when the poet tells us that "All things move faster than time and make a stillness thereby."

Note, too, the specificity of the details, how they populate the poem with real creatures, real flowers, real stars. There is the "white spider on a peony bud," the doe that "continues to grow all night long," violets lifting to the rain, a brook growing louder, a German farmer asleep, flowers opening beneath stars, mint growing high, and finally the leaves that "bend in the sunlight as the rain continues to fall." At the dramatic center of the poem is the narrator herself going out and coming in, kneeling with a light in the darkness to watch the spider, the narrator who has nothing to give but her splendid ability to "Praise this wildness that does not heed the hour."

If one were to list this poem's internal sound echoes, the list would look something like this:

> *day/taken/delay/say/rain/praise/rain*
> *each/complete/beauty/leans/peony/heed/degree/asleep*
> *thing/in/nothing/rushing/things/thing/spring/flourishing*
> *grow/go/go/knows/go/growing/doe/grow/go/opening/grows*
> *by/time/fire/thereby/my/mind/wildness/high/violets*

For a short poem that is a rather astonishing amount of sound repetition!

One needn't be in a "natural environment" to write a poem in praise of the natural world. The houseplant thriving in midwinter, the bowl of fruit on the table, the potato that sends out shoots in a dark cupboard are all reminders that however much we mask the natural world with our buildings and artifacts, it remains there before us if we are awake enough just to look. One opens an old book and spies, crawling slowly across the page, the tiniest living creature:

> **"I do not know who is hoarding all this rare work."**

> Old One the dog stretches stiff legged,
> soon he'll be underground. Spring's first fat bee
> buzzes yellow over the new grass and dead leaves.

226

What's this little brown insect walking zigzag
across the sunny white page of Su Tung-p'o's poem?
Fly away, tiny mite, even your life is tender—
I lift the book and blow you into the dazzling void.

—Allen Ginsberg

Composed while reading a translation of the Sung poet Su Tung-p'o, Ginsberg's poem "Returning to the Country for a Brief Visit," of which the above lines comprise a brief section, captures the quiet grace and poignance of Chinese poetry and demonstrates the tenderness toward nature's beings that characterizes so much of the poetry of China and Japan. The first principle of Hindu, Buddhist, and Jain beliefs is *Ahimsa*: compassion for and harmlessness toward all sentient beings. In this little poem, Ginsberg grants full beingness to—acknowledges the actual life of—both the old dog stretching stiff legged and that tiny creature walking across the page. Here is another poem that pays homage to the smallest and most unacknowledged of lives:

Meeting of Mavericks

Milkweed grows by my fence.
Don't ask me to pull it.
Weeds were my friends in childhood—
emerald explosions
in the dull cinders of train track,
green lace at the sleeves
of our water trough.
Eyes starved for color
were well fed by fireweed
elbowing tin cans aside
to take over the dump.

I live in the city now,
but claim kinship whenever
the uncombed head of a dandelion
pops up like a gopher
in the midst of a groomed lawn,
or a purple thistle—
remembered from roadside ditches—
looms insolent
in an enclave of roses.

Today a prickly thing
I don't know the name of
is exploiting a crack
in our sidewalk.
I greet it as friend:

"Hello, I too
like to challenge the fissures
in my firmament,
squeeze through, sometimes,
more often fracture my skull."

My new acquaintance braces his spine
along the crack, and shoves.
Cement crumbles.

I think tonight
I will sneak out and water
this one!
                    —LoVerne Brown

In a world seen without prejudice or ego there are no weeds, only wild flowers.

To acknowledge the natural world which everywhere surrounds us is to transcend our human-centered perspective and to expand our ability to empathize with all of creation. In the following poem the light spirited tone does not keep the piece from becoming a reverent investigation of the most disdained of life forms:

Cat Puke And Flies Poem

I feed Marcello a can of Liver and Chicken.
He bolts it down too fast, as usual.
Two minutes later he throws up
on the back patio.
The first fly shows up within seconds,
ecstatic over life's bounty.
Within minutes, the word's out
somehow, the brothers and sisters
coming in fast.

The sun creeps along the cement floor.
Pretty soon, half the cat puke is in light,
the other in shadow, like sunrise
on a volcanic island.
At least thirty flies have gathered by now,
walking around and eating
what they're walking around on.

I move in closer.
Such organization and grace—
no fuss, no fighting. There's obviously always
enough for everyone in the fly world.
And plenty of time to get off a quickie
with your neighbor.

228

I'm now on my hands and knees,
my face within inches
of the calm feeding of at least fifty flies
(give or take arrivals and departures).
None seem to notice me,
the sun glinting off their emerald thoraxes
and through their purple wings.

—Al Zolynas

To approach flies on vomit not as something disgusting but as something interesting enough to draw us down on our hands and knees for a closer look! And how well the author observes it all—and observes himself observing it! Is it that tone of voice, the off-handedness of the narrator commenting that the flies are "ecstatic over life's bounty," the irreverent humor of being told that in the fly world there's always "plenty of time to get off a quickie with your neighbor," that disarms us and allows us to delight in his observations, allows us to share his admiration over "their organization and grace" while delighting in the gross comedy of the situation? In "Power," Corrine Hales told us that she couldn't stop watching. Linda Gregg feels compelled to go out even at night to see all she can of the world. And how true that is for Zolynas's narrator as well!

In the following poem, Walt Whitman enumerates the creatures of the sea, allowing us to participate in his wonder at the whole of creation:

The World Below the Brine

The world below the brine,
Forests at the bottom of the sea, the branches and leaves,
Sea-lettuce, vast lichens, strange flowers and seeds, the thick
    tangle, openings, and pink turf,
Different colors, pale gray and green, purple, white, and gold,
    the play of light through the water,
Dumb swimmers there among the rocks, coral, gluten, grass,
    rushes, and the aliment of the swimmers,
Sluggish existences grazing there suspended, or slowly
    crawling close to the bottom,
The sperm-whale at the surface blowing air and spray, or
    disporting with his flukes,
The leaden-eyed shark, the walrus, the turtle, the hairy sea-
    leopard, and the sting-ray,
Passions there, wars, pursuits, tribes, sight in those ocean-
    depths, breathing that thick-breathing air, as so many do,
The change thence to the sight here, and to the subtle air
    breathed by beings like us who walk this sphere,

The change onward from ours to that of beings who walk
 other spheres.

—Walt Whitman

Few poets can handle long inventories with Whitman's musical
grace and dramatic power. It is worth noting how the details of this
poem are organized: after his introductory line, he begins with the life
forms at the bottom of the sea, describes the colors, the objects, and
vegetation around which the swimmers move, then the creatures them-
selves, those "sluggish existences" that graze or crawl at the bottom.
The poet then lists several of the sea's larger, better known creatures,
after which he calls attention to the communities of sea creatures rather
than individuals ("wars, pursuits, tribes"). He then reminds us of our
relationship to those creatures by telling us that they are "breathing
that thick-breathing air," which leads him to make explicit the close
relationship between them and ourselves by commenting on the
change from their sphere to ours, where we breathe "the subtle air."
This leads to his final assertion that there are surely beings who walk
other spheres.

The movement of the poem then is from the bottom of the sea
upwards toward the surface, onto the land, and finally into the cosmos.
It is, for all the poem's apparent chaos and energy, a well-ordered, lin-
ear progression upwards in space. Whitman was not only a visionary, a
poet of consistently cosmic perspective, but a master of phrasing as well
as a superb musician of the language. Like all of Whitman's best poetry,
this short piece is well worth taking time to analyze musically, some-
thing that by this point you should be able to do easily on your own.

Here is another poem about the natural world that explicitly repre-
sents a compassionate empathy for its objects and creatures. Unlike the
others in this section, it has a traditional structure: rhymed iambic
quatrains, sometimes called *heroic quatrains*:

A Bright Day

My windows now are giant drops of dew
 The common stones are dancing in my eyes;
The light is winged, and panting, and the world
 Is fluttering with a little fall or rise.

See, while they shoot the sun with singing Larks,
 How those broad meadows sparkle and rejoice!
Where can the Cuckoo hide in all this light,
 And still remain unseen, and but a voice?

230

Shall I be mean, when all this light is mine?
Is anything unworthy of its place?
Call for the rat, and let him share my joy,
And sit beside me here, to wash his face.

—W.H. Davies

In a consciousness that experiences the world without prejudice, with joy that "all this light is mine," the rat is, of course, but a fellow being.

The spiritual structure of such poems as these—poems whose authors show a deep identification with their humble subjects—is illuminated by the following remarks about Zen brush painting:

> The fact is, however, that even such homely objects as stones, grass, and vegetables—a cucumber, for example, or an eggplant—may pictorially be represented with no less *ch'i yün* [essence, spirit, life-force] than a grand-scale landscape with mountains and streams, if only the painter knows how to concentrate his spiritual energy upon seeing into the nature of the thing he intends to paint, to harmonize his spirit, so to speak, with the spirit of the thing, and then to infuse it into his work through the power of his brush. If he succeeds in doing this, then, as a result, the spirit of the object will be rendered in such a way that it moves, alive, on the paper in perfect consonance with the pulsation of the inner spirit of the artist.... Let us suppose that a Far Eastern painter now intends to draw a black and white picture of a bamboo. He is not primarily interested in representing the likeness. For he is first and foremost concerned with penetrating into the inner reality of the bamboo and letting its very "spirit" flow out of his brush as if it were a natural effusion of the bamboo. In the tradition of Far Eastern aesthetics, a complete self-identification of the painter with the "soul" of his motif, i.e., his becoming perfectly at one with the spiritual significance of his motif, is considered an absolutely necessary condition for any high achievement in this sort of painting.

—Toshihiko Izutsu

Though all the poems in this chapter are about the natural world, the observations that engendered them require little specialized knowledge or experience. Don't imagine that urbanites and suburbanites cannot write about nature. One doesn't have to write about Mount Kilimanjaro to write about such matters. One finds mites and flies and weeds and common stones in the most urban of environments. There are birds and sunsets and splendid dawns and blooming flowers everywhere, even in our cemented-over cities. One need only have one's senses alert and one's heart attuned.

231

Exercise — A Walking Meditation

Take a walk by yourself through a relatively natural environment, a field or wooded area or around the margins of a lake. If you are in the city and such an environment is not accessible to you, a large park might serve, or even a tree-lined suburban street.

As you walk, focus your mind on forms and colors. Keep scanning your visual field, moving from things that are close to you to things that are further away and then back. But focus on specific spots. Notice a particular spot on a branch, on a fence, on a flower, on a stone. Don't "think" about these things, don't keep a running monologue in your head—but simply perceive their colors and forms, looking at one thing, then another, then another. Don't spend more than a second or two on each particular spot that you notice, and do not get trapped in the mind's chatter. Of course, the mind will chatter away regardless. It will judge, fantasize, comment, argue, conceptualize. You will talk to yourself endlessly, as you always do. That is only natural, for those are the things the chatterbox-mind does incessantly of its own accord. But on this occasion do not permit it to take over. Do not get trapped in those bubbles. Be vigilant and when you find yourself thinking, notice that you have done so and return to your process of looking at things as you walk. Do not be surprised if the mind continues to wander. Do not fight with the mind. Every time you are aware enough to catch those stray thoughts, just bring yourself back to the present moment of perception, and continue noting colors and forms. Remember, you are not writing a poem or taking notes for one in your head. To the contrary, your job is not to get lost in the mind's continual blather.

When smells and sounds enter your perceptual field that is perfectly fine just so long—once again—as you do not begin thinking of them. Simply smell the smell, hear the sound, feel the breeze, and return to your task of noticing the colors and forms of things in your visual field. For those without sight, this meditation can be done successfully by focusing on sounds or smells, but for those with sight this exercise should be done precisely as described.

If this task is done with concentration over a period of time—it might take anywhere from twenty to ninety minutes—there is a good likelihood that you will disconnect from those incessant thoughts and find yourself fully in the present, the chatterbox-mind having either noticeably quieted down or miraculously turned itself off. If that happens, your senses will function with an unsuspected acuteness.

Performed with attention and commitment, the exercise is capable of producing rather spectacular results.

Poem 65: In Praise

Write a poem in praise of something in the world of nature that is not commonly praised: flies, cockroaches, mold growing on bread, maggots crawling over a garbage pail. Describe the subject of your poem closely and lovingly the way Ginsberg, Zolynas, and LoVerne Brown do. Yet another model of this sort of poem, "Perfection" by William Carlos Williams, will be found in the next chapter.

Avoid a response that reflects the typical repugnance or indifference of those who prefer not to look at the world very closely. LoVerne Brown does it by remembering the wild flowers of her youth, Zolynas and Williams by a sort of droll and engaging curiosity. Whitman's strategy—and to some extent that of Linda Gregg—is to enumerate the objects of their admiration. Make sure you find a way of showing your compassion and excitement without indulging in false or sentimental posturing.

Poem 66: An Inventory

Try your hand at a poem like Whitman's, in which you catalogue all the creatures and objects in a particular space. Perhaps it will be your back yard, or a beach you walk along at night, or a vacant lot near your house, or an alley, or a small plot of land. Perhaps, if you are ingenious and ambitious, you can take something as small as a flowerbox and describe dozens of minute objects and creatures—from small pebbles and ants crawling on the leaves, to the colors of a single weed and the curled form of a desiccated leaf. Before you begin, it would be a good idea to make a list of at least two dozen items that exist in that place. The first several will come quickly, but you will have to open your eyes and look closely to see the rest. Try for strong pace and a rhythm based on "The World Below the Brine." Be specific, concrete and precise—but do not dwell on any one item for more than a line or two. Make your list, like both Gregg's and Whitman's, exuberant in both description and language.

27

Poetry and the Awakened Life

Every writer finds a new entrance into the Mystery.
—Lu Chi, The Art of Writing
(Translated by Sam Hamill)

L.A. Morning

Maybe it's Ian. Maybe walking with him
to the sitter's, a kind of
religious exercise, his singing
counterpoint to mine as we walk
wakens the gods.
The fog dances more gently
into the trees. This ripest of
moments gives birth to amazement
so pure it hurts. That the world
arranges itself so vividly before me!
That all things, trees, houses,
weeds, stones, roses,
even porched pigeons and a flat
gray sky, everything
glows! And my woman loves me
and my son adores me
and these marvels were set out for us to
stroll through and for one sweet minute
I have absolutely nothing to regret.

—Austin Straus

We have all experienced the world suddenly transformed into something ineffably exquisite and perfect. It might happen when walking peacefully through the woods, or awakening early in the morning during a trip to the mountains or the desert. Perhaps one is simply walking through a field of poppies or has suddenly come upon a beautiful stream or is driving to work or sitting on one's own back porch at sunset. For no reason whatsoever, you find yourself suddenly filled with a sense of blissful serenity: everything is perfect, interconnected, unitary, exactly as it should be. There is not a leaf, not a speck of dirt that does not participate in the perfection of the moment. Internally, one is still; it is a moment free of the mind's endless monologue. There is only the majesty of that very moment, in the presence of which one feels awe, love, acceptance. At such moments there is no longing, no desire. There is nothing to be sought, nothing to strive for. It is a world no longer clouded by busy distraction. Our thoughts have stepped aside. There is nothing to block our view of this magnificent world.

To some extent, all poetry, however complex or "negative" its specific emotional content, is ultimately celebratory. The experience that momentarily stops the internal jabberer, the internal complainer, the internal anxiety engine and planner and dreamer and intellectualizer, is indeed "the ripest of moments," a moment that awakens the gods and in which the world suddenly arranges itself vividly before us. It is not improbable that behind all the themes of art is this theme, so simply and eloquently expressed in "L.A. Morning."

The walking meditation you undertook when we were dealing with the poetry of the natural world is an expedient method of bringing you into touch with this deeper, more loving reality, an ability to see the world free from the mind's chatter. All activity done in a meditative spirit has the goal of awakening us to this very moment.

Here is another poem that records an occasion of awakening into the ordinary miracle of our lives:

Dusk in the Cuyamacas

It was the tangerine
& golden sepia light
spilling over the Cuyamacas
—each leaf
of the manzanita
chiseled in space—
that shook me out of my dreams,
till I woke again
to my own life:
everything shimmering.
Everything just as it is.

—Steve Kowit

235

Without the obsessively judging and discriminating mind, the world, in even the most quotidian of its details, is subject enough for reverence and awe:

> I believe a leaf of grass is no less perfect than the journey-
> work of the stars,
> And the pismire is equally perfect, and a grain of sand, and
> the egg of the wren,
> And the tree-toad is a chef-d'oeuvre for the highest,
> And the running blackberry would adorn the parlors of
> heaven,
> And the narrowest hinge in my hand puts to scorn all
> machinery,
> And the cow crunching with depress'd head surpasses any
> statue,
> And a mouse is miracle enough to stagger sextillions of
> infidels.
>
> —Walt Whitman

Surely one of poetry's sacred aims—indeed, one of the central aims of all art—is to lift us out of our sleep into the actual world of this present moment. Art, then, is a way of remembering our real selves, of stepping out of the busy mind and back into the real world of trees, birds, clouds, people, chairs—the extraordinary, unspeakable presence of everything that exists—the sense of our identity with all creation. And once we do enter the present, we are apt to see the world more vividly, more wholly, our emotions open to the miraculousness of the ordinary. William Blake expresses the same cosmic consciousness that Whitman does when he writes, at the beginning of "Auguries of Innocence":

> To see a World in a Grain of Sand
> And a Heaven in a Wild Flower,
> Hold Infinity in the palm of your hand
> And Eternity in an hour.

Blake's poem continues with a series of striking symbolic correspondences that suggest the interrelatedness of all things—a series of moral equations between our treatment of the animal kingdom and the fate of our own lives. Though the poem is too long to quote in full, here are a few of the inspired couplets that follow the four lines already quoted:

> A Robin Red breast in a Cage
> Puts all Heaven in a Rage.
> A dove house fill'd with doves & Pigeons
> Shudders Hell thro' all its regions.
> A dog starv'd at his Master's Gate

Predicts the ruin of the State.
A Horse misus'd upon the Road
Calls to heaven for Human blood.
Each outcry of the hunted Hare
A fibre from the Brain does tear....
He who shall hurt the little Wren
Shall never be belov'd by Men.
He who the Ox to wrath has mov'd
Shall never be by Woman lov'd.
The wanton Boy that kills the Fly
Shall feel the Spider's enmity.

—William Blake

How precious all of this life is, poetry says again and again in its million voices: how singular and extraordinary. To appreciate our own life and the lives around us—to see, suddenly, out of that larger, non-ego-centered perspective!

In the following excerpt from his notebook, the eighteenth-century poet Christopher Smart describes his cat Jeoffry, the sole companion during his years of confinement in a madhouse. A profoundly religious poet, Smart imbues his greatest work with an ecstatic sense of the presence of God. His praise of his cat, humorous and charming, is also, quite clearly, yet another way for the poet to praise the divine. Since the work was not published until 1939, it is not known whether Smart, a brilliant metricist and technician, considered this unrhymed, unmetered, highly experimental composition to be a poem, rather than notes toward a poem or journal entries, or some kind of personal testament. Its music, like that of Blake and Whitman, was clearly inspired by the antiphonal music of parts of the Old Testament. "Jubilate Agno" (Rejoice in the Lamb) is closer in its cadenced, free verse, anaphoric lines to modern poetry than it is to anything that was being written in Smart's own day. Here is a short excerpt from that remarkable poem:

For I will consider my Cat Jeoffry.
For he is the servant of the Living God, duly and daily
    serving him.
For at the first glance of the glory of God in the East he wor-
    ships in his way.
For is this done by wreathing his body seven times round
    with elegant quickness.
For then he leaps up to catch the musk, which is the blessing
    of God upon his prayer.
For he rolls upon prank to work it in.
For having done duty and received blessing he begins to
    consider himself.

237

For this he performs in ten degrees.
For First he looks upon his fore-paws to see if they are clean.
For Secondly he kicks up behind to clear away there.
For Thirdly he works it upon stretch with the fore-paws
  extended.
For Fourthly he sharpens his paws by wood.
For Fifthly he washes himself.
For Sixthly he rolls upon wash.
For Seventhly he fleas himself, that he may not be
  interrupted upon the beat.
For Eighthly he rubs himself against a post.
For Ninthly he looks up for his instructions.
For Tenthly he goes in quest of food.
For having consider'd God and himself he will consider his
  neighbor.
For if he meets another cat he will kiss her in kindness.
For when he takes his prey he plays with it to give it a chance.
For one mouse in seven escapes by his dallying.
For when his day's work is done his business more properly
  begins.
For he keeps the Lord's watch in the night against the
  adversary.
For he counteracts the powers of darkness by his electrical
  skin & glaring eyes.

—Christopher Smart

The following poem is another example of a visionary composition constructed out of the most common and domestic of subjects. If we perform the most commonplace of household chores in a meditative spirit, doing it with a concentrated awareness that prevents us from fading into the hypnotic slumber of the spinning mind, it becomes a meditation. Everyday work as a form of meditation is integral to the discipline of Zen. Hence the title of the following poem:

The Zen of Housework

I look over my own shoulder
down my arms
to where they disappear under water
into hands inside pink rubber gloves
moiling among dinner dishes.

My hands lift a wine glass,
holding it by the stem and under the bowl.
It breaks the surface
like a chalice
rising from a medieval lake.

Full of the grey wine
of domesticity, the glass floats
to the level of my eyes.
Behind it, through the window
above the sink, the sun, among
a ceremony of sparrows and bare branches,
is setting in Western America.

I can see thousands of droplets
of steam—each a tiny spectrum—rising
from my goblet of grey wine.
They sway, changing directions
constantly—like a school of playful fish,
or like the sheer curtain
on the window to another world.

Ah, grey sacrament of the mundane!

—Al Zolynas

From the very beginning, when he looks over his own shoulder, the poet presents himself as an objective observer of his own actions—as though he were taking an exterior view of his body. The details are crisply visual: how clearly the reader sees those hands in water, inside "pink rubber gloves, moiling among dinner dishes." The chalice evokes not only the ceremonial cup for the sacred wine of the church, but—at the genesis of that ritual—the cup that Jesus used during the Last Supper and, in the Middle Ages, the object of the legendary Arthurian quest. By that one piece of figurative language, the poem has been lifted into the realm of the mythic: the soiled wine glass in the sink has become the Holy Grail.

Notice that the poet then expands the poem's visual field the way a movie camera might pull away from a tight close-up to reveal the landscape. With the visual release into a more spacious perspective, our own inner, emotional space is likely to grow larger too, and there will be some sense of emotional release. We are no longer looking into a sink full of dirty dishes; once the wine glass has become the Grail, we are transported to a sylvan sunset landscape, at once ceremonial and contemporary. And then the poet closes up the visual field, moving in for a microscopically tight close-up as we focus in on the thousands of droplets of steam, each of them colorful, moving, playful, alive. How cleverly the poet has brought us into the minutiae of the actual moment, the tiniest, most discrete and elemental of miracles. But it is a full universe, however small, and the poet's words allow us the expansiveness of that cosmic and microcosmic perspective. Just as Whitman has chosen the smallest, most humble creatures as evidence of the awesome mystery and miracle of creation, so too does Zolynas celebrate the miracle of this world with the minutest of phenomena—the droplets of steam rising from a dirty glass in the sink. "Ah, grey sacrament of the mundane!" How nicely the final line, without being in the least commonplace, ties together his theme.

To see in what we normally perceive as our "mundane" experience the holy, awesome, and sacramental! Is that not what great art so often attempts to do?

William Carlos Williams, one of the most influential American poets of the twentieth century, chooses in the following poem a no less surprising object of meditation and praise—a rotting apple. He too uses the most banal of objects to exemplify the most solemn of mysteries:

Perfection

O lovely apple!
beautifully and completely
rotten,
hardly a contour marred—

perhaps a little
shrivelled at the top but that
aside perfect
in every detail! O lovely

apple! what a
deep and suffusing brown
mantles that
unspoiled surface! No one

has moved you
since I placed you on the porch
rail a month ago
to ripen.

No one. No one!

—William Carlos Williams

Williams tends to break his lines in the middle of phrase units, enjambing the lines to keep the poem quickly paced and full of little surprises. He stops line two on the word *completely*, thus letting the word *rotten* on the next line come as something of a shock. Most of us have been taught to be circumspect with the exclamation point, but in this short poem Williams uses it no fewer than five times. And note, too, that he is not reticent to use the poetic "O." In lesser hands, how forced and artificial that archaic poetic gesture might have become! There is a strong, individual voice behind this poem, and one hears the poet's passion and his half-humorous intensity throughout.

William Carlos Williams, who spent his life in Rutherford, New Jersey, as a country physician, loved not just those parts of the world which are obviously beautiful and noble, but also those parts of it which seem to conventional consciousness sordid and ugly. Looked at with innocent eyes, what does "rotten" mean but that the fruit is at a stage past ripeness. Is that stage any less beautiful, any less perfect? That doesn't mean that he shut his eyes to pain, greed, meanness, and suffering. For him, the world could be perfect and perfectly awful at once! This "perfection" that Williams speaks of is the perfection that Zolynas sees in the droplets of steam and that Linda Gregg means, too, in "Praising Spring" when she speaks of "The beauty in every degree of flourishing." It is the perfection that Austin Straus sees as he walks through the L.A. morning with his son, that Blake sees in a grain of sand, and that Whitman sees always and everywhere. It is the fruit of that visionary consciousness of the masters and mystics and yet, at the same time, it is also nothing but a rotten apple, the ordinary egg of a wren, the stretch of a cat with its forepaws extended, the sight of flies feasting on vomit.

The poetry we have been looking at in this chapter does not tend to call attention to itself, intent instead on bringing its vision to life. Reflecting on a letter by D.H. Lawrence, T.S. Eliot once remarked:

> This speaks to me of that at which I have long aimed, in writing poetry; to write poetry which should be essentially poetry, with nothing poetic about it, poetry standing naked in its bare bones, or poetry so transparent that we should not see the poetry, but that which we are meant to see through the poetry, poetry so transparent that in reading it we are intent on what the poem *points at*, and not on the poetry, this seems to me the thing to try for. To get *beyond poetry*, as Beethoven, in his later works, strove to get *beyond music*.
>
> —T.S. Eliot

Exercise

Spend half an hour at your ordinary daily tasks, but with your mind focused entirely on what you are doing, witnessing, as much as possible, instant by instant, exactly what is going on at that very moment. If you are driving a car, drive the car, being conscious of your movements and the sights all about you; if you are walking down a hall, walk down a hall, being conscious of your feet lifting from and touching the ground, of the sounds and sights around you; if you are vacuuming the rug, pay attention to the feel of the handle of the vacuum vibrating in your hand, to the sight of the rug as you sweep it clean. If you are eating lunch, be conscious of raising the fork to your mouth, chewing, and tasting. Eat more slowly than usual, tasting every bite. Be awake as well to the mind's incessant penchant for wandering off into la-la land. When the mind wanders—as it continually will—gently bring it back to the moment. If you do this with concentrated energy and determination, there are apt to be luminous moments when the senses are heightened, colors are brighter, forms sharper—moments when your perceptual field widens, your feelings deepen, and the humdrum noise about you becomes a kind of exquisite music. But if none of that happens, do not be too disappointed. The purpose is not to experience anything special but to awaken to your life. It is from an hour or month or decade of such practice that a poetry of wisdom and genuine vision might spring.

Poem 67: The Zen of Housework

As a result of the previous exercise, you should be able to write your own version of "The Zen of Housework," a poem about the experience of doing—fully doing, with complete presence—the most trivial and pedestrian of household tasks. Perhaps it will be about washing the car or scrubbing a floor or taking out the garbage. Describe yourself performing this task. Find one or two details that will help you to intensify or enlarge the perspective. See if you can't describe your task in such a way that it and the world become magical before our eyes. Bring back from that awakeness what you have seen and felt. You might try shifting the visual field, opening it up to the surrounding vista and then, like "The Zen of Housework," moving into the magic of a microscopic perspective.

Poem 68: An Epiphany

Almost every day there are moments when we awaken, if only to some small degree, out of our internal chatter and into the present moment. When that happens, the world becomes vivid and luminous. "L.A. Morning" records one such moment. So do "Dusk in the Cuyamacas" and "The Zen of Housework." Write about one such moment in a brief poem. Let it transform itself into a song of joy to the world. Keep it simple and detailed. Be careful of getting abstract, grandiose, or philosophical.

Poem 69: An Enlightened Poem

Pretend that you are an enlightened being, a fully realized soul, one who is utterly at home in the world, filled with empathy and compassion and a sense of the inexpressible oneness of all creation. Then take a short walk, describing whatever you see with wonder, affection, a sense of its kinship with yourself. Move from small objects such as wild flowers or potted plants, to large vistas—cities, nations, galaxies, nebulae—and then return to small objects. Let us see you, too—scratching yourself, or getting hungry, or grinning over the world. Make it at once an honest poem and a visionary poem. Keep it large and embracing without getting grandiose and overbearing. Let us see a genuine love for the world, a compassion for your fellow beings, a spirit that transcends the petty concerns of the ordinary ego. It might be a good idea to read twenty or thirty minutes of Whitman—preferably aloud—before embarking on this poem.

Nuts and Bolts

28

The Pleasures—and Pitfalls— of Poetry Workshops

Emily Dickinson Attends a Writing Workshop

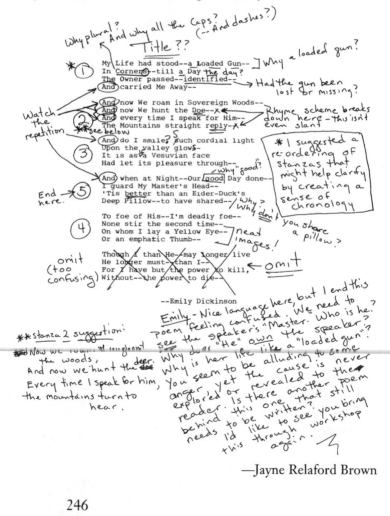

My Life had stood--a Loaded Gun--
In Corners--till a Day
The Owner passed--identified--
And carried Me Away--

And now We roam in Sovereign Woods--
And now We hunt the Doe--
And every time I speak for Him--
The Mountains straight reply--

And do I smile, such cordial light
Upon the valley glows--
It is as a Vesuvian face
Had let its pleasure through--

And when at Night--Our good Day done--
I guard My Master's Head--
'Tis better than an Eider-Duck's
Deep Pillow--to have shared--

To foe of His--I'm deadly foe--
None stir the second time--
On whom I lay a Yellow Eye--
Or an emphatic Thumb--

Though I than He--may longer live
He longer must--than I--
For I have but the power to kill,
Without--the power to die--

--Emily Dickinson

—Jayne Relaford Brown

Earlier in this book, we suggested nurturing one or two friends from whom you could get useful feedback about your poems. If you've done that and it's helped, that might be all you need—at least at the moment: one or two good critics who are willing to tell you what they feel about your poems in progress. On the other hand, formal poetry-writing workshops—the sort taught at adult schools, community colleges, universities, university extension programs, and writing conferences around the country—can be of enormous use. Although people with fragile egos or low self-esteem about their writing, or who for one reason or another find such situations annoying, threatening, or distracting might be better off avoiding such workshops, those who are intent upon making rapid progress, and who are able to tolerate an unindulgent and critical environment, are likely to find them a wonderful tool for learning. It's an opportunity to meet fellow poets, get the kind of support and feedback that will help you develop, and expose yourself to new ideas and a variety of critical points of view.

Here's how they generally work. The poet whose turn it is to be critiqued hands out copies of a poem in progress so that everyone can see it on the page. Then, either the poet or someone else in the group reads the poem aloud, after which participants start discussing it with a view to helping the poet with the next draft. It's important—and usually an iron-clad rule in such situations—that the poet whose work is being discussed doesn't talk. The poet's job is to listen as attentively as possible. That doesn't mean the poet has to accept everything that people say. But it is important to hear it all without spending one's energy trying to defend the poem that is being critiqued.

In a good workshop, people feel free to say what they want to, and very little time is spent in the polite formalities. Beginning the discussion with positive remarks—comments about what works best in the poem—is often helpful and keeps the discussion from becoming overly focused on the poem's problems.

One of the rewards of a decent workshop is listening to intelligent people discuss poetry. Another is being forced to begin articulating your own judgments and tastes. A third, of course, is getting useful feedback on poems in progress. But beware: poetry-writing workshops can also be confusing, frustrating, and discouraging. It is easy to be thrown off course by a group's concerted opinions. One can take others' misguided comments and suggestions too seriously and find oneself in a muddle of confusion. If you are in a group that doesn't have a knowledgeable facilitator, it's relatively easy for the group to lose its way—giving poor advice and counterproductive suggestions.

The Murder-Incorporated Workshop   Neither a workshop in which there is only praise nor one in which there is only negative criticism is likely to be helpful. Sometimes workshoppers get so enamored of the process that they want nothing more than to pick every phrase to death. In such groups, participants have lost their ability to appreciate anything. Then, too, there are some workshops—most often found in graduate writing programs—in which everyone is so ambitious that the frigid chill of competitive savagery permeates the room; polite smiles notwithstanding, no one wants anyone else to succeed, and no one has anything good to say about anyone's poems—except their friends'. Here is one poet's droll comments on the humorous terrors of such workshops:

In the Workshop After I Read My Poem Aloud

All at once everyone in the room says
nothing. They continue doing this and I begin to know
it is not because they are dumb. Finally

the guy from the Bay Area who wears his chapbook
on his sleeve says he likes the poem a lot
but can't really say why and silence

starts all over until someone says she only has
a couple of teeny suggestions such as taking out
the first three stanzas along with

all modifiers except "slippery" and "delicious"
in the remaining four lines. A guy who
hasn't said a word in three days says

he too likes the poem but wonders why
it was written and since I don't know either
and don't even know if I should

I'm grateful there's a rule
I can't say anything now. Somebody
I think it's the shrink from Seattle

says the emotion is not earned and I wonder
when is it ever. The woman on my left
who just had a prose poem in *Green Thumbs and Geoducks*

Says the opening stanza is unbelievable

and vindication comes for a sweet moment
until I realize she means unbelievable.

But I have my defenders too and the MFA from Iowa
the one who thinks the you is an I
and the they a we and the then a now

wants to praise the way the essential nihilism
of the poem's occasion serves to undermine
the formality of its diction. Just like your comment

I say to myself. Another admires the zenlike polarity
of the final image despite the mildly bathetic
symbolism of sheep droppings and he loves how

the three clichés in the penultimate stanza
are rescued by the brazen self-exploiting risk.
The teacher asks what about the last line

and the guy with the chapbook volunteers it suits
the poem's unambitious purpose though he has to admit
it could have been worded somewhat differently.

—Don Colburn

"Emily Dickinson Attends a Writing Workshop" by Jayne Relaford Brown which opened this section is another pointed comment not only on the penchant for critical overkill but on the danger of critiquing out of one's most conventional sense of what a poem should be—forgetting that poets who write wonderful poems often break all the rules. These remarks, however, should not be used to strengthen one's defenses against criticism. The more open you are to hearing and considering the opinions of others, the better your poems will ultimately be.

The Isn't-That-Wonderful Workshop The opposite sort of workshop is the one in which every poem, no matter how puerile, is effusively praised, encouraging the poet to write more poems of the same sort— entire volumes of banality and slush. This sort of mutual admiration society can be useful at an early stage in one's practice, especially if one needs a good dose of encouragement and confidence. But for poets who need honest feedback and assistance, such a setting will prove of limited value.

How to Choose a Workshop Any city or medium-sized community is likely to have a community college or adult education program that offers poetry-writing workshops. Almost every university will offer such courses as well. It is the rare citizen who lives more than an hour away from a school that offers writing workshops. The advantage of community college and adult education courses is that they're cheap. On the other hand, the local university might very well have some excellent and well-established poets facilitating their courses—though keep in mind that the teaching itself is not necessarily going to be better simply because it takes place at a university. Universities tend to hire more on the basis of professional reputation and publication than on the ability to teach. If there are several people who teach poetry-writing courses in your community, study with them all! They'll all have something different to teach you.

Even if you get nothing else from a workshop, it will force you to produce poems, and you'll get to meet fellow poets who live in your community. More than likely you'll get a good deal of value from such situations and find yourself richly rewarded for having taken the risk.

Graduate Programs If you take a graduate level course in poetry-writing, you are likely to find yourself among serious poets working at a high level of accomplishment. There are any number of graduate programs in writing poetry. Two of them, schools with excellent reputations—Warren Wilson College in North Carolina and Goddard College in Vermont—are "low-residency" programs that demand only twenty days a year of attendance. The rest is done through correspondence. Almost all the others are traditional semester-long (about fifteen-week) or quarter-long (about ten-week) courses. The degree program usually requires about two years to complete.

There are also any number of summer conferences—most of them lasting a week—in which you will find yourself in an intensive writing situation and working under the guidance of well-known writers. You can find these conferences and many of the graduate programs in creative writing advertised in *Poets and Writers* and the *AWP Chronicle* (addresses can be found in the final chapter), as well as in various other magazines devoted to serious contemporary literature.

In large cities there are often individuals—often well-published poets themselves—teaching privately. They tend to advertise in weekly newspapers or local poetry magazines and newsletters.

Organizing Your Own Workshop If you are interested in organizing informal workshops, you can simply call up your poet-friends and invite them to bring a poem to your apartment next Friday at seven. Or you can put an ad in an appropriate newspaper, inviting local poets to send you two samples of their work for a possible workshop. Screen those responses and invite the ones who sound promising to a first meeting—perhaps at a local luncheonette or coffee shop—so you can make plans for getting a workshop started.

Computer Workshops In the age of cyberspace, it didn't take long before poetry workshops were being conducted via modem. The ability to chat with others around the country on computer networks makes such long-distance workshopping a perfectly comfortable and relatively inexpensive alternative. Check your CompuServe, America OnLine, Prodigy, and Internet services to see what groups are exchanging poetry; if those groups don't work for you, put the message out that you'd like to talk to fellow poets and start a little group to share and critique poems.

Using This Book in Informal Workshops If you do form or participate in a poetry-writing workshop, a book such as this might prove useful in giving the group both impetus and structure. You might wish, for example, to discuss one chapter at each meeting, the suggested poems in that chapter becoming the "assignment" for the following meeting.

Hiring a Poet-Teacher Another way to build structure into such a group is to occasionally invite a well-respected poet to conduct a meeting of your group. There are many fine poets all across America, and if you know who's in your area, or who will be passing through, it's not so difficult to get them to do a workshop in your community for a modest honorarium.

A Reminder Please keep in mind that many developing writers never participate in workshops. Some are simply afraid to take the risk, as we have already indicated, for it can be hard on the ego. But others find that process irrelevant to their development or, for one reason or another, counterproductive. Reading this book a second time and writing the suggested poems that you did not do the first time around (or using the same writing suggestions to generate additional poems) might be a productive way to continue your progress. Reading collections of poetry more assiduously and seriously would certainly pay dividends in terms of your own progress. There are a great many works of poetry criticism that will help you as well. In our short final chapter, you will find the names of a number of such books that might prove helpful.

29

Getting Your Poems into the World

However private the creative process itself might be, the finished poem is usually meant to be a form of public communication. Ultimately, one writes both for oneself and for other people. On the other hand, the joys of writing are usually private ones, and the discipline of writing will be rewarding whether or not you ever decide to publish your work. But if you do wish to reach an audience, then you'll eventually have to point some of your efforts in that direction.

Obviously, the best way to reach a large audience is by getting your work into print. If you publish your poem in a large, general circulation magazine like the *Atlantic* or the *New Yorker*, you will reach tens of thousands of people. If you publish in literary journals you will reach a much smaller audience but an audience seriously interested in contemporary literature. But the competition in the most prestigious literary magazines is stiff, and if you insist on sending your poems only to such journals you might go years without an acceptance. On the other hand, if you lower your sights a bit and start to send to magazines that are not quite so well known, you are more likely to find your work being greeted with an occasional letter of acceptance. There are scores of respect-worthy literary magazines, both in print and online, that are looking for excellent poetry. Although they might not always have a large readership, they have a discerning and appreciative one made up largely of fellow writers. Many of these magazines, though utterly unknown to the general public, are important venues for contemporary literature.

It's not a bad idea to send some of your work to small local magazines, or magazines that have advertised that they're hungry for work, or magazines run by your friends—or yourself. A few acceptances from publications of that nature can do wonders for the damaged ego, restoring your confidence and your resolve. These are perfectly respectable places for poets to publish, and it's not unusual to find fine, well-known poets publishing in such small-press publications. Besides, you can never be sure who's reading even the smallest circulating magazines. I recall a friend of mine, a writer who has just started publishing her work in the past few years, telling me that she had received a letter from a TV station on the East Coast that wanted permission to use a poem of hers on a show devoted to women artists in America. They had found it in a small California poetry journal—the sort that probably doesn't have a readership of more than a few hundred. A friend and former student had a poem published in a major anthology the same way—because it had been noticed in a small magazine.

The two books most useful for finding magazines in which to publish poetry are *Poet's Market* and *The Directory of Poetry Publishers.* Those two books will supply you with the names and addresses of hundreds of magazines that publish poetry, the names of the editors, what kind of poetry each is looking for, how long they tend to keep poems before responding (sometimes as long as a year!), the size of their circulation, how to order a sample copy, and other useful information. You will find the addresses of those two resources in the next chapter. Use a search engine like Google to find "literary journals" online.

Of course, if you are somewhat familiar with the magazine you're submitting your work to you are better off. Editors of magazines, often poets themselves, tend to have strong biases. Each is likely to favor poems of a particular sort (often, not surprisingly, the sort they themselves write), and is likely to overlook or undervalue poems written in a different manner. Why submit a charming sonnet to a magazine that is relentlessly avant-garde or an experimental poem to a journal that is looking for poems in traditional form? Although some editors favor poems by poets whom they know or who they know are well published, a great many editors delight in finding new talent and in publishing work they admire by poets of whom they have never heard. Online literary journals will usually allow you to read a few poems, stories, and essays from previous issues, and in that way you can see the sort of material they publish.

253

Format for Submissions Once you have the name and address of the magazine, submitting material is simple: send a cleanly typed copy of three to seven poems with a very brief cover letter and a self-addressed, stamped envelope. Without a self-addressed, stamped envelope you are unlikely to hear from the editor. Magazines do not generally spend their own money to return submissions. Many journals allow you or require you to submit online and almost all literary magazines have a website that will contain submission guidelines.

The cover letter is a mere courtesy, a way of introducing yourself. It usually says something as simple as: "Dear Editor: I'm enclosing four poems for submission and a self-addressed, stamped envelope. Thanks for considering them. Sincerely...." That's it! If you have recent work coming out in other magazines or have recently published other work, you might want to make brief mention of that. But "brief" is the operative word. The last thing you want to do in a cover letter is try to "sell" the enclosed poems by telling the editor that they are "true stories," or "the best things I've done," or by going into autobiographical detail. This is just what editors do not want to read, and it can only prejudice them against your work.

When you submit poems, you should generally send three to seven pages of work. Magazines want to get some sense of your voice, and a single short poem might not be enough to establish the work for them. On the other hand, they are even less interested in receiving a twenty-page batch of your work and are likely to be disposed against liking any of it from the start. It is a good idea to put your name and address in the upper right margin of each page: editors receive hundreds of manuscripts, and it's not difficult for the envelope with your name and address to be misplaced. Many literary and poetry magazines permit you to make multiple submissions, so long as you inform them that the work has also been submitted elsewhere and then immediately inform them if it is accepted elsewhere. Whether a particular magazine accepts multiple submissions will be in their online guidelines and in *Poet's Market*.

The Rejection Slip—and Its Dangers What you will receive in response to your submission is either a form rejection slip politely thanking you; a form rejection slip on the bottom of which the editor has scrawled a few words either of apology or encouragement ("be glad to look at more..."); a personal note of encouragement suggesting that the magazine would be delighted to read more of your work; or a note saying they are happy to accept your poem "Sweeney Among the Butterflies" and will send you, as payment, two copies of the issue in which it appears.

Here's the real danger. A great many beginning poets are so frightened of getting rejected that they dare not send their poems out to magazines in the first place—or if they do, that first rejection slip is so painful they never send work out again. If you are to get your work published you must learn to keep submitting despite the inevitably painful emotions that a rejection slip brings. So that you will be forewarned, those emotions are anger, resentment, confusion, sadness, humiliation, and uncertainty about your talent. For an hour or two or a day or two after receiving the rejection slip, you are likely to feel deflated, tired, disgusted, certain you're a lousy poet, certain they're a lousy magazine, and certain that you need a stiff drink, cigarette, piece of apple pie, good cry, and/or a quiet evening in front of the boob tube watching something brainless. There is nothing wrong with those responses. They are perfectly normal. Normal and healthy. The trick is to allow yourself to have those feelings and still get those poems—or others—back into the mail! Not giving up in the face of rejection is one of the chief skills that a writer needs to nurture.

Practicing Being Rejected The Greek philosopher Diogenes, the one who lived in a barrel and is known for having gone around Athens with a lamp looking for an honest man, understood the business of rejection perfectly. It is said that early one cold winter morning he was seen in a public park, his begging bowl held at arm's length, entreating a statue for money or food. When accosted by a curious throng later in the day and asked why he was begging of a statue, Diogenes replied that he was practicing being refused. That is what you, too, must do.

Get Rich Quick Not with your poetry you won't! Most magazines, if they accept poems, will pay you nothing but two copies of their magazine. The bigger, more prestigious magazines might pay you ten or twenty dollars for a poem, maybe even a few dollars per line. You are unlikely to make an appreciable sum of money on a well-received volume of poetry, let alone on a few poems in a magazine. If poets ever make any money, it's from grants, awards, lectures, readings, and whatever gainful employment they have apart from their life as a poet.

255

Vanity Presses It is generally a good idea to avoid vanity publications. They advertise in newspapers and popular magazines and often suggest that they are putting out an anthology and looking for new poets. If they accept your poem—and they accept just about everything submitted—they are likely to cajole you into ordering a copy of the gilt-edged anthology in which your work will appear—at a price of only $49.95. Don't fall for the bait. Anyone whomakes you pay out money to have your poem published is publishing something in which you do not want to appear! No one reads such anthologies except the contributors themselves.

On the other hand, some fine poets have decided to publish a first collection with a vanity press in hopes that their work would get some notice. If you do sign a contract for such a book, make sure you know exactly what you're getting for your money. You should know how much money will be spent on advertising, how many copies will be distributed (not just printed), how those copies will be distributed, and how many copies you will get—and for what price. The more questions you ask, the better.

Publishing a Book of Poems After you have published a number of poems—perhaps twenty or thirty, or a few hundred—it will be time to think about publishing a book. *Poet's Market* and *The Directory of Poetry Publishers* will give you the names and addresses of numerous publishers who are interested in seeing book-length manuscripts. Once you start reading collections of poetry, you will begin to become familiar with the better-known poetry presses in the United States. Although many of the major publishing houses publish collections of contemporary poetry, they usually take on very few, if any, new poets each year. Many university presses publish collections of poetry, as do a great many "small" presses. By "small" we do not mean that they are unknown or unheralded, but simply that they are not mega-publishing houses or associated with universities. Many such "small" presses—publishing houses like Graywolf, BOA Editions, City Lights, and Copper Canyon—are among the most prestigious poetry publishers in the nation. There are several other publishers of that order and many, many smaller houses that also do fine publishing.

A volume of poetry usually contains between forty-eight and eighty pages of poetry, though many small presses publish poetry "chapbooks," books that are stapled or sewn and which are not bound with a spine. These books usually run from fifteen to forty pages in length. Manuscripts should be neatly typed and numbered with never more than one poem on any page. The typed manuscript should contain a table of contents and an acknowledgments page, which lists the magazines and anthologies in which the poems first appeared. Editors want to see the sort of clean printing on manuscripts that is produced by a decent laser or inkjet printer, though good photocopies of well-printed poems are perfectly acceptable.

The best places to learn about publishers and book contests are in the bimonthly magazine *Poets and Writers* and the bimonthly *Writers Chronicle*. Many publishers hold national competitions for collections of poetry, and these contests will be listed in those two magazines with all pertinent facts included for submission of manuscripts.

Each issue of those two magazines will also tell you what literary magazines and anthologies are looking for material, and present pertinent information about awards and prizes being offered around the country for individual poems or groups of poems. They are the central magazines of the American literary community, and no serious writer should be without one or the other. Their addresses will be found in the next chapter. Check their current price by calling their toll-free number and send one or the other a check for a subscription. The amount of useful information you'll receive with each issue will be well worth the price.

If you are making multiple submissions of your book-length manuscript, let the publisher know that in your cover letter. If you are submitting to a major publishing house, it is a good idea to call them first to find out to whom your manuscript should be addressed. Needless to say, enclose a self-addressed return envelope with sufficient postage for the return of your manuscript if that is requested. Often, these days, such manuscripts are recycled under the assumption that the authors have a copy of the manuscript on their computer.

Self Publishing Many poets—including Walt Whitman—have published their own books. Putting together a small chapbook is a relatively inexpensive project to undertake, and for well under two hundred dollars you can often print fifty copies of such a book. If you do the printing on your own computer and just use a quick-copy store to print the cover and staple the pages, you can do a considerable number of copies for less than one hundred dollars. There are several books on

257

self-publishing that will walk you through the process of creating such a book. Your poetry book will be inexpensive enough that you can afford to give copies away to people to whom you would like to show your work. You can also sell those books at your poetry readings or on consignment at local literary bookstores. "Print on Demand" companies allow you to print as few copies as you want and are often a worthwhile investment so that you do not find yourself with a closet full of undistributed copies of your book. You can find names and addresses online with a simple search.

Poetry Readings There are, of course, other ways to publish one's work. Giving public poetry readings allows you to present the poems before a live audience. Just about every medium-sized city in the United States has a few coffee houses or bookstores that feature weekly readings. If there are open-mike readings, readings in which all members of the audience are encouraged to read, you should consider participating. They are often fun, generally everyone is friendly and supportive, and you will gain valuable experience in reading your work. Practice at home so that when you get up before an audience you can present your work effectively.

If you attend solo readings where one or two poets perform their work, you will soon enough get to know the people in charge of organizing such events and, when you feel ready, can probably manage to wangle yourself a reading. Keep the reading short and appealing by reading only your best work and by reading it well. The biggest sin is mumbling your poems, or reading in a monotone. But the second biggest sin is reading at too great a length. It's the rare poet who can entertain an audience for more than twenty minutes.

The important point is to find an audience when you feel ready to do so. Beginning to publish can be a great impetus to increasing your devotion to your craft and making you a more accomplished poet.

30

Resources

The following two publications list magazines and publishers looking for poetry. They will also give you the addresses of literary magazines to which you might wish to subscribe:

Poet's Market is published in an updated version each year by Writer's Digest Books. It is carried by many libraries and bookstores and is available from online bookstores such as Amazon.com or from the volume's publisher at WritersDigest.com.

The Directory of Poetry Publishers is published in an updated version each year by Dustbooks at PO Box 100, Paradise, CA 95967. Or order online from dustbooks.com or from any online bookstore or call Dustbooks at 800-477-6110.

Poets and Writers, Inc., is a national organization of poets and literary writers. They put out a biannual *Directory of American Poets and Fiction Writers* and a bimonthly magazine *Poets & Writers*, which is of great use to poets. It lists almost all the poetry manuscript competitions, most literary prizes and awards available, and usually contains a listing of magazines and anthologies currently looking for submissions. It also contains many articles of interest to poets. The organization also publishes a number of short books that poets and small-press publishers will find of use. Their address is 72 Spring Street, New York, NY 10012. Their New York phone number is 212-226-3586. Their toll-free number is 800-666-2268.

The AWP Official Guide to Writing Programs is a list of graduate and undergraduate creative writing programs in the United States and also describes over 200 writers' conferences, colonies, and centers. The Associated Writing Programs is an organization that provides many services for writers and teachers and also puts out a useful bimonthly magazine, the *AWP Chronicle*, that contains lists of prizes and book competitions plus a great deal of information for poets. Located at Old Dominion University, Norfolk, their website is awpwriter.org and their phone number is 703-993-4301.

A Google search for "Poetry Contests" should give you several useful links. Or try www.writing-world.com for links to a great many poetry contests as well as contests for all other literary genres. That site also contains a wealth of other information.

There are many books designed to help poets develop their skills. I can recommend *The Poet's Companion: A Guide to the Pleasures of Writing Poetry* by Kim Addonizio and Dorianne Laux, but there are, by now, scores of other such books that poets at various stages will find useful. Look them up under "poetry writing books" on Amazon.com. There are a large number of them.

There are also numerous books about poetic form, such as *Patterns of Poetry: An Encyclopedia of Forms*, by Miller Williams, *The Book of Forms: A Handbook of Poetics*, by Louis Turco, and *Poetic Meter and Poetic Form* by Paul Fussell. Amazon.com and other online bookstores will give you the names of and particulars about many others.

There are a great number of anthologies of poetry available. Any literary bookstore or good-sized library should have anthologies from many countries and cultures. You can read, in translation, the poetry of ancient Egypt and of modern China—and just about everything in between. You can read anthologies of younger American poets, American women poets, twentieth-century American poets, innovative American poets, formalist American poets, and just about any other category of poetry that might interest you. If your library doesn't have what you're looking for, use their interlibrary loan service or check *Books in Print* and order the book from the publisher. We list here only a handful of recent anthologies of American poetry:

The Best American Poetry, published by Scribner, is an annual, guest-edited by a different poet each year.

The Pushcart Prize Anthology is another annual book that attempts to publish the best poetry, fiction, and essays from the previous year's literary journals and small presses. They are invariably excellent collections.

Shaking the Pumpkin: Traditional Indian Poetry of the Americas, by Jerome Rothenberg, published by University of New Mexico Press. All of Rothenberg's anthologies are recommended. It would be well worth getting your hands even on the ones that are out of print. They widen our perspective on the world tradition.

Against Forgetting: Twentieth-Century Poetry of Witness, edited by Carolyn Forché, published by Norton. One of several anthologies of twentieth-century world poetry. It includes many of the major figures of the past hundred years.

An Invitation to Poetry: A New Favorite Poem Project Anthology by Robert Pinsky and Maggie Deitz is an excellent anthology of both contemporary and classical poetry, comes with a wonderful DVD of people discussing and reading their favorite poem.

A Book of Luminous Things by Czeslaw Milosz, published by Harcourt Brace, is an excellent international anthology.

Poetry Like Bread: Poets of the Political Imagination, published by Curbstone Press, edited by Martin Espada.

Poetry 180: A Turning Back to Poetry and *180 More*, edited by Billy Collins, published by Random House.

The Face of Poetry, edited by Zack Rogow, published by the University of California Press, is a lively multicultural anthology that comes with a CD on which you can hear many of the poems being read by their author.

Every Shut Eye Ain't Asleep is an anthology of African American poetry edited by Michael S. Harper and Anthony Walton, published by Back Bay Books. Two even more recent anthologies are *Every Goodbye Ain't Gone: An Anthology of Innovative Poetry by African Americans*, edited by Lynn Nielsen and Lauri Ramey and published by the University of Alabama Press, and *Rainbow Darkness*, edited by Keith Tuma and published by Miami University Press.

Burning Down the House: Selected Poems from the Nuyorican Poet's Café's National Poetry Slam Champions by Roger Bonair-Agard, Stephen Colman, Guy LeCharles Gonzalez, and Alix Olson, published by Soft Skull.

100 Great Poems of the Twentieth Century, edited by Mark Strand and published by Norton.

100 Essential Modern Poems, selected by Jay Parisi and published by Ivan R. Dee.

Stand Up Poetry: An Expanded Anthology, edited by Charles Harper Webb, published by University of Iowa Press. This is a very readable collection of highly accessible recent poetry.

The Maverick Poets, edited by Steve Kowit, published by Gorilla Press, PO Box 404, Potrero, CA 91963. An anthology of accessible contemporary American poetry illustrated by Charles Bukowski and others and edited by the author of this book.

As I mentioned in the last chapter, there are hundreds of literary magazines in America that are either devoted exclusively to poetry or that publish poetry as well as fiction. A good library or bookstore will probably have some of the better-known ones, magazines such as *Poetry*, the *American Poetry Review*, the *Paris Review*, the *Kenyon Review*, *Grand Street*, and the *Partisan Review*. However, the vast majority of poetry magazines are not likely to find their way into bookstores and must be purchased through the mails. *Poet's Market* and *The Directory of Poetry Publishers*, or a brief online search, will give you the addresses of the *Boston Review*, *Exquisite Corpse*, *Five Points*, *Home Planet News*, *Literal Latté*, *Open City*, *Ploughshares*, *Rattle*, the *Tampa Review*, the *Sun*, and scores of other literary journals in which serious contemporary poets are publishing their work.

Each year sees the publication of many critical works on American poetry. Any issue of *Poets and Writers*, the *American Poetry Review*, or other large literary journals is likely to carry ads for such recent volumes. There are numerous critical studies of famous twentieth-century authors and literary movements. The reference librarian at your library or a brief online search will help you find] such works. A few of the many writers who have written well about contemporary American poetry include Charles Altieri, Paul Breslin, Dana Gioia, Robert Hass, Alicia Ostriker, Marjorie Perloff, Robert Pinsky, M. L. Rosenthal, Timothy Steele, Helen Vendler, and Alan Williamson. Their books on the subject of American poetry are worth reading.

There are few better ways to become a more effective poet than by reading a great deal of poetry—from all cultures—and by reading books of criticism about poetry. If you have always admired the work of John Keats, why not begin by reading one or two of the recent studies of Keats's life and poetry? If Emily Dickinson fascinates you, there are any number of provocative recent books investigating her life and suggesting new approaches to her poetry. If some of the poets included in this book excite your interest and curiosity, see if their books are available in your library or bookstore. These days, the interlibrary loan service of most libraries can have books that you request sent to your library from around the country. *Books in Print* (or for some small-press titles, *Small Press Books in Print*), or a brief Google search will help you find titles that are still in print—books that can be ordered from any good bookstore.

By all means become strongly influenced by poets you admire and read everything you can about their lives. If, under their influence, you find your poetry changing and growing, you are on the right track. There is nothing like finding a wonderful poem or discovering a splendid poet to inspire new work of your own. The more poetry you read, the more poetry you are likely to write. If you want to study poetry with the best teachers, study the works of the great poets. It would be a good idea to start collecting poems that move you deeply, compiling a personal anthology of poems to which you can turn for inspiration. And finally, the best resource is your own desire to keep writing, keep learning, keep perfecting your skills.

Future Work

"Please send future work"
 —Editor's note on a rejection slip

It is going to be a splendid summer.
The apple tree will be thick with golden russets
expanding weightily in the soft air.
I shall finish the brick wall beside the terrace
and plant out all the geranium cuttings.
Pinks and carnations will be everywhere.

She will come out to me in the garden,
her bare feet pale on the cut grass,
bringing jasmine tea and strawberries on a tray.
I shall be correcting the proofs of my novel
(third in a trilogy—simultaneous publication
in four continents); and my latest play

will be in production at the Aldwych
starring Glenda Jackson and Paul Scofield
with Olivier brilliant in a minor part.
I shall probably have finished my translations
of Persian creation myths and the Pre-Socratics
(drawing new parallels) and be ready to start

on Lucretius. But first I'll take a break
at the chess championships in Manila—
on present form, I'm fairly likely to win.
And poems? Yes, there will certainly be poems:
they sing in my head, they tingle along my nerves.
It is all magnificently about to begin.

—Fleur Adcock

Afterword
The Mystique of the Difficult Poem

Publisher's note: This essay was originally published in Poetry International *#3 in 1999. We are grateful to Mary Kowit, Steve's wife and literary executor, for permission to reprint it here.*

When I was about fifteen I fell in love with Hart Crane. The poems in *White Buildings, The Bridge,* and *Key West* shimmered with the most fragile and delicate poignance. It was the very music of the soul's anguish. As for Crane's suicide, that was icing on the cake: it made the work even more tragic, more unbearably gorgeous. The fact that I had only the vaguest idea what he was talking about, and sometimes not even that, bothered me hardly at all until I was in my twenties and the pure music of Crane began to seem less enticing than the work of poets who, in addition to their engaging linguistic skills, actually seemed to have something coherent to say.

Although Crane's pervasive obscurity was more tolerable than that of poets who were less exquisite musicians, I had by then read enough incomprehensible poetry to know that I wanted something more. I wanted marvelous music to be sure, stunning figures, an imaginative linguistic playfulness that was everywhere inspired and surprising, but I also wanted poems that spoke to me with thrilling precision and insight.

The "ambiguities" that the New Critics imagined to be at the center of poetic craft seemed almost always to weaken rather than strengthen my experience of the poem. Though my first reading of a poem is likely to take pleasure in the language, the tonalities, the music and linguistic sparkle, the intelligence and taste behind the phrasing, nonetheless I find myself unlikely to finish reading a poem if it becomes apparent that the poet has no intention of communicating much of anything beyond all that language, all that music. Far be it from me to invade his privacy. If I want pure music I can listen to Palestrina and Sam Cooke.

At about the same time as my uneasiness over modernist incoherence was growing, Allen Ginsberg, himself still a young man, was beginning to publish a poetry that was more fierce, emotionally charged, and appealingly human than anything I had read from his more staid and conventional contemporaries. And not the least of his virtues was that he was perfectly coherent. The stuff wasn't filled with footnotable literary allusions and hopelessly gnarled syntax and untrackable metaphoric acrobatics. "Howl" opened up a territory, at least for me, that the modernists had spent the first half of the century trying to close off. Suddenly the doors of possibility had been flung wide open. There was plenty of freedom, plenty of room to move around and to do what the avant garde had never dared to do—write poems in coherent English.

And then, when I was twenty-seven, I moved to the West Coast and picked up Robinson Jeffers, and was stunned anew. He was as wonderful a musician as any of the modernists I'd read, easily as fine and conscious a craftsman, but his poems, like Ginsberg's, were perfectly understandable. Jeffers' music was certainly not as ecstatic or intoxicating as Hart Crane's, but then again he never seemed ornamental, precious, histrionic; he was never without flesh and substance. Jeffers not only had something of moment to say, but he managed to say it, as had Ginsberg, without resorting to a hundred subterfuges, misdirections, ambiguities. Moreover, Jeffers' vision was larger by far than that of his contemporaries, those high modernists who had dominated American poetry during the first half of the twentieth century.

Of course, in the background of my life, there had always been Whitman: larger and wiser than any poet had been before or has been since, and everywhere luminously clear. But somehow, perhaps because he was not of my century, or because he was a poet

266

of such singular genius, his ability to speak with the utmost clarity about even the most subtle and all but inexpressible matters hadn't been able to serve me as a model. Under the influence of Whitman, Ginsberg, and Jeffers, the canonical American poets, with their inordinate love of difficulty, began to lose their luster. I became profoundly suspicious of the whole modernist enterprise. As a fledgling poet I had written enough high-flown gibberish myself to know its seductions. Though I would continue to read occasional poems and passages in poems that were thrilling, however inexplicable, the business of writing incoherent poetry seemed tiresome, and I wanted nothing to do with it.

This, I fully realize, is a minority opinion, at least among poets, academics, and critics. Though I imagine the vast bulk of the reading public feels much as I do—hence their indifference to contemporary poetry—I suspect many in the trade will find such an attitude appalling, for impenetrability is still widely admired.

A recent review in *The New York Review of Books* claims, for example, as though it were a sign of the poet's talent and distinction, that Eugenio Montale "will lead commentators into all kinds of difficulty when it comes to establishing the content of many of the poems." The reviewer, discussing at length a particular twelve-line poem from Montale's early collection, *Cuttlefish*, happily admits that he has almost no idea what it means, though it is one of Montale's "simplest" lyrics. "What, overall, is the poem about?" he asks. "Even with this simplest of lyrics, the essential nub winds off into a cloud of possibilities." But this unclarity at the "essential nub" of so many Montale poems is, so the reviewer assures us, among the poet's chiefmost virtues. The genius of Montale's work is achieved through "a prodigious density encouraging ever more complex levels of consciousness, and evoking the finest shadings of emotion colored by every variety of thought."

The reviewer, Tim Parks, is a knowledgeable reader of Montale's poetry, and his praise of poetic incomprehensibility is not at all unusual among those who read poetry seriously. Nonetheless, if you look at his assertion closely, you will see that it is little more than a sophisticated version of the bemused college freshman's belief that a poem isn't really supposed to mean anything at all, so that the reader can have the pleasure of making it mean whatever he wants it to mean. When Tim Parks reminds us that "poetry in this century has become more cryptic, more private, more untranslatable," there is, in his voice, no hint of reproach. This assertion, that "difficulty" is one of modernism's defining virtues, has been so frequently injected into the body of contemporary aesthetics that it has become an unchallenged and toxic part of its bloodstream.

In *The Best American Poetry of 1990*, Jorie Graham makes perhaps the most eloquent, lengthy and detailed recent defense of difficult and indeterminate verse. In one typical passage she writes:

> When we experience a loosening of setting or point of view, and a breakdown of syntax's dependence on closure, we witness an opening up of the present-tense terrain of the poem, a privileging of delay and digression over progress. This opening up of the present moment as a terrain outside time—this foregrounding of the field of the "act of the poem"—can be explained in many ways. We might consider the way in which the idea of perfection in art seems to be called into question by many of our poets. On the one hand, some might argue today, the notion of perfection serves ultimately to make an object not so much ideal as available to a marketplace, available for ownership—something to be acquired by the act of understanding.

In this passage, Graham is recommending not just the virtues of being "indefinite" about the poem's setting, but the value of employing a syntax that guarantees that the reader will be confused about anything the poet might be trying to say. The tactical advantage of this seems to be that if readers have no idea what you're talking about and are unable to pay attention to either the narrative or the ideas (because, in fact, the poet has refused to articulate any), they will be forced to attend to "the field of the 'act of the poem,'" that is, I take it, to the manner of its saying: the phrasing, juxtapositions, music, diction, imagery and such. This, I assume, is what she means by "an opening up of the present-tense terrain of the poem," and what she means by suggesting, in a phrase that seems somewhat inflated for its occasion, that such poems are "outside time."

Apparently, if there is no narrative, no temporal instance that is being described, the poem is, therefore, "timeless." Finally, she seems to suggest that the idea of a "perfect" poem, or the attempt to write such a poem, produces something that, by virtue of being accessible to the general reader, becomes no more than a contemptible "commodity." This notion betrays a patrician haughtiness that one imagines Graham would be loathe to confess more directly. Elsewhere in that essay she writes:

> The genius of syntax consists in its permitting paradoxical, "unsolvable" ideas to be explored, not merely nailed down, stored, and owned; in its permitting the soul-forging pleasures of thinking to prevail over the acquisition of information called knowing.

For Graham, thinking and exploration seem to mean no more than being vague and ambiguous enough so that neither the author nor the reader can recognize, let alone explore, any genuine idea or perception. This, of course, is not what we tend to mean by genuine exploration of ideas but is only the facade of such exploration, and indeed what is being recommended in her essay seems nothing but a poetry of facades. Her introductory essay, made up almost entirely of this sort of piffling, goes on for some fourteen pages, all to glorify the lofty desire of the poet to resist making sense. This is the open-ended, exploratory, multivoiced, indeterminate, opaquely textured, disjunctive and defamiliarizing, closure-free world of postmodern poetics. And if it promotes a poetry that is "free of any user," it augurs as well a poetry that is likely to be free of many readers.

While Graham wants others to share her heady excitement over such verse, it is apt to prove a difficult sell, though her own experience of such poetry, she insists, is nothing short of redemptive. Here, in her somewhat overheated prose, she captures (or invents, depending on your view of her credibility) the rapturous, revival-meeting spirit that overcomes her when she listens to the glossolalia of incomprehensible verse:

> [T]he motion of the poem as a whole resisted my impulse to resolve it into "sense" of a rational kind. Listening to

the poem, I could feel my irritable reaching after fact, my desire for resolution, graspable meaning, ownership . . . . It resisted. It compelled me to let go. The frontal, grasping motion frustrated, my intuition was forced awake. I felt myself having to "listen" with other parts of my sensibility, felt my mind being forced back down into the soil of my senses. And I saw it was the resistance of the poem—its occlusion, or difficulty—that was healing me, forcing me to privilege my heart, my intuition—parts of my sensibility infrequently called upon in my everyday experience in the marketplace of things and ideas."

Mercifully less decorative is Graham's discussion, near the beginning of her essay, wherein she admits—though only, I would guess, as a rhetorical ploy—that she feels some uneasiness about the enterprise of writing poetry that resists being understood. Here, it is interesting to note, the misty cerebral romance of the rest of her essay is nowhere to be found. Here she writes in cogent English— perhaps because she has something unequivocal to say:

Yet surely the most frequent accusation leveled against contemporary poetry is its difficulty or inaccessibility. It is accused of speaking only to itself, of becoming an irrelevant and elitist art form with a dwindling audience . . . . For how can we hear that "no one reads it," or that "no one understands it," without experiencing a failure of confidence . . . . We start believing that it is essentially anachronistic. We become anecdotal. We want to entertain. We believe we should "communicate."

In the lexicon of modernism, "anecdotal," "entertain," and "communicate" are indeed beneath contempt. They stand with "self-expression" and "sincerity" as the sort of sorry business in which only the novice and the inept engage. But if poets have far more noble goals, as Graham assures us they have, than to concern themselves with so tawdry a matter as making their poems intelligible, whatever these goals might be they seem too ephemeral and rarefied to attract the common reader, who is likely to find behind the claim little of substance and nothing of interest.

Jorie Graham, one of our most praised contemporary poets, represents the aesthetic thinking of those who, like Parks, find difficulty a decided virtue. Indeed, she envisions a poetry that is not merely difficult but indeterminate, that is to say, incomprehensible. And if Graham's rationale seems a bit murky, what is one to say of something like this, the opening half-sentence of an essay by Charles Bernstein, a leading "theoretician" among the American postmodernists:

> Not "death" of the referent—rather a recharged use of the multivalent referential vectors that any word has, how words in combination tone and modify the associations made for each of them, how "reference" then is not a one-on-one relation to an "object" but a perceptual dimension that closes in to pinpoint, nail down (*this* word), sputters omnitropically (the in in the which of who where what wells), refuses the build up of image track/projection while, pointillistically, fixing a reference at each turn . . . .

More reasoned and modest than Jorie Graham's, and far less silly and dismissable than Bernstein's, is the defense of difficult poetry recently set forth by Donald Justice, who argues that certain kinds of obscurity in poetry are "not altogether destructive" ["Benign Obscurity," from *Oblivion: On Writers and Writing*, Story Line Press, 1998]. The least persuasive of his arguments is the curious notion that a poem without "hidden meanings" is likely to be trivial or frivolous, an assertion that he makes in passing and does not bother either to explain or defend. Nor does it seem likely, from anything his essay suggests, that he would be able to.

Though he distinguishes a "benign" sort of obscurity from that form of obscurity for which he has less indulgence—what he characterizes as the "blanketing fog that can creep over everything"—he seems to be saving his approval, for the most part, for a poetry of magnificent music which makes the obscurity of its text seem not only palatable but perfectly appropriate, a part of the poem's necessary texture—a quality without which the poem would be something less imposing and less memorable than it is. Justice, who makes such suggestions in the most provisional and tempered language, argues that "one may be led on, and cheerfully enough at times, by precisely one's failure to grasp what is being said. And there is the excitement, meanwhile, of being in beyond one's depth."

Though it is possible, I suppose, that an opaque passage or phrase in an otherwise clear text can be intriguing, and can add a certain color and excitement to a poem, I am not fully convinced of it. Though the joy of pure poetic music and language certainly has its rewards, they seem ultimately smaller rewards than such poetry would have were the same quality of language tethered to intelligible subject matter and perception. Imagine Hart Crane, for example, writing a poetry of the same verbal richness and intensity, but one that was filled with brilliant and fully lucid descriptions, narratives, characterizations, and insights. I hardly imagine it would be a lesser poetry.

Justice makes an even more interesting argument about the success of many of the more obscure poems of Hopkins, Hart Crane, and Dylan Thomas when he suggests that "the singular power of such poems seems to penetrate the emotional system directly, without ever having to pass through the understanding." But this, it seems to me, is to make too much of the fact that one can catch the flavor, subject, attitude, and emotional tone of a passage with only a few verbal cues. That certainly seems true. But with the exception of a few heady examples—poets of glorious musical skill such as the ones Justice cites—it is hard for me to think of many poets who can carry the day on their musicianship alone. It is to suggest, I think, that the content of poems really is an unimportant aspect. Perhaps that is true for Justice. I know it is not true for me.

His third argument is that the obscurity of a narrative poem such as E. A. Robinson's "Eros Turanos" might, perhaps, be "expressive of the very understanding the poem is intended to carry." By this he seems to mean that the poem's narrative unclarity might be rooted in—that is, it might be a consciously formal or strategic correlative for—the moral complexity of the situation it purports to describe. I confess at once that the suggestion seems farfetched, and the very fact that Justice himself is so uneasy about postulating it leads me to believe he's about as unconvinced by it as I am.

I suspect, rather, that he so much admires both those parts of the Robinson poem that are clear and the prosodic and writerly skill of the whole that he has allowed his good common sense to be swayed by a number of other critics who admire the poem, in part, for the very reason that it doesn't entirely make sense.

To my taste, Robinson's best poems are, however subtle in their narrative strategies, nonetheless perfectly clear. When he fails, which is often enough, it is because of an inability or unwillingness to tell his story with sufficient clarity. "Eros Turanos" has fine passages and, here and there, admirable moments of complex psychological portraiture, but, in the end, the poem collapses beneath the weight of its unclarity. Although Justice wonders if those critics might be right that its very unclarity is a virtue, he seems uneasy about the proposition and not entirely convinced, and his essay ends with the most modest of claims. For certain poems or certain kinds of poems a degree of obscurity, he posits, is simply unavoidable, and with such poems "the obscurity is no handicap, perhaps even has its uses—can we claim this much?"

It seems to me that the widespread critical belief that poetry needn't communicate has had disastrous consequences for the art, and that a shockingly large part of the poetry of our own time is, with its blanketing fog of obscurity, altogether unreadable. In the end, neither avant-garde Language Poets like Charles Bernstein nor well-meaning postmodernists like Jorie Graham are to be blamed for this mess.

Children of the age of theory, the postmodernists argue that communication isn't really possible anyhow and that no reading of a "text" can be "privileged" over any other: that is to say, language itself is indeterminate. But this idea is by no means the radical break with the modernist tradition that it might at first seem. It is, rather, its natural extension: postmodernist "indeterminacy" being the logical extension—or at least the reductio ad absurdum—of the defining modernist penchant for difficulty. It wasn't Charles Bernstein, after all, but T. S. Eliot who suggested that "meaning" was a questionable expedient that we could well do without, nothing more than meat thrown to the watchdogs while the burglar robbed the house.

It need be said at once that Eliot never practiced quite so radical a poetics as his remark suggests. At its best, which is a good deal of the time, his poetry, however nonlinear, is brilliantly coherent. Though the various settings of a poem like "Prufrock" continue to shift disconcertingly, in Eliot's controlled hands the collaged, unanchorable narrative, a fusion of interior anxieties and exterior perceptions and assertions, remains, however complex and novel, brilliantly intelligible.

By the Forties, the fashion for the difficult had become so pervasive that the subject of incoherence and indeterminacy rarely arose as a significant issue in critical discourse. And although a good number of our best poets are no longer engaged in that sort of enterprise, and take pleasure in writing a poetry that, however wild, subtle, and surprising, is perfectly lucid, indecipherability is still much in vogue, as one can prove by glancing through just about any contemporary anthology or poetry journal.

This opacity, which has effectively killed off any possibility of a large American readership, has been a reigning fashion in conventional poetry for almost a century now, and while it is still common to hear the virtues of difficulty extolled in the critical literature, it is exceedingly rare to find even the most tepid dissent. If there are serious poets and critics who are appalled by this facet of the contemporary aesthetic, they have been politic enough to keep their mouths shut. But its absence from serious consideration is probably less a matter of conscious decision than the fact that the ideology is so pervasive it has become an all but unchallengeable assumption, as if difficulty were a necessary function of what poetry is, a fundamental condition of the art itself.

Which is why, I suppose, the issue has not been a significant feature of any of the poetry pie fights of the past few decades. Fought out at the edges of the Great American Kulturkampf—that low-intensity protracted warfare between an ascendant conservatism and a liberalism that dare not speak its name—these periodic skirmishes, often emblematic of the larger national conflict being waged over America's soul, reveal a good deal about who we are and what we believe. A few years back, for example, Joseph Epstein, in a bit of conservative nostalgia, provoked an amusing squabble by suggesting that our verse had notably degenerated since the era of Eliot and Stevens.

Another battle raged over the "neo-formalists," who wish to return us to the prosodic rigors of the past. At the same time, there was the marginally memorable flap over the deconstructionist aesthetic of the Language Poets who were either registering a monumental epistemic breakthrough, as they themselves loudly proclaimed, or were merely "long on theory," as Allen Ginsberg once pointedly suggested. Apparently, many mainstream poets who smirk at the relentless incoherence of those avant-gardists delude themselves with the comforting notion that their own brand of highly complex, disjunctive, and imagistically dense poetry is, if one only reads sensitively enough, perfectly intelligible.

In the latest poetry brouhaha, Harold Bloom, a tireless advocate of difficulty in poetry, has registered his pique at the new multicultural barbarism that is undermining the Western intellectual tradition. With the universities' urgency to teach an inclusive, gender-conscious, multi-ethnic curriculum, it is Bloom's fear that the "major" poets and novelists of the English tradition will be abandoned by the academy in favor of undistinguished figures whose only virtue is that they are representatives of various "underrepresented" minorities. At the same time, so Bloom would have it, the critical establishment has been seriously undermined by poststructuralist and decidedly anti-canonical notions of literature, language, and culture. American poetry is self-destructing, he insists, under the influence of "the French diseases, the mock-feminists, the commissars, the gender-and-power freaks, the hosts of new historicists and old materialists."

In his essay, which appears as his introduction to *The Best of the Best American Poetry: 1988–1997* (a later volume of the same series in which Jorie Graham's essay appeared), Bloom is indignant at the dumbing-down of the university curriculum as indicated by the widespread sanctioning of cultural studies departments: that is to say, all those Black, Hispanic, Feminist, and Queer *arrivistes* who have managed to elbow their way into seats at the academic banquet. More particularly, he is in a dither over the likes of Lady Mary Chudleigh and Anne Killigrew having insinuated themselves into those hernia-inducing tomes that undergraduates are forced to lug from building to building on Tuesdays and Thursdays. This reprehensible attack on

275

the Western canon, he assures us, is a byproduct of "cultural guilt" and successful hectoring by "The School of Resentment."

Apparently, in tilting toward affirmative action set-asides—toward homosexuals, women, undeserving poets of color, the politically correct and hyphenated-Americans—these offending anthologies have been insidiously undermining the foundations of our civilization. Not surprisingly, in the many rejoinders that have been made to his broadside—most notably in the Spring 1998 *Boston Review*, which was devoted to such responses—he is roundly attacked by a number of poets for his cultural conservatism and, by a few postmodernists, for his aesthetic conservatism. Carol Muske, in the brightest and most eloquent of those published responses, defends the revisionist Heath and the revised Norton by recalling, during her college days, paging through anthologies of poetry, in vain, looking for the names of women. Surely there was some other female writer besides Dickinson or Sappho? Maybe the Countess of Pembroke? How thrilling it was, back then, to find a female name, even if it was attached to a relatively uninspiring poem. It was thrilling just to see that women wrote, were published. So room had to be made for these other voices—beyond the best. And beyond The Best of.

Several of the other *Boston Review* respondents take Bloom to task for one or another of his blind spots. But it seems to me both significant and lamentable that not a single essayist responding to Bloom took issue with what I take to be his most pernicious assertion: "Authentic American poetry," he declares in that bilious introduction, "is necessarily difficult. . . our situation needs aesthetic and cognitive difficulty. . . it is our elitist art, though that elite has nothing to do with social class, gender, erotic preference, ethnic strain, race, or sect. 'We live in the mind,' Stevens said."

This insistence on poetic opacity is questioned only by those postmodernists among the *Boston Review* respondents who insist that poetry ought to be more incomprehensible yet. Apparently what Bloom finds objectionable among the deconstructionist critics, those pernicious purveyors of "the French diseases," is their subversively anti-hierarchic beliefs about literature and culture, and has nothing to do with the macaronic density of their language. This is hardly surprising: the love of jargon-saturated, dizzyingly complex rhetorical footwork which those infected with the "French diseases" find so attractive is not, after all, so different from the kind of academic flapdoodle upon which his own critical reputation rests.

As for his insistence on the very necessity for difficulty, Bloom is in the absurd position of having to claim that even Walt Whitman was, "above all else, a very difficult poet," while asserting with a straight face that Wallace Stevens, T.S. Eliot, and John Ashbery are Whitman's true heirs. In order to spin Whitman in the image of poets so utterly inimical to his spirit, he simply stands Whitman on his head. On an earlier occasion he had declared that Whitman's statement of ecstatic longing, "To touch my person to some one else's is about as much as I can stand," was the poet's confession that he found human touch repulsive. An unreconstructed Freudian, Bloom is capable of making any statement mean what he wishes it to mean. Freud's main technique for this kind of convenient fast shuffle was "reaction formation," a putative psychic mechanism that transformed things into their opposites. When a patient said or dreamed something that confounded the analyst's interpretation, it was simply a reaction formation: that is, the patient's meaning was the very opposite of what it seemed to be.

Thus, according to Bloom, "Whitman's poetry generally does the opposite of what he proclaims its work to be: it is reclusive, evasive, hermetic, nuanced, and more onanistic even than homoerotic." This, of course, is embarrassing nonsense. As for living in one's head, à la Wallace Stevens, that is precisely what Whitman is at pains to warn us against. When he tells us that he is "Both in and out of the game, and watching and wondering at it"—a line Bloom quotes in his essay—it is not, as that critic assumes, to register the kind of self-conscious alienation from life that his favorite modernists display. Rather, the poet is declaring that he does not live in thrall to the common delusions of the ego, but has awakened into the unmediated world: that he is not an intellect filled with attitudes and opinions, but an empty, observing awareness.

As for "difficulty," Whitman proclaims: "I will not have in my writing any elegance or effect or originality to hang in the way between me and the rest like curtains. I will have nothing hang in the way, not the richest curtains." Against the corollary modernist principle that poems are made of words, not ideas, he memorably declares: "The words of my poem nothing, the drift of it everything."

But the case of Whitman also offers to us the cautionary example of the dangers of canonical literary judgments: Our "best" poets and critics, blind to his genius, dismissed him as a vulgar eccentric, until the zeitgeist shifted in mid-century and everyone suddenly noticed his bearded figure towering above our literature.

However, the most curious and provocative portion of Bloom's essay was not his attack on multiculturalism or his absurd revision of Whitman, but his attack on Adrienne Rich, whose *Best American Poetry of 1996* was the only one of David Lehman's annual series from which Bloom did not draw work for his *Best of the Best*. Rich's anthology is emblematic for Bloom of the wretched state of literary affairs, exemplifying everything that's wrong with the new affirmative action poetics. "It is of a badness not to be believed, because it follows the criteria now operative: what matters most are the race, gender, sexual orientation, ethnic origin, and political purpose of the would-be poet. I ardently wish I were being hyperbolical, but in fact I am exercising restraint . . . . Bursting with sincerity, the 1996 volume is a Stuffed Owl of bad verse, and of much badness that is neither verse nor prose."

With this judgment at least three of the *Boston Review* respondents unequivocally concur: one, J. D. McClatchy, is an enthusiastic advocate of difficult poetry. The other two, Marjorie Perloff and Reginald Shepherd, disdain meaning altogether. Perloff finds many of Rich's choices "relentlessly PC . . . maudlin, self-righteous, boring, and ultimately just plain incompetent." A tireless champion of the poetry of impenetrability, it is hardly surprising that she would find Rich's penchant for the accessible, emotional, and socially engaged antithetical to her tastes. For Perloff, any poetry that doesn't exhibit an uncompromising indeterminacy smacks of the platitudinous and sentimental: soap opera masquerading as art.

Not surprisingly, Perloff faults Bloom, too, for his reactionary poetic tastes, his inability to appreciate the "genuinely radical poetry now being written," by which she means the unabashedly incomprehensible writers whom she has been championing for the past many years. McClatchy's criticism, less idiosyncratic than Perloff's, is more telling for the fact that it shares Bloom's particular elitist predilections. The first poem in Rich's volume, written by a prisoner at the Pelican Bay State Prison serving a twenty-two year sentence for burglary, is, he declares, a piece of "utter banality" and symptomatic of her volume as a whole. With its "clutter of clichés, sentimentality, confused syntax, and flailing gestures," it is a poem that McClatchy finds downright campy. An attempt to express the dehumanizing horror of a prison notorious for its systemic brutality, "In the Tombs," by Latif Asad Abdullah, is indeed an unsuccessful poem, but not because of sentimentality or platitudes. Rather, its flaw is a more common one: the inability to make its case with the incisive power that its subject demands. On the other hand, McClatchy's use of the word "campy" to characterize a poem about such enormous personal anguish strikes me as rather chilling, and perfectly typical of the crippling emotional disability that he shares with many of his fellow academic poets and literary critics.

For such writers any unarmored feeling is to be avoided at all cost, a need that is likely to make the distancing strategies of obliqueness and opacity seem appealing. Given that pathology, one understands why to such writers "sincerity"—a word that both McClatchy and Bloom use as a smirking pejorative—would seem threatening.

Actually, Abdullah's poem about Pelican State—one of her collection's few unpolished pieces—is not at all symptomatic of the Adrienne Rich anthology, while the weaknesses of Bloom's book can, I believe, be fairly characterized by McClatchy's own lengthy contribution to that collection. Like one of those wits who imagines himself endlessly amusing, McClatchy's poem, "An Essay on Friendship," rambles on for some two hundred and seventy lines in that excruciatingly sophisticated, three-martini tone peculiar to the academic gentility. More ruinously, the poem's narrative thread is willfully obscure. McClatchy, who is by no means an untalented writer, and whose poems, though sometimes uninteresting are almost always skillfully composed, tells us in his little explanatory note at the end of the volume that certain sections of "An Essay on Friendship" will only be understood by readers familiar with Renoir's film, *Rules of the Game*. Clearly, then, the poet has only the most minimal interest in communicating much of anything with his reader: whether or not he is understood is of little concern to him.

Not far from McClatchy's endnote in the Bloom anthology is another telling one, in which Richard Wilbur wryly reports that

279

after his wife had read his poem "Lying," she remarked, "Well, you've finally done it; you've managed to write a poem that's incomprehensible from beginning to end." But immediately Wilbur assures us that on second reading she found it "quite forthright" (no doubt with a little cuing), and then tells us that he makes no apology for the fact that the poem requires several readings. "Provided it's any good, a poem which took months to write deserves an ungrudging quarter hour from the reader."

But Wilbur's scolding the reader for not spending enough time puzzling out his poem misses the point. One is reminded of Norman Mailer's apology, some decades back, for having used as an epigraph to one of his early collections of essays the admonition: "Do not understand me too quickly." Older and wiser, Mailer had come to understand that if even experienced readers were misapprehending him, the fault was his own: clarity is the writer's responsibility, not the reader's. Surely when Richard Wilbur's poems are a joy to read, as they so often are, it is because that exquisitely deft versification is the brilliant vehicle for ideas and arguments rendered with lapidary clarity. Here, for example, are the final stanzas of that wonderful "Aubade," in which he argues to his beloved that staying in bed is the most reasonable of her options:

> Think of all the time you are not
> Wasting, and would not care to waste,
> Such things, thank God, not being to your taste.
> Think what a lot
> Of time, by woman's reckoning,
> You've saved, and so may spend on this,
> You who had rather lie in bed and kiss
> Than anything.
> It's almost noon you say? If so,
> Time flies, and I need not rehearse
> The rosebud-theme of centuries of verse.
> If you must go,
> Wait for a while, then slip downstairs
> And bring us up some chilled white wine,
> And some blue cheese, and crackers, and some fine
> Ruddy-skinned pears.

Though he believes adamantly that "strong poetry is always difficult," it is noteworthy that Harold Bloom includes in *The Best of the Best* a good number of poems that are perfectly clear, and these are the poems that are most likely to raise the hair on the back of one's neck: poems by May Swenson, Kay Ryan, Amy Clampitt, Allen Ginsberg, Ed Hirsch, Philip Levine, and Molly Peacock, among others. Donald Justice is represented with a memorable elegy for Henri Coulette in which the poet asks his friend to "Come back and help me with these verses/ Whisper to me some beautiful secret that you remember from life." Although Donald Hall has a strained exercise in vatic rage, an ersatz-Ginsbergian rant that strikes a note decidedly false, it is followed by one of his exemplary poems, this one about Jane Kenyon's dying, a poem that is the very model of simplicity, clarity and unadorned honesty. The two poems together make a fine study in the dangers of the postured and the virtues of the sincere, the authentically felt. Also of note are two stunningly powerful and perfectly accessible pieces by Louise Glück. In "Vespers," the narrator argues with God for having let her tomatoes die:

> ... I doubt
> you have a heart, in our understanding of
> that term. You who do not discriminate
> between the dead and the living, who are, in
> consequence,
> immune to foreshadowing, you may not know
> how much terror we bear, the spotted leaf,
> the red leaves of the maple falling
> even in August, in early darkness: I am
> responsible
> for these vines.

All told, Rich's anthology is just about as good as Bloom's, its major virtue being that she has a lively eye for the coherent and the unashamedly human, the openly emotional and exuberant kind of engaged poetry that many American poets have been writing since the 1960s. Were there anthologies filled exclusively with the work of such writers, American poetry would have a fighting chance of regaining its rightful audience. Rich assuredly does not agree with Bloom that the aesthetic is an autonomous realm independent of political and cultural ideologies, or that poetry is ruined by social engagement, or that a less rarefied, intellectualized poetic is the death blow to our literary culture. Not surprisingly, there is a good deal less here of the mannered rhetoric that pervades Bloom's choices and a good deal more of a poetry awake to the world outside of the poet's head.

Since a good two-thirds of Rich's offerings are by well-known, well-respected poets, and since her volume contains, as he grudgingly acknowledges, the work of several of the same writers that appear in his own, Bloom's claim against it is seriously undermined. Surely it was not discerning taste but sheer petulance that kept him from being able to acknowledge how many fine poems she has brought together in her collection. He might not have been able to appreciate the emotional power of Raymond Patterson's "Harlem Suite" or Luis Alberto Urrea's long, rhapsodic, open-hearted elegy for his father, not because he harbors any racism—he most likely does not—but because that sort of gritty, heart-centered, anti-intellectualized poetry, which owes nothing to the tradition of Wallace Stevens, is the sort for which he has little patience.

Though Bloom's abhorrence of explicit social compassion might have made him immune to the powerful, history-drenched poems of Alicia Ostriker and Wang Ping, and to the fine, socially engaged ones of Ann Winters, Chase Twitchell, Gary Soto, and Alma Villanueva—for compassion, like sincerity and accessibility, is not a modernist virtue—there are several pieces in her anthology that would undoubtedly have interested him had he not been in such high dudgeon. He would likely have been drawn to W. S. Merwin's "Lament for the Makers," with its nicely jagged, Dunbar-esque rhythms and off-rhymed couplets, especially given its generous sprinkling of literary gossip, and it is hard to believe he wouldn't have given serious consideration to "Touch Me," a Stanley Kunitz love poem that is surely going to find its way into numerous anthologies of twentieth-century verse. Both poems share the traditional metrical skills that Bloom, for all his admiration for Ashbery, most admires.

Rich's anthology also contains finely made pieces by Reynolds Price, Jane Kenyon, Naomi Shihab Nye, Yusef Komunyakaa, and half a dozen others that would certainly have merited his attention. She is to be congratulated for looking beyond the rhetorical commonplaces of conventional poetry and including pieces that are far removed from the academic mainstream. Not the least of the poems she chose for her anthology is a sestina by Katherine Alice Power, an antiwar radical who is presently serving an eight- to twelve-year sentence for participating in a bank robbery back in 1970 which ended in the murder of a policeman. Her surrender in 1993 provoked enormous national publicity and debate. Power's impressive and touching sestina for her son is a useful example of how to employ a form that even in the hands of competent poets tends to sound forced, formulaic, and insincere.

On the other hand, the clunkers in the Rich anthology share with Bloom's clunkers the same overriding flaw: they're incomprehensible. And by this I do not mean to suggest that clarity determines the quality of poetry: most emphatically it does not. Surely much of the most hilariously inept and amateurish verse being written is perfectly intelligible. What I am asserting is that although clarity is by no means a sufficient condition for successful poetry, it is, in all but the rarest of cases, a necessary one. And yet for certain poets and critics of our time, as I have been at pains to point out, obscurity is an overriding virtue.

What kind of poetry is it, then, that they want? What might it look and sound like? In the texts I have been examining, the most explicit answer to that question comes from Reginald Shepherd, the third *Boston Review* correspondent who, implicitly at least, can find little merit in a poetry that is coherently engaged in the world beyond language. Shepherd, like Marjorie Perloff, rejects any poetry that makes so much as a grain of sense, for such poetry, according to him, refuses to "honor language," something that is done, apparently, by treating it as an end in itself. Shepherd wants a poetry of "strangeness and opacity," one that exhibits a "resistance to communication . . . which restores language to itself," criteria with which Perloff would surely agree.

Understandably, Shepherd is reticent to attack Adrienne Rich's anthology because it contains one of his own poems, so his example of what poetry should not be is drawn instead from Bloom's *Best of the Best*. He faults Bloom for canonizing Amy Clampitt, whom he characterizes as an erudite and amiable writer, but one "for whom language has no independent existence: she has something of greater or lesser interest to 'say' and she says it more or less well. But poetry is not versified thought . . . nor is it amiable or well mannered." In reiterating the aesthetic stance of the Language Poets, it seems curiously off-point for Shepherd to single out Amy Clampitt rather than a less exuberant poet. Surely one hopes there was a reason for his choice beyond the cute pun on her name, just the sort of sophomoric "word-play" that postmodernists are often unembarrassedly given to. But Shepherd could not have chosen a more inappropriate example, for there are few contemporaries who seemed as utterly in love with the succulence of words, the intoxicating pleasures of language. If anyone of our era ought by rights to have been characterized as a poet who was language-centered, it is surely Amy Clampitt, a poet who manages to be wildly intoxicating with her language while remaining perfectly intelligible. This is how "My Cousin Muriel," a poem about her dying cousin that Bloom wisely chose for *The Best of the Best*, begins:

> From Manhattan, a glittering shambles
> of enthrallments and futilities, of leapers
> in leotards, scissoring vortices blurred,
> this spring evening, by the punto in aria
> of hybrid pear trees in bloom (no troublesome
> fruit to follow) my own eyes are drawn to—
> childless spinner of metaphor, in touch
> by way of switchboard and satellite, for
> the last time ever, with my cousin Muriel . . .

But this sort of delicious and truly language-centered writing makes far too much sense for Reginald Shepherd, who tells us in his essay that poetry ought to be an escape from meaning. Shepherd concludes his brief essay with four lines from a contemporary poem that he admires "because something is happening in them that happens nowhere else." This is his exemplary excerpt:

Vagrant, back, my scrutinies
The candid deformations as with use
A coat or trousers of one dead
Or as habit smacks of certitude.

In the presence of such writing it is difficult to know what to say. Surely in the prison house of language, poets writing in this manner have opted for solitary confinement. If one is going to "escape from meaning" and foreground other qualities, one would imagine that either music, striking linguistic and figurative invention, or deft and original phrasing would be evident. If one is going to be excruciatingly difficult or downright incomprehensible, we need in compensation other virtues. One needs, at the very least, the intensity and profound musical and linguistic skill of authentic poetic composition. One thinks of the evocative, heartbreaking music of Hart Crane, or the coryambic and often rigorously measured verse of Dylan Thomas, or the syntactically wrenched and passionate strangeness of Vallejo, or the hypnogogic dream-swirling Dionysian difficulties of Hopkins or Berryman or Rimbaud or Cesaire, or of Robert Lowell's early work with its headlong velocity and gorgeously gnarled intensities, or of the strange, disquieting magic we encounter in someone like Antonin Artaud, for whom surrealism was not so much a novel technique as a desperate means of plumbing his tormented depths.

"Resistance to communication" the passage Reginald Shepherd has quoted certainly exhibits. But flattened of affect and bereft of music, this kind of silliness doesn't even have the virtue, any longer, of novelty. That such lines restore language to itself seems questionable—to put it mildly. Given that the defining property of language is communicability, shouldn't this sort of thing be called "Anti-Language Poetry"?

Although poetry often attempts to transcend the limits of language, in an attempt to invent such an idiom legions of twentieth-century poets have mistaken mystification for mystery. The real mystery of poetry is that it inexplicably opens the reader to that which is all but inexpressible. It is as though one had used a ladder to climb onto a roof with a spectacular view and then discovered that the ladder upon which one had climbed does not, in fact, exist—to use Ludwig Wittgenstein's provocative metaphor. But mystification, whether of the modernist or post-structuralist variety, is simply the pretense of having climbed anywhere.

Poetry, when it is at its most ineffable, transports us to places we had no reason to believe language could take us. What is needed for this task is the most luminous vision, the most receptive spirit and the most crystalline possible clarity of presentation. Our period's infatuation with the opaque has been, in the end, a seriously misdirected effort. The most eloquent response to that wrong turning was made by Robinson Jeffers more than seventy years ago, when the modernist agenda had hardly begun and long before its eccentric notions had come to dominate aesthetic discourse. Prescient as ever, Jeffers wrote in the introduction to his 1938 Random House *Selected Poetry*:

> Long ago, before anything included here was written, it became evident to me that poetry—if it was to survive at all—must reclaim some of the power and reality that it was so hastily surrendering to prose. The modern French poetry of that time, and the most "modern" of the English poetry, seemed to me thoroughly defeatist, as if poetry were in terror of prose, and desperately trying to save its soul from the victor by giving up its body. It was becoming slight and fantastic, abstract, unreal, eccentric; and was not even saving its soul, for these are generally anti-poetic qualities. It must reclaim substance and sense, and physical and psychological reality .... Another formative principle came to me from a phrase of Nietzsche's: "The poets? The poets lie too much." I was nineteen when the phrase stuck in my mind; a dozen years passed before it worked effectively, and I decided not to tell lies in verse. Not to feign any emotion that I did not feel; not to pretend to believe in optimism or pessimism, or unreversible progress, not to say anything because it was popular, or generally accepted, or fashionable in intellectual circles, unless I myself believed it; and not to believe easily. These negatives limit the field; I am not recommending them but for my own occasions.

Let us, by all means, have a poetry of the most incandescent verbal pyrotechnics, of the most restlessly experimental and original design. Let us have poems that astonish the reader at every turn. Let our poets attend to making it new with nearly as much fervor as they attend to making it true. But on those occasions when we fail to communicate, let us no longer imagine we have succeeded at something larger and grander.

Let us not blame our failures on the intellectual poverty of our readers, or on their inability to register complex ambiguities, or on their irritable reaching after fact, or on the ineptitude of their teachers, or on the seductions of the media, or on crass materialism, or on the philistine vulgarity of our culture, or on—well, whatever else seems convenient to blame for our own failures. Let us no longer be gulled into imagining that rhetorical sophistication and verbal panache in the absence of genuine, communicated perception can create a poetry that is genuinely complex, textured, multilayered, exploratory, intuitive and profoundly insightful, a poetry worth careful study. They create, rather, poems that are hardly worth reading through once. Harold Bloom notwithstanding, our situation demands aesthetic and cognitive clarity.

"They have the numbers, we the heights" is the heroic epigraph Bloom uses for his dyspeptic rant against those who would open the doors of what he calls our "elitist art" and let in some air. They are words attributed by Thucydides to the Spartan commander at Thermopylae. No doubt Bloom, our self-appointed Keeper of the Canon, imagines himself the heroic captain of the last small band of stalwart Western aesthetes, holding the gates of the Temple of Art against the raucous assaults of the parti-colored resenters, the Great Unwashed. But the very mean-spiritedness of his attack belies the pretense that he represents some nobler and higher ground. The only heights that the defenders of the aesthetic of difficulty have to offer us are the heights of arrogance, exclusivity, and self-aggrandizement, and the only effect of composing one's poetry from such heights is to insure that it remain chilly, windy, and unlikely to be heard.

Acknowledgments

The author wishes to thank Deborah Harding, Lloyd Hill, Dorianne Laux, Victor Margolis, and Fred Moramarco for reading sections of this manuscript and making valuable suggestions, many of which found their way into the text. Mark Melnicove's close reading of the entire manuscript and his suggestions concerning both organization and content were of enormous use, and Mary Kowit's keen editorial eye, which helped make this book considerably more straightforward and graceful, was as important as her constant support. My thanks to them for their generous assistance.

Translations and adaptations that are unacknowledged in the text are by Steve Kowit.

"Future Work," from *Selected Poems*, by Fleur Adcock, Oxford University Press, 1983. ©1983 by Fleur Adcock, reprinted by permission of Oxford University Press. ■ "Therapy," by Kim Addonizio, ©1995 by Kim Addonizio. Excerpt from "Night Feeding" by Kim Addonizio, ©1987 by Kim Addonizio and reprinted by permission of the author. ■ "Lot's Wife," by Anna Akhmatova, translated by Richard Wilbur from *Walking to Sleep: New Poems and Translations*, ©1969 by Richard Wilbur, reprinted by permission of Harcourt Brace & Company. ■ Passage by Matsuo Basho ("You can learn about the pine..."), translated by Nobuyuki Yuasa. From Nobuyuki Yuasa's introduction to *The Year of My Life: A Translation of Issa's 'Oraga Haru.'* ©1972 The Regents of the University of California and reprinted by permission of University of California Press. ■ "People Who Died," from *So Going Around Cities*, by Ted Berrigan, published by Blue Wind Press. ©1980 and 1986 by Ted Berrigan. Reprinted by permission of the Estate of Ted Berrigan. ■ "Phone Call to Rutherford," from *The Selected Poems of Paul Blackburn*, edited by Edith Jarolim. ©1989 by Joan Blackburn. Reprinted by permission of Persea Books. ■ "White Cessna and seagull..." by Will Boland. ©1995 and printed by permission of the author. ■ "Emily Dickinson Attends A Writing Workshop," by Jayne Relaford Brown, ©1995 by Jayne Relaford Brown and reprinted by permission of the author. ■ "Meeting of Mavericks," "A Very Wet Leavetaking" and "A Sunday Morning After A Saturday Night" from *The View from the End of the Pier*, by LoVerne Brown. ©1983 by LoVerne Brown and reprinted by permission of the author. ■ "The Burning of the Books," from *Selected Poems*, by Bertolt Brecht, translated by H.R. Hays, ©1947 by Bertolt Brecht and H.R. Hays and renewed 1975 by Stefan S. Brecht and H.R. Hays. Reprinted by permission of Harcourt Brace & Company. ■ Excerpt from "The Man with the Beautiful Eyes," ©1992 by Charles Bukowski. Reprinted from *The Last Night of the Earth Poems*, with the permission of Black Sparrow Press. ■ Excerpt from "Good Field, No Hit," from *Get Some Fuses for the House*, by Bobby Byrd, published by North Atlantic Books, ©1987 by Bobby Byrd and reprinted by permission of the author. ■ "The Parrots," by Ernesto Cardenal, translated by Jonathan Cohen, ©1986 by Jonathan Cohen and reprinted by permission of Jonathan Cohen. ■ "After-Glow," from *A New Path to the Waterfall*, by Raymond Carver, ©1989 by the Estate of Raymond Carver and reprinted by permission of Grove/Atlantic, Inc. ■ Excerpt from "Notes on a Return to the Native Land," by Aimé Césaire, translated by Ellen Conroy Kennedy, from *The Negritude Poets*, ©1975 by Ellen Conroy Kennedy and reprinted by permission of Thunder's Mouth Press. ■ Line from Lu Chi's *Wen Fu* translated by Sam Hamill from *The Art of Writing*, Milkweed Editions, 1991. ©1991 by Sam Hamill. Reprinted by permission of Milkweed Editions and the author. ■ "My Wicked Wicked Ways," from *My Wicked Wicked Ways*, by Sandra Cisneros. Published by Third Woman Press, Berkeley, California. ©1987 by Sandra Cisneros and reprinted by permission of Third Woman Press. ■ Excerpt from "The Inner Source," from *Comrade Past & Mister Present*, by Andrei Codrescu, Coffee House Press. ©1986, and reprinted by permission of the author. ■ "In the Workshop After I Read My Poem Aloud," by Don Colburn, ©1989 by Don Colburn. Originally appeared in *The Iowa Review* and is reprinted by permission of the author. ■ "Untitled," from *African Sleeping Sickness*, by Wanda Coleman. ©1990 by Wanda Coleman and reprinted by permission of Black Sparrow Press. ■ "Memento Mori," from *Questions About Angels*, by Billy Collins. ©1991 by Billy Collins and reprinted by permission of William Morrow & Company, Inc. "Flames" from *The Apple that Astonished Paris*, by Billy Collins, University of Arkansas Press, ©1988 by Billy Collins and reprinted by permission of the author. ■ "OAS" and "Ars Poetica 1974," from Roque Dalton's *Poems*, translated by Richard Schaaf, Curbstone Press, 1984. Translation ©1984 by Richard Schaaf. Reprinted with permission of Curbstone Press. Distributed by InBook. ■ "A Bright Day," from *The Complete Poems of W.H. Davies*, ©1963 by Jonathan Cape Ltd., Wesleyan University Press, by permission of the University Press of New England. ■ "There is a pain so utter..." and "My life has stood—a loaded gun..." from *The Complete Poems of Emily Dickinson*, edited by Thomas H. Johnson, ©1929, 1935 by Martha Dickinson Bianchi; © renewed 1957, 1963, by Mary L. Hampson. By permission of Little, Brown and Company. Additional lines of these poems reprinted by permission of the publishers and the Trustees of Amherst College from *The Poems of Emily Dickinson*, Thomas H. Johnson, ed., Cambridge, Mass.: The Belknap Press of Harvard University Press, ©1951, 1955, 1979, 1983 by the President and Fellows of Harvard College. ■ "The Gift I Never Got," by Vincent B. Draper, ©1995 by Vincent B. Draper and reprinted by permission of the author. ■ One sentence from *Myths, Dreams and Mysteries*, by Mircea Eliade. ©1957 by Librairie Gallimard. English translation ©1960 by Harville Press. Copyright renewed. Reprinted by permission of HarperCollins Publishers, Inc. ■ "The farewell," ©1992 by Edward Field. Reprinted from *Counting Myself Lucky: Selected Poems 1963–1992*, with the permission of Black Sparrow Press. ■ "Reunion," from *The Country Between Us*, by Carolyn Forché, ©1978 by Carolyn Forché. Reprinted by permission of HarperCollins Publishers, Inc. ■ Quotation from Sigmund Freud, translated by Dr. A. A. Brill, is reprinted from *The Interpretation of Dreams*, by permission of Gioia Bernheim and Edmund Brill, owners of 1938 copyright. Copyright © renewed 1965. ■ "At their raucous meeting...," by Malika Fusco, ©1995 by Malika Fusco, and printed by permission of the author. ■ "Pulling tissues...," by Nina Garin, ©1994 by Nina Garin and printed by permission of the author. ■ "New Hampshire Marble" and "Divorce" from *Monolithos*, by Jack Gilbert, ©1982 by Jack Gilbert, and "Michiko Dead," from *The Great Fires: Poems: 1982–1992*, by Jack Gilbert, ©1994 by Jack Gilbert and reprinted by permission of Alfred A. Knopf, Inc. ■ Excerpts from "Howl" and "Kaddish" and excerpt from "Returning To The Country For A Brief Visit," ("I do not know

Selected Poems, by Ted Kooser, by permission of the University of Pittsburgh Press. ©1980 by Ted Kooser. ■ "Dusk in the Cuyamacas," from *Lurid Confessions*, by Steve Kowit, ©1985 by Steve Kowit. "The Grammar Lesson" and the adaptation of Izumi Shikibu's "At the Temple Ceremony for Her Departed Daughter" by Steve Kowit, ©1995. ■ "The Portrait" is reprinted from *The Poems of Stanley Kunitz, 1928–1978*, by permission of the author and W.W. Norton & Company, Inc. ©1971, 1979 by Stanley Kunitz. ■ "The Tooth Fairy," "Girl in the Doorway," and "The Catch," ©1990 by Dorianne Laux. Reprinted from *Awake*, by Dorianne Laux. "This Close," ©1994 by Dorianne Laux. Reprinted from *What We Carry*, by Dorianne Laux. Reprinted with the permission of BOA Editions, Ltd., 92 Park Ave., Brookport, NY 14420. Foreword ©1995 by Dorianne Laux. ■ Lines from "Saturday Sweeping" from *New Selected Poems*, by Philip Levine. ©1991 by Philip Levine. Excerpt from "What Work Is" from *What Work Is*, by Philip Levine. ©1991 by Philip Levine. Reprinted by permission of Alfred A. Knopf, Inc. ■ "The Freedom Fighters," from *A Constituency of Dunces*, by Gerald Locklin. Slipstream Press. ©1988 by Gerald Locklin and reprinted by permission of the author. ■ "The Divorcing Men," from *Falling Short of Heaven*, by Suzanne Lummis published by Pennywhistle Press. ©1990 by Suzanne Lummis. Reprinted with permission of the author. ■ "I Think You're Wonderful," from *Memory's Handgrenade*, by Thomas Lux. Published by Pym-Randall Press. ©1972 by Thomas Lux and reprinted by permission of the author. ■ "Z3" is an excerpt from "5 Poems from and for Louis Zukofsky," by Jackson Mac Low. ©1994 by Jackson Mac Low and published by permission of the author. ■ "Memory from Childhood," by Antonio Machado, translated by Robert Bly. ©1973 by Robert Bly and reprinted by permission of Robert Bly. ■ "A Gift" and excerpt from "This is the Bodiless Night" originally appeared in *Sesame*, by Jack Marshall, Coffee House Press, 1993. Reprinted by permission of the publisher. ©1993 by Jack Marshall. Excerpt from "Chaos Comics" from *Chaos Comics*, published by Pennywhistle Press. ©1994 by Jack Marshall and reprinted by permission of the publisher. "Forced Entry" from *Bearings*, Harper & Row, Publishers. ©1969 by Jack Marshall and reprinted by permission of the author. ■ Excerpt from "Dirge" from *Nonesuch Creek*, by Al Masarik. ©1980 by Al Masarik and reprinted by permission of the author. ■ "Lie With Me Courage...," by H.S. Matthews. ©1995 by H.S. Matthews and printed with permission of the author. ■ "Living, standards, dependent on high levels...," "Fortunately, your impulse...," and "Each soul is a glowing spark...," by Mark Melnicove. ©1995 by Mark Melnicove and printed by permission of the author. ■ 'November 23" is a section from "Album of Dreams," ©1988 Czeslaw Milosz Royalties, Inc., from *The Collected Poems*, by Czeslaw Milosz, printed by The Ecco Press. Reprinted by permission. ■ "Dancing before him...," by Mirabai, translated by Andrew Schelling from *For Love of the Dark One: Songs of Mirabai*, published by Shambhala Press. ©1993 by Andrew Schelling. Reprinted by permission of Shambhala Press. ■ Passage from *Tropic of Capricorn*, by Henry Miller, published by Grove/Atlantic, Inc. ©1961 by Grove Press, Inc. and reprinted by permission of the publisher. ■ "A Traumatic Scene from Childhood," by Fred Moramarco. ©1994 by Fred Moramarco and reprinted by permission of the author. ■ "Ladies on the Beach," by Clare Nagel. ©1995 by Clare Nagel and printed by permission of the author. ■ "Very Like a Whale," by Ogden Nash from *Verses from 1929 On*, by Ogden Nash. ©1934 by The Curtis Publishing Company. Reprinted by permission of Little, Brown and Company. ■ "You Must Have Been a Sensational Baby" and excerpt from "In November," by Harold Norse. ©1974 by Harold Norse and reprinted by permission of the

and reprinted by permission of the author. ■ "Mementos, I," by W.D. Snodgrass. ©1987 by W.D. Snodgrass and reprinted by permission of the author. Stanza XV of Part V of "Stanzas in Meditation," by Gertrude Stein. © renewed 1956 by the Estate of Gertrude Stein and reprinted by permission of the Estate of Gertrude Stein. ■ "Behaving Like a Jew," by Gerald Stern, ©1990 by Gerald Stern and reprinted by permission of the author. ■ "L.A. Morning," by Austin Straus, ©1984 by Austin Straus and reprinted by permission of the author. ■ "The Uninvited," by Virginia R. Terris, ©1987 by Virginia R. Terris and reprinted by permission of the author. ■ "The Other Night," from *Weather Reports: New and Selected Poems*, by Quincy Troupe, Harlem River Press. ©1991 by Quincy Troupe and reprinted by permission of the author. ■ "Good Indications of Icy Loins" and "Six Rivers," by Cherry Vasconcellos. ©1995 by Cherry Vasconcellos and printed by permission of the author. ■ "After Sappho," by Anne Waldman is reprinted from *Makeup on Empty Space*, by Anne Waldman, published by The Toothpaste Press. ©1984 by Anne Waldman and reprinted by permission of the author. ■ "Retreat" by Charles Harper Webb, from *Everyday Outrages*, by Charles Harper Webb. ©1989 by Charles Harper Webb and reprinted by permission of the author. ■ "Perfection" from *The Collected Poems of William Carlos Williams, 1939–1962, Volume II*. ©1944 by William Carlos Williams and reprinted by permission of New Directions Publishing Corp. ■ "Considering the Accordion," "The Hat in the Sky," "Love in the Classroom," and "Cat Puke and Flies Poem" from *Under Ideal Conditions*, published by Laterthanever Press, 3751 First Avenue, San Diego, CA 92103. ©1994 by Al Zolynas. "The Zen of Housework" from *The New Physics*, Wesleyan University Press. ©1979 by Al Zolynas. Reprinted by permission of the author. ■

293

Index

Poets and Poems

Terms

Remembering Steve Kowit (1938–2015)

by Mark Melnicove

In September 1978, I was hired to teach photography at the College of the Atlantic in Bar Harbor. I was 26, and also a poet. As a way of getting my students to think about the pictures they were making, I had them read, discuss, and write poems about photography. I compiled a small classroom anthology of the poems I shared with them and thought about publishing it, since I could find no book like it.

In early 1979, I sent out a call for more poems to *CODA*, the then-magazine of Poets and Writers in New York. In response to that four-liner in the free classifieds, I received hundreds of poems from all over the country. Steve Kowit, a San Diego poet I had never heard of, sent me a hand-sized, stapled booklet of poems he had written and published in a small edition about his parents on the occasion of their fiftieth wedding anniversary the previous year. I chose one of those poems, "Golden Anniversary," for my anthology. The poem was autobiographical; in it Steve reminisced about his parents by recalling a night he and his wife, Mary, had looked through his family's photo album, "back home in Brooklyn," at pages that crumbled "like confetti" and fell "like tears" beyond "the joy & tenderness & passion of these early snapshots."

I came to call the anthology *Poets on Photography,* and published it in 1981 under my own, newly invented imprint, The Dog Ear Press. Steve loved the book, not only for the poems, but also the collages I made to illustrate them; this was a tremendous boon to me at the time. I had taken a gamble by printing 1,000 books and sold them all.

Steve and I became letter writing buddies. Like his poems, Steve's letters were full of wit and passion for what he was doing. I got to know him through these letters, where we exchanged news, poems, ideas, and dreams. Both he and I had been active in the anti–Vietnam War movement, and we remained politically engaged on opposite sides of the continent, spurring each other on. This was when he founded the first animal-rights organization in the San Diego area, a cause he worked for tirelessly, as he did throughout his life for everything he believed in.

As I was putting the finishing touches on *Poets on Photography*, he sent me a book-length manuscript of his, a series of 100 poems inspired by Sanskrit, Bengali, Maithili, and Tamil love poems. With the exception of some small pamphlets Steve had published himself, he had yet to publish a book of his poems. As Steve made clear, these were not translations—he did not know any of those languages—nor were they even adaptations, but what he called "new poems on ancient themes." The short poems were sexy and graphic, but also nearly chaste in their wisdom. It was a powerful combination. We immediately corresponded about doing a book: the result, was Dog Ear's 1982 *Heart in Utter Confusion,* a small gem of a book. I printed the poems in brown ink on sensuous, cream-colored paper, using linocuts by Richard Denner. Steve dedicated the book to Mary.

> All night we lay in each other's arms.
> The words spilled forth
> as if language itself
> had come into being
> there,
> with our love.
> We talked about everything...
> nothing...
> not even dawn stopped us.

Heart in Utter Confusion quickly went out of print, due in part to Steve's efforts at selling it at his readings on the West Coast. It was the first of a number of books of his poems that other small presses published in the 1980s, such as *Cutting Our Losses* (1982), *Lurid Confessions* (1983), and *Passionate Journey* (1984). Steve would send me his books as they came out along with some of the broadsides and pamphlets he continued to publish himself.

We kept up our correspondence and book sharing as the years went on. One of his most important books was *The Maverick Poets* (1988), an anthology he edited and published of decidedly non-academic poets who wrote in a direct style about everyday topics, nature, politics, and love—the things that mattered. In this book I discovered the work of the poet Billy Collins for the first time.

In 1991, Dog Ear and Harpswell Press merged to form Tilbury House Publishers. In addition to books about Maine, we published children's books and poetry. Our books were now appearing in editions of 5,000–20,000 copies. In 1993, Steve sent me a proposal for a how-to book about poetry, to be written in an engaging second-person style that would distill the essence of what he had been teaching with great success to his university and workshop students in San Diego over the prior two decades. It was fun working with him on a book again. He'd send me chapters as he finished them, and I'd write back with comments (mostly glowing praise) and some suggestions for developing this or that.

As the book took shape we brainstormed titles and settled upon *In the Palm of Your Hand: The Poet's Portable Workshop*, which was fine until Viking Publishers wrote me a very official letter saying we could not use that subtitle, since they had a well-known and lucrative line of books with the word "portable" in their titles: *The Portable Faulkner, The Portable Steinbeck, The Portable Hemingway*, etc. I fired back a letter, with Steve's encouragement, telling Viking his book was absolutely different from theirs, and they backed off once they were convinced we were not a threat.

Later on, Steve wrote an essay, "The Mystique of the Difficult Poem," that laid out his credo of the "accessible" poem, the kind he wrote, taught, and promoted. This essay is one of the best poetry manifestoes ever written by anyone from any era, and is included in this edition of *In the Palm of Your Hand*. I suggest you read it if you haven't already. You may never think of poetry quite the same way again.

In the Palm of Your Hand is still in print 20 years later and still selling strong. It's one of the press's best-selling books of all-time. Among poets and poetry teachers it is considered one of the most insightful and useful poetry how-to books ever written. One of the delights of the book are the poems Kowit uses as models for the writing prompts in each chapter. Early on in the book he declares:

> The belief that good poetry is necessarily dense and obscure is a misconception. To the contrary, lucidity is almost always a great virtue in writing.
>
> Many inexperienced poets also imagine that the language of poetry must be ultra-romantic and theatrical, but a poetry which is too richly embellished with hyperventilated language, inflated sentiments, and abstruse verbiage is in grave danger of sounding artificial or just plain foolish.

Steve Kowit died in his sleep on April 2, 2015. I learned of his passing on Facebook within hours of its happening. It is hard to believe that this generous teacher and man, and incredible poet, is gone. Luckily, he has left behind not only his masterpiece of a poetry-writing manual, but also a dozen or so books of some wonderful poetry. Never in denial about the inevitability of death, he knew his time was limited; he certainly epitomized what is meant by "seize the day." He brought out the best in people, loved his wife dearly, and assembled a body of work that will keep his spirit and teachings alive for a long time.

He was one of the funniest people I knew and also among the most skeptical, to say the least, about what he called "the silliness of the human ego." I keep coming back to his widely anthologized poem "Notice" as I try to make sense of what we've lost with his death, and what we gained by having had him among us as a teacher, poet, activist, publisher, essayist, friend. Pass it on, as he writes in "Notice," pass it on.

NOTICE

This evening, the sturdy Levi's
I wore every day for over a year
& which seemed to the end
in perfect condition,
suddenly tore.
How or why I don't know,
but there it was: a big rip at the crotch.
A month ago my friend Nick
walked off a racquetball court,
showered,
got into this street clothes,
& halfway home collapsed & died.
Take heed, you who read this,
& drop to your knees now & again
like the poet Christopher Smart,
& kiss the earth & be joyful,
& make much of your time,
& be kindly to everyone,
even to those who do not deserve it.
For although you may not believe
it will happen,
you too will one day be gone,
I, whose Levi's ripped at the crotch
for no reason,
assure you that such is the case.
Pass it on.

About the Author

 Born in New York in 1938, Steve Kowit was part of the Lower East Side poetry scene in the early 1960s; later, attracted by the intellectual freedom of the Beat poets, he moved to San Francisco's Haight Ashbury. Celebrated for his lively, entertaining readings and dynamic poetry workshops, he taught at San Diego State University, San Diego City College, UC San Diego, and the College of Southern Idaho; he relocated to the Southern California backcountry near the Mexican border with his wife, Mary.

He edited the anthology *The Maverick Poets*, translated a volume of Pablo Neruda's political poetry, wrote two collections inspired by the erotic love poetry of India (*Sringararasa*), and published eight other volumes of poetry. His work has appeared in numerous anthologies and magazines, including the *Los Angeles Times*, the *New Yorker, Ploughshares,* the *Sun*, and *Yoga Journal*. Among his awards are a National Endowment fellowship, two Pushcart Prizes, and the 2006 *Tampa Review* Poetry Prize. Steve described himself as a "poet, essayist, teacher, workshop facilitator, and all-around no good troublemaker." After retiring from Southwestern College in Chula Vista, he continued to conduct poetry workshops in San Diego until he died in his sleep in 2015, days before his latest volume of poetry was published by Tampa University Press.